Power,
Violence
and Justice

SAGE STUDIES IN
INTERNATIONAL SOCIOLOGY

Series Editor Chaime Marcuello Servós (2016–ongoing)
Editor, Department of Psychology and Sociology,
Zaragoza University, Spain

Recent books in the series
Journey to Adulthood: East Asian Perspectives
Chin-Chun Yi & Ming-Chang Tsai

Power, Violence and Justice: Reflections, Responses and Responsibilities
Edited by Margaret Abraham

Sociologies in Dialogue
Edited by Sari Hanafi & Chin-Chun Yi

Global Childhoods in International Perspective:
Universality, Diversity and Inequalities
Edited by Claudio Baraldi & Lucia Rabello De Castro

Key Texts for Latin American Sociology
Edited by Fernanda Beigel

Global Sociology and the Struggles for a Better World: Towards the
Futures We Want
Edited by Markus S. Schulz

Sociology and Social Justice
Edited by Margaret Abraham

Facing An Unequal World: Challenges for Global Sociology
Edited by Raquel Sosa Elizaga

Power, Violence and Justice

Reflections, Responses and Responsibilities

Edited by **Margaret Abraham**

SSIS SERIES SAGE STUDIES IN INTERNATIONAL SOCIOLOGY: 69

Los Angeles | London | New Delhi
Singapore | Washington DC | Melbourne

Los Angeles | London | New Delhi
Singapore | Washington DC | Melbourne

SAGE Publications Ltd
1 Oliver's Yard
55 City Road
London EC1Y 1SP

SAGE Publications Inc.
2455 Teller Road
Thousand Oaks, California 91320

SAGE Publications India Pvt Ltd
B 1/I 1 Mohan Cooperative Industrial Area
Mathura Road
New Delhi 110044

SAGE Publications Asia-Pacific Pte Ltd
3 Church Street
#10-04 Samsung Hub
Singapore 049483

Library of Congress Control Number: 2022940363

British Library Cataloguing in Publication data

A catalogue record for this book is available from the British Library

Editor: Natalie Aguilera
Assistant editor: Rhoda Ola-Said
Production editor: Vijayakumar
Copyeditor: Christobel Colleen Hopman
Proofreader: Benny Willy Stephen
Indexer: TNQ Technologies
Marketing manager: Ruslana Khatagova
Cover design: Francis Kenney
Typeset by: TNQ Technologies

ISBN 978-1-5296-0981-3
ISBN 978-1-5296-0980-6 (pbk)

Contents

About the Editor   vii

About the Contributors   ix

Introduction   1

Margaret Abraham

1 Power, Violence and Justice: Reflections, Responses and
  Responsibilities   14

  Margaret Abraham

2 Indigenous Land Appropriation and Dispossession in
  Australia: In Search of Justice   32

  Maggie Walter

3 Surveilling Blackness in the 21st Century USA: Modernity/
  Coloniality, Objectivity and Contemporary Forms of Injustice   46

  Natalie P. Byfield

4 Socio-Ecological Violence, Resistance and Democratization
  Processes   65

  J. E. Castro

5 The Moral Crusade on 'Gender Ideology': Alliances Against
  Sexual and Reproductive Rights in Latin America   87

  Richard Miskolci

6 The Arc of Justice in the Era of Routinized Violence   100

  Bandana Purkayastha

7 Sociology's Bipolar Disorder   123

  Michael Burawoy

8 The Iron Bars Get Closer: Anormative Social Regulation   130
   Margaret S. Archer

9 The Rise of National Populism in Western Democracies   145
   Alberto Martinelli

10 Mapping Violence: A Comprehensive Perspective   159
   T. K. Oommen

11 Moral Capital: A Much Needed Resource   175
   Piotr Sztompka

12 Preventing and Exiting Violence: A Domain for Sociology? 189
   Michel Wieviorka

13 White Women in the War on Immigrants: Framing
   Anti-Immigrant Discourse Against Migrant Mothers   206
   Mary Romero

14 A Case for Academic Justice: Universities as Sites of
   Violence, Power (and Justice?)   229
   Nandini Sundar

Index   243

About the Editor

Margaret Abraham is Professor of Sociology and the Harry H. Wachtel Distinguished Professor at Hofstra University, USA. She is the past President of the International Sociological Association (2014–2018). Her teaching and research interests include social justice, gender, ethnicity, citizenship, globalization, migration, intersectionality and domestic violence. Margaret has been involved in research and activism for over 3 decades. She has published several articles and her books and special issues include *Speaking the Unspeakable; Contours of Citizenship; Sociology and Social Justice; Interrogating Gender, Violence, and the State in National and Transnational Contexts* and *Making a Difference: Linking Research and Action*. She serves on community board organizations, journal editorial boards and is an advisory board member on projects addressing gender-based violence. She has been honoured for her work by community-based and academic organizations. For further details see http://margaret abrahamonline.com

About the Contributors

Margaret Abraham is Professor of Sociology and the Harry H. Wachtel Distinguished Professor at Hofstra University, USA. She is the past President of the International Sociological Association (2014–2018). Her teaching and research interests include social justice, gender, ethnicity, citizenship, globalization, migration, intersectionality and domestic violence. Margaret has been involved in research and activism for over three decades. She has published several articles and her books and special issues include *Speaking the Unspeakable; Contours of Citizenship; Sociology and Social Justice; Interrogating Gender, Violence, and the State in National and Transnational Contexts*; and *Making a Difference: Linking Research and Action*. She serves on community board organizations, journal editorial boards and is an advisory board member on projects addressing gender-based violence. She has been honoured for her work by community-based and academic organizations. For further details see http://margaret abrahamonline.com

Margaret S. Archer studied at the London School of Economics and as a post-doc at the École Pratique des Hautes Études, Paris, also working with Pierre Bourdieu. She first developed her 'morphogenetic approach' in *Social Origins of Educational Systems* (1979 re-printed 2013). She was Professor of Sociology at the University of Warwick from 1979 until 2010, writing and editing over forty books, including *The Reflexive Imperative in Late Modernity* (2012), *Making Our Way Through the World: Human Reflexivity and Social Mobility* (2007), and *Realist Social Theory: The Morphogenetic Approach* (1995). In 2011 she became Professor of Social Theory at École Polytechnique Fédérale de Lausanne and Directrice of Centre d'Ontologie Sociale. She continues to develop her 'morphogenetic approach' as the explanatory framework of Critical Realism's social ontology. She was

President of the International Sociological Association (1986–90); a Trustee of the Centre for Critical Realism; a founding member of FAcSS; the British Nominee for the Balzan Prize, 2013; and a founder member of the Pontifical Academy of Social Sciences, becoming its President in 2014. She has recently been awarded Honorary Doctorates (honoris causa) by the Uniwersytet Kardynala Stefana Wyszynkiego, Warsaw, and the University of Navarra, Pamplona, Spain.

Michael Burawoy teaches sociology at the University of California Berkeley. He is also a research associate of SWOP at the University of Witwatersrand, South Africa. These days he is writing about W.E.B. Du Bois and canonical dialogues.

Natalie P. Byfield is the Founding Director of the Institute for Critical Race & Ethnic Studies and a Professor in the Department of Sociology and Anthropology at St. John's University. She explores language use in a variety of cultural objects as a way to study systemic racism and its associations with other inequities, e.g. as gender, class and sexuality. Her studies of newspapers, newsrooms spaces, research methodologies, law enforcement systems and algorithmic-based technologies trace their histories to slavery, coloniality of power and empire. Dr. Byfield is the former Editor-in-Chief of *Language, Discourse & Society*, a journal of RC 25 of the International Sociological Association. She is the author of the monograph *Savage Portrayals: Race, Media, and the Central Park Jogger Story* and several peer-reviewed journal articles and book chapters. Her current book project is titled *Minority Report: Place, Race, and State Surveillance in New York City*.

José Esteban Castro is Emeritus Professor of Sociology at Newcastle University, United Kingdom. He is a Principal Researcher at the National Scientific and Technical Research Council (CONICET), based at the National University of General Sarmiento (UNGS), Argentina, and is a regular visiting scholar at universities in Brazil, Colombia, Mexico and Spain. He coordinates the international research network WATERLAT-GOBACIT (www.waterlat.org) dedicated to research, teaching and practical action in relation to the politics of water. Copies of most of his publications are available from Newcastle University's e-prints collection (http://eprint.ncl.ac.uk/author_pubs.aspx?author_id=78329).

Alberto Martinelli is Professor Emeritus of Political Science and Sociology and former Dean of the Faculty of Social and Political Sciences, University of Milan. He is past-President of the International Social Science Council, and International Sociological Association. He is President of AEM Foundation (a2aGroup), and Vice-President of Science for Peace of the Umberto Veronesi Foundation. He is member of Lombardy Academy of Sciences and Grand Officer of the Order of Merit of the Italian Republic. His present research interests focus on transformations to sustainable development; European Union's response to COVID-19; social and political cleavages in American society; nationalism and populism; states, markets, communities and global governance; and the social integration of immigrants. His main recent publications in English are *European Society* (with A. Cavalli), Boston, Brill, 2020 and *When Populism Meets Nationalism*, Milan, ISPI, 2019. His other publications include *Transatlantic Divide. Comparing American and European Society*, Oxford University Press, 2008 (Italian edition, 2011); *Global Modernization. Rethinking the Project of Modernity*, Sage, 2005 (Italian edition 2010, Russian edition, 2006, Chinese edition 2011); and *Economy and Society* (with N. Smelser), Sage, 1990.

Richard Miskolci is Full Professor of Sociology at the Federal University of São Paulo (UNIFESP), Brazil. Miskolci is also a researcher of the CNPq (National Council for Scientific and Technological Development) and member of the Research Committee Futures Research of the International Sociological Association. He was one of the first scholars to introduce a queer perspective to Brazilian gender and sexuality studies. He was a visiting scholar in the University of Chicago, University of Michigan and University of California. Miskolci is also a specialist on digital sociology and his ongoing research is about disinformation on the new technomediatic ecosystem. His last book is *Batalhas Morais* (2021), an analysis of the moral frame that has shaped the battles between advocates of sexual and reproductive rights and their adversaries in the new public sphere under the hegemony of digital social media.

Bandana Purkayastha is a Professor of Sociology and Asian and Asian American Studies, and Associate Dean of Social Sciences, at the University of Connecticut. Her research on human rights, intersectionality, transnationalism, migrants, violence and peace appears in books, articles, and chapters published in many countries, including in translation. She has been recognized for research excellence and teaching and mentoring, including two career awards: the Contribution to the Field award for her work on Asian and Asian Americans, and American Sociological Association's Jessie Bernard award, 'which recognizes significant contributions to improving the lives of women'. As President of Sociologists for Women in Society in 2013 she initiated a move towards decolonizing knowledge. She serves on the executive committee of ISA. For further details see https://sociology.uconn.edu/person/bandana-purkayastha/

Mary Romero is Professor Emerita, Justice and Social Inquiry in the School of Social Transformation at Arizona State University. She served as the 110th President of the American Sociological Association. She is the 2022 recipient of the ASA W.E.B. Du Bois Career of Distinguished Scholarship Award, the 2017 recipient of the Cox-Johnson-Frazier Award, 2015 Latina/o Sociology Section Founders Award, 2012 Julian Samora Distinguished Career Award, the Section on Race and Ethnic Minorities 2009 Founder's Award and the 2004 Study of Social Problems Lee Founders Award. She was selected as the 2021 SWS Distinguished Feminist Lecturer. She is the author of *Introducing Intersectionality* (Polity Press, 2018), the *Maid's Daughter: Inside and Outside the American Dream* (NYU, 2011), and *Maid in the U.S.A.* (NYU, 1992). She is the editor and co-editor of eight books, and numerous social science journals and law review articles.

Nandini Sundar is Professor of Sociology at the Delhi School of Economics, Delhi University. Her research interests include constitutionalism, academic freedom, intellectual history, democracy, law, inequality and agrarian ecologies. Her recent publications include, *The Burning Forest: India's War Against Maoists* (Verso 2019), which has been translated into Gujarati, Tamil, and Telugu; two edited volumes, *A Functioning Anarchy* (co-edited, Penguin, 2021), and *Reading India: Selections from Economic and Political Weekly 1991–2017* (co-edited, Orient Blackswan, 2019), as well as journal articles on democracy, authoritarianism and academic freedom. She was awarded the M.N. Srinivas Memorial Prize, 2003, the Infosys Prize for Social Sciences (Social Anthropology) in 2010, the Ester Boserup Prize for Development

Research, 2016 and the Malcolm Adiseshiah Prize for Distinguished Contributions to Development Studies, 2017. Her media articles are available at http://nandinisundar.blogspot.com.

Piotr Sztompka is Professor of Theoretical Sociology (Emeritus) at the Jagiellonian University at Krakow, Poland. He is a member of the Polish Academy of Sciences, Academia Europaea (London) and American Academy of Arts and Sciences (Cambridge, MA). Between 2002 and 2006 he served as President of the International Sociological Association (ISA). In 1995 he was awarded a major international award New Europe Prize. He is the honorary doctor of five universities in Poland and abroad. He has been a frequent visiting professor at in the United States, Mexico, Argentina, Australia and Europe. His most important books in English include *System and Function* (1974), *Sociological Dilemmas* (1979), *Robert Merton: An Intellectual Profile (1986), Society in Action: The Theory of Social Becoming.* (1991), *The Sociology of Social Change* (1993) translated into eight languages, *Trust: A Sociological Theory* (1999) translated into four languages, and *Cultural Trauma and Collective Identity* (coauthored 2005).

T. K. Oommen is at present Professor Emeritus at the Jawaharlal Nehru University, from where he retired in 2002 after being a professor for 26 years. He was President of International Sociological Association as well as that of Indian Sociological Society. He was a Visiting Professor/Research Fellow at several universities including University of California, Australian National University, Institute of Advanced Studies at Budapest and Uppsala. He has authored and edited 33 books. His latest book is *Contemporary Society:* Concerns *and Issues* (2019). He is a recipient of the V.K.R.V. Rao Prize in Sociology (1981), G. S. Ghurye Prize in Sociology and Social Anthropology (1985) and the Swami Pranavanda Award in Sociology (1997). He was a National Fellow at the Indian Council of Social Science Research, 2008–2010. Oommen was conferred the Padma Bhushan in 2008 in recognition of his contribution to higher education.

Michel Wieviorka is Professor at the École des Hautes Études en Sciences Sociales (Paris), where he has been Director of the Centre d'Analyses et d'Interventions Sociologiques (CADIS, 1993–2009). He has been the President of the Fondation Maison des Sciences de l'Homme (Paris, 2009–2020). He is founder and co-editor of *Violence: An International Journal,* and *SOCIO*. He has been the President of the International Sociological Association (ISA, 2006–2010), and a member of the scientific board of the European Research Council (ERC, 2014–2019). His main research focus is on social movements, democracy, multiculturalism, racism, anti-semitism, terrorism and violence. His books (in English) include: *The Arena of Racism* (SAGE); *The Making of Terrorism* (University of Chicago Press); *Violence: A New Approach* (SAGE); *The Lure of Anti-semitism* (Brill); and *Evil* (Polity Press).

Maggie Walter (PhD; FASSA) is *Palawa,* a member of the Briggs Aboriginal family and Distinguished Professor of Sociology (Emerita) at the University of Tasmania. Her research interests encompass inequality, race relations and Indigenous Data Sovereignty. Maggie is founding member of the Indigenous Data Sovereignty group in Australia (Maiam nayri Wingara) and an executive member of the Global Indigenous Data Alliance (GIDA). Her recent books include *Indigenous Children Growing Up Strong: A Longitudinal Study of Aboriginal and Torres Strait Islander Families* (with. K.L. Martin and G. Bodkin-Andrews, Palgrave McMillan: London 2017)*;* Indigenous *Data Sovereignty and Social Policy* (with T. Kukutai; S.R. Carroll and D. Rodriguez Lonebear, Routledge, 2020) and *The Oxford Handbook of Indigenous Sociology* (with T. Kukutai; A. Gonzales and R. Henry. Oxford: New York 2022).

Introduction

Margaret Abraham

Sociology has always been concerned with power, violence and justice, yet current social, economic and political challenges have enhanced their relevance. As capitalist globalization expands and deepens, corporate power increases, exacerbating inequality at all levels of society. New geo-political power configurations and confrontations are emerging, with violence being used as a tool to oppress as well as resist oppression. Colonial histories and contemporary land appropriations reflect the structures and cultural processes that perpetuate violence against indigenous and minority communities. The failure of states to meet their responsibility to provide basic resources is often deflected by divisive tactics that cast blame upon the most vulnerable sectors and communities. Both global-economic and geo-political processes create crises and massive displacements of people, and, at the same time, fuel racism, nationalism and xenophobia. Fear has become a powerful tool used by states, corporations and other institutions to generate popular support for the curtailing of freedom in the name of security. Efforts to curtail the flow of desperate refugees, attest to the reinforcement of national and racialized borders. Despite visible progress on equality issues, violence against women and intersectional violence point to the entrenchment of the gender border around the world. Equally significant is the need to consider the role of state and institutional power relations in ongoing everyday violence. Amid this increasingly exposed ugliness, however, there is a growing response to the ongoing forms of disempowerment, violence and injustice. We have witnessed nonviolent movements, humanitarian interventions and peace processes around the world working to empower communities, reduce violence and promote a justice that is inclusive. Diverse communities have built solidarities outside the neo-liberal frames of the state–global–capital nexus, and this is where we can find some hope for the future.

In the last decade there has been considerable focus placed on understanding the complexity and interaction between power, violence and justice. These concepts have been discussed, debated and contested by generations of social scientists (Bhambra, Bourdieu, Connell, Crenshaw, de Sousa Santos, Della Porta, Du Bois, Durkheim, Fanon, Mies, Marx, Rege, Ritchie, Sen, Sundar, Walby, Weber). Framing and examining the structural dimensions of power and violence, including looking at the major socio-historical institutions through which they operate, are vital. Questions that require our attention include how does power flow through institutions, and what is the importance of structure for understanding the broader context of violence? What are the contradictions and fault lines? Where and how can we expect human agency and emerging struggles for justice to be successful?

Power, defined as the capacity to influence or control the behaviour and conduct of others, has largely determined the historical trajectory that leads us to where we stand today. Power is a critical component in all human interactions. It can be creative, and it can be destructive. History tells us many stories of contestations for power in the multiple arenas of human interaction. We cannot address power, violence and justice without pointing to the ways that colonial histories and contemporary land appropriation reflect the structures and cultural processes that perpetuate ongoing violence against indigenous and minority communities. We see how state and corporate power often collude in both overt and subtle marginalization. Understanding the historical processes of colonial and contemporary land dispossession; the persistence of past inequalities and violence, as well as contemporary forms of extraction, unequal development and displacement, with implications for labour markets, gender relations, families, household, culture and nation are the key to creating forms of contestation, resistance and agency. It is also needed to address and rectify injustices for social transformation.

Global-institutional and techno-bureaucratic transformations have seen the dominance of socio-economic and political matrices that produce forms of inequalities and oppressions at the level of everyday life. The lens of power, violence and justice provides and captures the devastating effects of the processes of globalization and neo-liberalism, which have led to displacements, dislocations and differentiations across lines of gender, class, religion, age and nationality. These merit critical sociological engagement as an ethical-moral project.

Historically and in our world today, the role of violence in the production and reproduction of inequalities and exclusion is undeniable. Violence is frequently represented in terms of resistance to (legitimate) forms of governmental and institutional power. However, these very structures tend to constitute a form of violence directed against the racialized other. Structural violence is used to secure and reproduce inequality by manipulating local populations against stigmatized others within their midst. Migration, violence, dislocation and displacement show us the social and political efforts made towards producing more democratic and just societies, as well as how these have engendered different forms of violence that generates migration and displacement. As such, the structures, processes and impact of physical, moral and political inclusion, exclusion and forced containment of minorities and migrant populations require our sociological attention.

Violence, in all its forms threatens social cohesion, even at the level of micro aggressions and invisible biases. Gender and intersectional violence focus on violence as being the extreme form of exercising power. Here, violence takes on various forms through action, inaction, erasure and invalidation. We see this in both historic and contemporary contexts. Individuals and groups occupy multiple social positions within local, national and global systems of inequality. Often gender-based violence is complicated, brought on and exacerbated by stereotypes, social constructions and discriminatory social practices based on various forms of social divisions. The consequences of such intersections of inequalities and oppressions are often devastating at the micro, meso and macro level. Examining the role of violence in reinforcing social constructions and raising questions of resistance, agency and social justice is key for social change and social transformation.

In addressing injustice, we must look at the connections between power and what power deems to be justice. It is imperative to understand in which contexts state and nonstate institutional processes inhibit or enhance the possibilities of justice and for whom. The corollary to which is examining the forms of power that constrain justice. In various parts of the world there has been rising populism, a consolidation of authoritarian rule, a decline of democracy with institutions of justice being compromised or decimated. Increasingly, we see how notions of security have been made into a state priority, both domestically and internationally. The state has increasingly subjected individuals and their associates to extreme levels of state surveillance under the guise of "protection". The very nature of information and surveillance within these efforts puts marginalized individuals, groups and organizations at risk. At the same time, the power of some social movements is playing a significant role in the resistance to these forms of oppression, speaking out against what is in fact injustice, and thus contributing to social change.

Together, the authors in this book provide sociological insights, theoretical perspectives and glimpses into their research in the diverse contexts that contribute to a deeper understanding of the complexities of power, violence and justice. Although primarily grounded in sociology, many of the authors draw across disciplines. The spectrum of topics covered within their diverse contexts, their varied perspectives, and the authors' writing styles is intentional. The scope of the author contributions offers different foci in terms of an emphasis on theoretical, historical, analytical, descriptive and contextually applied topics. This includes diverse insights on a range of topics including colonialism, migration, race, gender and intersectionality, social movements, security, environment and education. Within all of these floats the open question: What is the role that sociology plays and can play in moving us forward? Through their insights, this collection of articles stimulates us as academics and human beings, to reflect, respond and share in the responsibility of countering the forces that perpetrate violence, subvert equality and dilute the notion of justice.

The Chapters

This book had its genesis in the XIX ISA World Congress of Sociology in 2018. It brings together 14 articles from the presidential and plenary sessions that addressed the themes of the conference: Violence, Power, and Justice. Although presented prior to the global COVID-19 pandemic, the theoretical perspectives and applied contexts showcased by the authors in this collection contribute to a much-needed conversation around the roles played by power, violence and justice in our world today, which have been exacerbated, highlighted and increased by the climate crises and the various effects of the global pandemic. The 14 articles have deliberately not been prearranged or slotted into sections to avoid an imposed, predetermined grouping of theories, concepts and contexts. Instead, it is arranged so that the reader may draw upon individual chapter concepts and contexts, and weave between diverse perspectives making connections that can enhance our understanding of the issues raised.

Chapter 1 explores some the issues that are most relevant to a discussion of power, violence and justice. The hope is that our sociological enquiries, reflections and responses to these issues will help build a better understanding and contribute to framing policies and actions that will make for a less violent, more just and enduring world. Starting with a brief introduction on the state of our world, emphasis is brought to the violence being used against vulnerable sections of the population who have been identified by the state, in one way or another, as being "the Other". The chapter highlights the rise of illiberal democracies; the direct nexus between the rise of right-wing populist nationalism across the world and the international disregard for human rights violations of ongoing violence against women, gender and intersectional violence. Also noted is the power of the media and how no discussion on power, violence and justice today would be complete without factoring in the enormous influence of the knowledge and misinformation that is disseminated, distorted or dismissed by the media. This chapter mentions the role of protest movements, concluding with an emphasis that sociology matters and can forge pathways towards a better present and a hopeful future for a more just world.

In Chapter 2, Maggie Walter draws our attention to how land justice and societal justice are co-dependent. She emphasizes how relationship with land is the foundation of Indigenous social order and discusses the historical appropriation of Indigenous Land and Dispossession in Australia. She shows how in 1788, by the simple act of raising the British flag at Possession Island in North Queensland, the British claimed an entire continent. She emphasizes how the British deemed Aboriginal and Torres Strait Islander peoples to be 'without a sovereign or system of land tenure thereby making the country "un-owned"' (terra nullius). How despite protracted frontier wars, this legal fiction supported the Euro-Australian myth that

Australia was settled, not invaded. She underscores that although Terra Nullius was formally overturned in 1993, the quest by Aboriginal and Torres Strait Islander peoples to regain even a small semblance of their rights to traditional county has been slow and contested. Using 2016 census data, Walter empirically links Aboriginal and Torres Strait Islander's socio-economic and political disenfranchisement with both historical and contemporary dispossessions. Framed within Australian socio-cultural discursive realities, and inclusive of the *Uluru Statement from the Heart* (the 2017 Indigenous message to Australian political leaders), the strong relationship between 'country' and Indigenous well-being is made.

In Chapter 3, Natalie P. Byfield carefully and compellingly addresses contemporary constructions of blackness in the digital age, in which the emergent era of policing in the United States focuses on security and risk management and incorporates a variety of surveillance tools and technologies, such as data analytics and algorithms. This requires us to critically think about the lessons of US history concerning the role of science – particularly the social sciences – in creating associations between blackness and criminality. She compellingly argues that all these are or have been part of the state or empire's strategies for survival and 'development'. Byfield examines the incorporation of all these considerations in an assessment of the increasingly digitally based approach to policing New York City neighbourhoods, and aptly reveals the ways in which the forces of modernity/coloniality create new approaches to objectivity and develop new types of injustice.

In Chapter 4, J. Esteban Castro discusses the significance of violence in the emergence, maintenance and erosion of socio-ecological orders. He focuses on the interconnection between violence against marginalized communities and the rapid expansion and accumulation of neoliberal capitalism. Using examples from Latin America, this chapter discusses the global impact of environment-related conflict and violence, primarily related to the expansion of extractivist activities and the unequal distribution of impacts from extreme geophysical and weather-related events. Castro focusses on the production of structural inequality and injustice through systemically organized violence and the criminalization of social actors who try to defend the land, their territories, livelihoods and even basic rights. He highlights the fundamental contradiction between the discursive commitment to democratic principles and processes made by governments and international institutions, and the illegal and violent atrocities that are committed on the ground against defenceless communities. The chapter also discusses the challenges encountered by social scientists to produce more advanced and complex understandings and explanations that may contribute towards the construction of more humane socio-ecological orders.

In Chapter 5, Richard Miskolci presents a thoughtful synthesis of a broad and complex situation on the reaction against advances in sexual and reproductive rights that have emerged in several Latin American countries showing common elements, among which is a shared vocabulary that labels such rights as "gender ideology". He notes how politicians and interest groups, acting as opportunistic moral entrepreneurs, have come to adopt the term as an electoral strategy by converting the grammar of the political dispute into the moral conflict between "good citizens" and others, often identified as feminists, homosexuals and trans people. Miskolci argues that such Latin American crusade against "gender ideology" in its different national manifestations as having already had various consequences and results, such as the impediment to the adoption of a gender perspective in educational policies, thus contributing to the maintenance of inequalities between men and women and above all to discrimination and violence against gays, lesbians, trans people and others.

Bandana Purkayastha, in Chapter 6, explores some critical questions in our understanding of the linkages between violence and justice. How is justice configured in an era of routinized violence? How do the dynamics of changing institutions around justice, and the various diverse segments of civil society, intersect to shape an arc of justice? Her chapter focuses on the questions of violence and justice by foregrounding the experience of migrants. To make the case, Purkayastha provides an array of different migrant populations. She argues that states are increasingly using routine violence, institutionalized violence, the facilitation of vigilante action and weaponized language, to shape the human insecurities of all those who are deemed immigrants. It is the nexus of justice and the treatment of migrants then, she argues, that shows either a state's commitment to principles of democracy, rights and freedoms, or the gap between state rhetoric and practice.

Michael Burawoy, in Chapter 7, draws our attention to sociology and the challenge that sociology faces with the world it studies. He notes that Sociology is engaged with the world it studies, it reflects the changing metaphysical pathos of the times. Therefore, Sociology swings between moods of optimism and pessimism. For Burawoy, the cure for what he calls this bipolar disease is the development of social theory. Here he explores how the ideas of Karl Polanyi may provide a deeper understanding of these swings by rooting them in capitalism. However, he qualifies this noting that Polanyi needs updating and revising. That it requires recognizing the importance not just of a ubiquitous commodification but also of the dynamics of capital accumulation that give rise to waves of marketization. For Burawoy, only by grasping the nature of capitalism can we appreciate the etiology of our bipolarity.

In Chapter 8, Margaret Archer discusses 'coercion' as the use of power to enforce compliance; emphasizing techniques whose intensification is employed to get other agents to do or to cease from certain actions. She explains anormative regulation increases significantly with the intensification of social morphogenesis – unbound from countervailing forms of morphostasis. She notes that approximately around 1980, bureaucratic regulation predominates over normatively based legislative control as the law cannot run fast enough to keep up with simultaneous social transformations. She argues that legal provisions tend to lag behind innovative malfeasance as morphogenetic variety stimulates more variety, outdistancing juridical control. In turn, there is a severance from past legal concern with legitimacy without any new preoccupation with social legitimation. Archer provides an eight point ideal type that encapsulates the regulatory quest for social coordination and unconcern with cooperation and re-distribution. She systematically discusses the ways that integrative Commons is overshadowed by the digital proponents of the situational logic of competition having made common cause with the political and corporate promoters of anormative social regulation.

Alberto Martinelli, in Chapter 9, focusses our attention on the critical problem of the rise of National populism in Western democracies in recent years, on both sides of the Atlantic. He notes that a growing literature is highlighting the increasing use of national-populist rhetoric and policies, for example, those of Donald Trump, and European leaders such as Marine Le Pen of Front National, Nigel

Farage of the UKIP, Matteo Salvini of Lega, Viktor Orban of Fidesz, Jaroslaw Kaczynski of Prawo i Sprawiedliwość and others. Martinelli's chapter carefully explores key member states of the European Union, arguing that the diffusion of both nationalism and populism are symptoms of a crisis in European democracies. The convergence of nationalist ideology and populist rhetoric is a major challenge that the European Union faces and it can be effectively countered by developing the political project of a truly democratic and supranational union. Martinelli outlines the distinctive features of nationalism and populism, and then analyses the major factors fostering the rise of national populism in European Union countries, concluding by discussing some more effective alternatives.

In Chapter 10, T.K. Oommen puts forth a conceptual history of violence, considering colonialism, the Cold War period and the current time. He provides a backdrop of different periods and examines the three 'cides', genocide, culturocide and ecocide, and their meanings for a comprehensive analysis of violence. In mapping violence, Oommen looks at the nature of colonialism and types of violence and this is followed by a discussion where he then lays out the emergence of the three-world schema. Oommen also discusses technology and violence at the micro level in the mapping of violence.

Piotr Sztompka, in Chapter 11, explores that much needed resource: moral capital, which he states is nothing else but what happens between and among individuals in the interhuman space. He argues that one of the crucial missing resources of societies pervaded with abuses of power, violence and poverty is social capital, the network of good relations among the citizens. However, for him, the core of social capital is moral capital, which consists of six fundamental relations: trust, loyalty, reciprocity, solidarity, respect and justice. These relations constitute a syndrome; they are logically and empirically interconnected and none can be realized alone. He argues that, together they create important prerequisites for the functional efficiency of the social whole, from the family to the nation, at the same time they make life of societal members more satisfying, fulfilling and happy. This chapter explores the idea of a common good as having become an abstraction replaced by rampant egoism. Abuse, hostility and violence. Injustice of all sorts prevails. It argues that without moral capital social development cannot be achieved.

In Chapter 12, Michel Wieviorka explains how and why preventing and exiting from violence is a crucial problem for the social sciences According to him, the knowledge on violence comes mainly from specialists, experts, lawyers, diplomats, heads of NGOs, psychiatrists and diplomats rather than social scientists. He argues that it is time to rectify this immense gap and make the prevention and exiting from violence a real field of sociology that covers a wide range of issues from addressing the individual level of victims and perpetrators, to major geopolitical issues, from the communities and groups concerned through to the level of the state. Wieviorka explains how the issues require considering different time scales, analysing different subjectivities and a reconstruction of subjects through a process of subjectivation. He also emphasizes that addressing these issues requires the social sciences to extend their approach to violence and to the actions that counter it.

In Chapter 13, Mary Romero contributes in important ways to the growing literature on the significance of white women in the United States in maintaining white supremacy and their participation in the war on immigrants. Critically reflecting on the role that white women have played in using their white motherhood to argue on behalf of the Trump administration's zero tolerance policy involving the separation of parents and children, this chapter examines research on Mothers Against Illegal Aliens' (MAIA) and its impact on normalizing racist hate speech by posing themselves as protecting their white families. Themes, images and metaphors used by MAIA, Romero notes, reappeared in white women's participation in the Trump administration's immigration policies. The children of immigrant mothers are positioned as economic and safety threats to white mothers' children. Romero persuasively concludes that the use of white motherhood in nativist movements contributes to normalizing hate speech and inhumane immigration policies.

Finally, in Chapter 14, Nandini Sundar compellingly turns the enquiry around themes of power, violence and justice inward, focusing on an important site, that is, academia itself. She insightfully points out that University-based scholars are used to directing their gaze outwards, reflecting on different manifestations of power, violence and struggles for justice in the world – civil wars, ethnic or religious conflict, in factories, in urban spaces, at resource frontiers, within the family etc. She suggests that this is because universities are our own workplaces, and any critique might implicate us or our own colleagues. Hence, she justifiably notes that there is much less attention to how universities encode their own forms of violence and power – as well as hold out particular forms of justice and injustice.

Through their writings, the questions that they pose and the theoretical frameworks they use, these authors compel us to consider a host of challenges, from the relevance and importance of sociology engaging in the debates and discussions for social transformation, to the ways in which we understand how sociologists frame and examine sites and contexts in which power, violence and justice are contested. These chapters expose both similarities and differences in the goals, processes and outcomes of power and violence. They provide a plurality of lenses through which to view issues that were relevant pre-pandemic and are now of critical importance. Most importantly, this collection of insightful articles draws attention to the need for continuous sociological engagement with conceptualizing, connecting and contextualizing power, violence and justice. Conceptualizing is complex and defies being reduced or slotted to a singular universally accepted definition.

Addressing the diverse perspectives and practices of justice in different contexts can lead to a greater understanding of what is entailed in crafting a more just world. Connecting concepts and practices of power, violence and justice through a critical understanding of some of the divisive dynamics that contribute to multiple forms of inequalities, exclusions and oppressions is vital. The authors highlight some of the systemic patterns of violence in our world. The contextualization they offer enables us to see the historical, geographical, economic, political and cultural contexts that shape perceptions and practices of power, violence and justice.

Acknowledgements

I am grateful to the many people who have helped make this book happen. A very special thanks to SSIS Series Editor Chaime Marcuello Servós, for his encouragement, sociological insights and steadfast support. Various unanticipated factors, including the pandemic, delayed its completion, but finally, we were able to bring it to fruition. My sincere thanks to the contributing authors, reviewers, ISA Publications Committee, ISA Executive Committee; to the SAGE team, especially Rhoda OlaSaid, Assistant Editor: Natalie Aguilera Publisher at SAGE; Vijayakumar, Production Editor; Christobel Colleen Hopman, Copyeditor; Benny Willy Stephen, Proofreader; Ruslana Khatagova, Marketing Manager; and to all involved in the book production. A very special thanks to Amanda Hester for her invaluable input and careful copyediting, and to Taisha Abraham for her incisive comments. My profound thanks to my family and friends and but most importantly to my life partner, Pradeep Singh, for being there in all ways. I am very grateful to Hofstra University for the immense support that I have received over many years.

References

Abdul Bari, M. (2018). *The Rohingya crisis: A people facing extinction.* Leicester: Kube Publishing.

Abraham, T. (2002). *Women and the politics of violence.* New Delhi: Har-Anand Publications.

Abraham, M. (2019). *Sociology and social justice. Sage studies in international sociology.* London: SAGE.

Abraham, M., Ngan-ling Chow, E., Maratou-Alipranti, L., & Tastsoglou, E. (Eds.). (2010). In *Contours of citizenship: Women, diversity and practices of citizenship.* Farnham: Ashgate.

Abraham, M., & Purkayastha, B. (2012). Making a difference: Linking research and action in practice, pedagogy, and policy for social justice. *Current Sociology, 60*(2), 123–141.

Abraham, M., & Tastsoglou, E. (2016). Interrogating gender, violence, and the state in national and transnational contexts: Framing the issues. *Current Sociology Monograph, 64*(4), 517–553.

Bhambra, G. (2007). *Rethinking modernity: Postcolonialism and the sociological imagination.* New York, NY: Palgrave Macmillan.

Bourdieu, P. (1991). *Language and symbolic power.* Cambridge, MA: Harvard University Press.

Bringel, B. M., & Domingues, J. M. (Eds.). (2015). *Global modernity and social contestation.* London: SAGE.

Burawoy, M. (2005). For public sociology. *American Sociological Review, 70*(1), 4–28.

Collins, P. H. (1990). *Black feminist thought.* New York, NY: Routledge.

Connell, R. (2011). Gender and social justice: Southern perspectives. *South African Review of Sociology, 42*(3), 103–115.

Crenshaw, K. (1989). *Demarginalizing the intersection of race and sex: A black feminist critique of antidiscrimination doctrine, feminist theory and antiracist politics.* University of Chicago Legal Forum 1989(1): Article 8.

Crenshaw, K. (1991). Mapping the margins: Intersectionality, identity politics, and violence against women of color. *Stanford Law Review, 43*(6), 1241–1299.

Della Porta, D. (2006). *Social movements, political violence, and the state: A comparative analysis of Italy and Germany.* Cambridge: Cambridge University Press.

de Sousa Santos, B. (2007). *Cognitive justice in a global world: Prudent knowledges for a decent life.* Lexington, MA: Lexington Books.

de Sousa Santos, B. (2015). *If god were a human rights activist.* Redwood City, CA: Stanford University Press.

Du Bois, W. E. B. (1903). *The souls of black folk.* Chicago, IL: A.G. McClurg & Co.

Durkheim, E. (2005). *Suicide: A study in sociology.* London: Routledge.

Fanon, F. (1963). *The wretched of the Earth.* New York, NY: Grove Press.

Finkelstein, C., & Skerker, M. (2018). *Sovereignty and the new executive authority.* Oxford: Oxford University Press.

Kannabiran, K., Kannabirān, K., & Kannabiran, V. (2002). *De-eroticizing assault: Essays on modesty, honour and power.* Mumbai: Popular Prakashan.

Marx, K., & Engels, F. (1967). *The communist manifesto.* London: Penguin.

Mies, M. (1986). *Patriarchy and accumulation on a world scale.* London: Zed Books.

Platt, J. (1998). *History of ISA: 1948–1987. International sociological association 50th anniversary publication.* Madrid: ISA.

Porta, D., Andretta, M., Mosca, L., & Reiter, H. (2006). *Globalization from below: Transnational activists and protest networks.* Minneapolis, MN: University of Minnesota Press.

Rege, S. (2006). *Writing caste/writing gender: Reading Dalit women's testimonios.* New Delhi: Zubaan.

Richie, B. (2012). *Arrested justice: Black women, violence and America's prison nation.* New York, NY: New York University Press.

Romero, M., & Stewart, A. J. (1999). *Women's untold stories: Breaking silence, talking back, voicing complexity.* New York, NY: Routledge.

Sen, A. (2006). *Identity and violence: The illusion of destiny.* New York, NY: W.W. Norton.

Sen, A. (2008). Violence, identity and poverty. *Journal of Peace Research, 45*(1).

Sundar, N. (2008). *Subalterns and sovereigns: An anthropological history of Bastar (1854–2006).* India: Oxford University Press.

Tastsoglou, E., & Dobrowolsky, A. (2006). *Women, migration and citizenship: Making local, national and transnational connections.* Farnham: Ashgate.

Walby, S. (2013). Violence and society: Introduction to an emerging field of sociology. *Current Sociology, 61*(2), 95–111.

Weber, M. (1946). *From max weber: Essays in sociology,* trans. and ed. HH Gerth and C Wright Mills. New York, NY: Oxford University Press.

Wieviorka, M. (2009). *Violence: A new approach.* London: SAGE.

Yuval-Davis, N., & Werbner, P. (1999). *Women, citizenship and difference.* London: Zed Books.

1

Power, Violence and Justice

Reflections, Responses and Responsibilities

Margaret Abraham

Introduction

The theme of the XIX International Sociological Association World Congress of Sociology revolved around the multiple forms of intersection that can arise between power and violence, and the implications this has for justice. We are at a critical juncture in our human journey, where the policies and actions of a powerful few have engendered inequality, conflict, harm, injustice and suffering on a stunning scale around the world. We sociologists need to step up now, with purpose, and draw upon our theories, research and practice in the best interests of humanity.

The ISA World Congress, held in 2018 in Toronto, Canada brought together the knowledge, talent and resources of sociologists from across the world to address the gamut of issues relating to these dynamics. The Congress theme was so immeasurably vast, complex and multifaceted that it probably was discussed and debated in all of the 1,200 sessions that were organized. For my part, I shared a few pertinent issues that I consider relevant and of critical importance to some of our deliberations that took place during the Congress. Hopefully, our sociological enquiries, reflections and responses will have helped to build a better understanding of the problems that beset our societies and will contribute to framing policies and actions that will make for a less violent and more just and enduring world.

Power, defined as the capacity to influence or control the behaviour and conduct of others, has largely determined the historical trajectory that leads us to where we stand today. Power is a critical component in all human interactions. It can be creative, and it can be destructive. As the character in George Orwell's 1984 says: 'We know that no one ever seizes power with the intention of relinquishing it. Power is not a means; it is an end . . . . The object of power is power' (Orwell, 1949). In our world today, this is too often the case.

History tells us many stories, of contestations for power in the multiple arenas of human interaction. It tells us of its uses and also of its corruption. In the context of nation states, we have seen the use of power that is coercive and uses military might or economic advantage to force and manipulate compliance. We have seen power through intimidation and persuasion on display on the world stage. We have witnessed how coercive power and violence go hand in hand, as force is consistently the preferred instrument of the powerful against the weak or vulnerable. One can find this in the interventions in Syria, Iraq and Afghanistan, Russia's annexation of Crimea, the nixed Nuclear deal, the travel bans from certain Muslim-majority nations and the imprisonment of immigrants in Texas as just some recent examples. History has repeatedly shown that such exercises of power and control sow the seeds for future conflict.

Violence, in all of its various forms, threatens social cohesion, even at the level of micro-aggressions and invisible biases. Decrying violence as being an unmitigated evil, however, is also problematic. Mahatma Gandhi, a proponent of non-violence, understood this dilemma when he observed: 'Though violence is not lawful, when it is offered in self-defense or for the defense of the defenseless, it is an act of bravery far better than cowardly submission' (in Prabhu and Rao, 1967). His reference point was colonialism, arguably the most formidable exposition of power in the last two centuries. It was a system that we can now recognize as being a persistent narrative of genocide, violence, suffering and injustice. Similarly, Frantz Fanon viewed violence in this context as being a necessary tool for the emancipation of the oppressed (Fanon, 1963). The contexts, connections and intersections that inform our understanding of power, violence and justice matter.

Weber (1946) described the State as having a monopoly on the legitimate use of violence or force, as a means of maintaining social order and cohesion. Bestowing such power to the State, however, has been challenged by aggrieved agencies within and outside the system, primarily on the grounds that the established order has been unjust to certain groups, and especially to those already disempowered. Imbued with such power, States have taken advantage of this monopoly to oppress and repress certain groups who then have no substantive recourse to justice. The discordance in interests and views of the State in relation to such groups has been a trigger for violence, irrespective of the form of the State apparatus in place. As Martin Luther King pointed out, 'there can be no peace without justice and without justice, there can be no peace'.

A particularly worrying feature of our present times is the way violence is being used against vulnerable sections of the population who have been identified by the State, in one way or another, as being 'the Other'. This has become a relentless tool of politicians and certain media outlets. It has become a form of targeting and controlling difficult or marginalized groups in many countries, often through some form of State collusion. The plight of the Rohingyas in Myanmar, ethnic Tamils in Sri Lanka, Muslims in India, Christian Copts in Egypt, Kurds in Iraq and Syria, Kurds and Armenians in Turkey, and immigrants and people of colour in Europe and America are only a few examples (*cf:* Abdul Bari, 2018; Arena, 2006; Baxter, 2017; Murray, 2017).

We live in an age of cataclysmic social change, economic misgivings and global tensions. The traditional bastions of liberal democracy have become pillars of uncertainty about the shape of things to come. The 'liberal' smugness implicit in theories like Francis Fukuyama's (1992) 'end of history', or Tony Blair's observation that the 'grand ideological battles of the twentieth century are over', now sounds particularly hollow and naïve, as was their optimism about the permanence of liberal democracy. What we are witnessing today is a counter-movement that is interrogating the structures and institutions celebrated as a bequest of Western liberal democracy and capitalism to the world. This is a movement that is deeply distrustful of the most basic liberal values of tolerance, inclusion and even human rights. It is challenging us to look at how these principles have been used to enable complacency and complicity in various forms of systemic exclusion and injustice. There is widespread frustration and anger at the mounting inequality and economic uncertainty that have created great cleavages within society; at the fragmentation and uprooting of lives caused by marketization and globalization; and at the vast numbers of migrants who have been displaced as a result of endless conflict and persecution.

Some of these frustrations have led to activism, some to despair and some have morphed into a shrill nationalism that is populist, xeno-phobic, ethnocentric and hostile to minorities and immigrants.

Illiberal Democracies

In 2014, Viktor Orban, Prime Minister of Hungary, captured the world's attention with what is known as his 'illiberal democracy' speech. To quote him: 'There is a race underway to find the method of community organization, the State, which is most capable of making a nation and a community internationally competitive ... The most popular topic in thinking today is trying to understand how systems that are not western, not liberal, not liberal democracies, and perhaps not even democracies, can nevertheless make their nations successful.'[1]

Orban implies that behind the veneer of democracy, a nation state can be a winner by rejecting liberal values and democratic norms – where only the end goal matters and not the methods deployed. Orban has given voice to a worldview that seems to be shared by an increasing number of populist leaders across the world. An issue of *TIME* magazine (3 May 2018) had a cover story titled 'Rise of the Strongman'. It describes the emergence of powerful populist leaders in countries across the world, those who care little for civil liberties or the rule of law.

A further devastation to the democratic dream was the tragic unravelling of the hope that had been engendered by the 'Arab Spring'. Egypt, which was at the heart of the upheavals towards democracy in 2011, but in 2018 was in the thrall of a dictator – Abdel Fattah el-Sisi. Likewise, it is significant that in a number of countries, including America, governments are encouraging and fostering schisms within society by playing on the fears and insecurities of ordinary citizens and targeting ethnic, religious, racial minorities, migrants and dissidents – effectively constructing 'the Other' to use as a target for discrimination, violence and repression.

The reality of economic and social setbacks have created a sense of loss and have instilled fear. For many groups in society, there is a pervasive sense that we are facing a bleak future. Society's fear, frustration, disenchantment and rage have all been manipulated and twisted by politicians for their own interests and power. What matters today is no longer the truth, but rather the ability to appeal to people's emotions, to align statements to correspond with, or even to develop, group anxieties.

The fear generated by the 2008 financial crisis devastated many economies, with consequences particularly for the common person and civil society. This was further exacerbated by the arrival of immigrants who had been displaced due to persecution, ongoing wars and conflicts, from countries such as: Syria, Afghanistan, South Sudan, Somalia and Myanmar. Terrorist attacks linked to Islamic fundamentalism then added to the fears and resentments that were growing against immigrants and 'outsiders'. This resulted in a turn towards nationalist, xenophobic, far-right, populist political positioning. Those who took up these positions in both the media and governance appealed to people's emotionality and perceived grievances, to their sense of insecurity and loss. The populist rhetoric resonated! Those who hold more liberal values have watched with dismay as populist leaders manipulate public sentiment in the direction of racism and hyper-nationalism. However, there is also a growing response to counter the promotion of anti-plurality and the erosion of democratic institutions. Proponents of social justice and social activism push against this tide of hate, and every day they are making ground for greater humanity, acceptance, inclusion and understanding.

Ironically, sections of the underprivileged, many of whom should be practical allies of liberal social policies, are increasingly supporting right-wing and xenophobic policies and forces. We may not be seeing the actual end of liberal democracy, but the dangers facing it are palpable. Across the world, authoritarian and autocratic populists have been gaining ground, consolidating and centralizing power and control. We are seeing the resurgence of the authoritarian personality, and the popular belief in the Strong State. We saw this in Turkey, with President Erdogan's victory, through democratic elections, which have allowed him to continue to consolidate his power and extend his authority over the legislature and judiciary. Indeed, we are seeing this story play out multiple times all over the world.

A deeply disturbing feature of our times is the majoritarian impulse gaining momentum even in acclaimed democracies like the United States and India. In both of these countries, leaders with an unmistakable majoritarian agenda have come to power, democratically, through the will of the people. These leaders have then undermined their countries' hard-won freedoms and have eroded democratic institutions and values. They have sought to buttress power by dividing their people and targeting those whom they see as either a threat or as an opportunity to victimize for political interests and gain. The problem with the majoritarian worldview is that it invariably excludes certain groups of civil society on the basis of race, ethnicity, religion, class and gender identity. Such exclusions, in turn, give rise to deeply polarized societies, which then perpetuate these tendencies.

At its core, social justice is premised on the principle that every human being matters and that every person has the right to equality and fundamental liberties, to security and dignity (Abraham, 2019). This is the essence of an egalitarian society. Although, in reality, equality has never been totally achieved. Today this basic postulate of democracy is under serious threat from a growing band of authoritarian and ethically compromised leaders and those who enable them. On his campaign trail for the US Presidency, Donald Trump violated the norms of civility and decency, indulged in blatant falsehoods and false equivalences, incited hatred, violence and distrust of minorities, including Blacks, Latinos, Muslims and immigrants. He exhibited misogyny and sexism, boasted on tape about sexual assault and yet he won enough of the Electoral College votes to gain the US Presidency.

His victory is attributed, on the one hand, to this pandering to the prejudice of white nationalists, and on the other hand, to a deep suspicion and dissatisfaction with the liberal elite and the existing establishment. The fears and realities of lost jobs, and absent opportunities, all have fed into the burgeoning xenophobia in America. The power of populist rhetoric to resonate with these fears and frustrations in a period of both perceived and real uncertainty should be of great concern. The power of the Presidency under Trump eroded key institutions in America, and in no way restrained Trump and his administration from initiating and executing extremely regressive and harmful policies. Limiting funding for women's reproductive health; providing massive tax breaks for the rich; preventing victims of domestic violence and gang violence from seeking asylum in the United States; and most recent and outrageous, the shocking, inhuman cruelty of separating illegal migrant parents from their children at the border.

Here is an example of power being used to inflict such careless suffering and misery on the vulnerable. We know from colonial histories in the United States, Canada and Australia, of the role the State

played in rationalizing and enacting the forced separation of indigenous parents from their children. We also know the horrific consequences of this, and the long road through the process of truth and
reconciliation. We are also witnessing the power that public pressure
can have in fighting against such violence, by challenging unjust laws,
policies and practices, and especially highlighting those that devastate
the lives of children, families and communities.

Donald Trump was admiring and wistful in expressing his views on
North Korea's dictator, Kim Jong-un. He publicly expressed appre-
ciation for other dictators across the world, such as Vladmir Putin,
Abdel Fatteh el-Sisi, and Rodrigo Duterte. Trump's public assertions
that he had the power to pardon himself, meaning that he considers
himself to be above the law, have triggered talk of an 'Imperial
Presidency' (Finkelstein and Skerker, 2018). His endless attacks on the
liberal media and his creation of 'fake news' also contributed to deep
and dangerous divides. The first half of 2018 saw his approval ratings
rise, and this was an important indication of the state of civil society.
It is one that we need to contemplate and to engage with skilfully.

As all of this and more has been going on, there has not been much
mention of what's been playing out in India in the past few years.
India today – the world's largest democracy – is a striking example of
an 'illiberal democracy', with a dangerous blend of power, violence
and injustice. The muted response of the Metropolitan States to the
creeping fascism and blatant human rights violations occurring in
India can be primarily linked to commerce. India is the largest
importer of armaments in the world. It is also a huge market for a
variety of imports from the developed countries. These countries that
dominate and define the international discourse on freedom and
human rights are strategically silent when it comes to policies or
practices in a country where they have significant economic interests.

To those who dispute the capacity of political leaders to remold
society in consonance with their worldview, the happenings in India in
the last few years are an ominous example of the use of power and
violence to undermine key democratic values. India has moved from
plurality to a deeply polarized, majoritarian State very quickly. India's
Prime Minister, Narendra Modi, came to power in 2014 with a
massive win through a free and fair election. Modi captured the public
imagination by promising a more decisive, powerful polity and an
equitable social order. But within months of taking office, it became

clear that he and his party planned to convert India into a homogenous, supremacist Hindu State – the Hindu Rashtra of Hindutva – where Hindus could claim to be the privileged community of India and where minorities, including Muslims and Christians, would live as second class citizens. There are many reports of lynching, gang rapes, vandalism and acts of religious desecration all with near impunity. A group of social activists who visited the sites of lynching and hate crimes across eight states of India were horrified to find that the police had lodged charges against the victims and their kin in these instances, whereas the actual perpetrators were treated leniently, their bail not opposed.

What is most disturbing is that it is not just India and the United States, but across the world we are seeing the complicity of State institutions in the persecution of marginalized groups. Even our justice systems, at times, succumb to the majoritarian pressures that victimize and oppress. Even when justice systems do hold strong, the populist rhetoric tenaciously erodes the legitimacy of institutions and processes that ensure justice.

One should not despair, however, for these atrocities and manipulations are stirring many who would otherwise remain complacent. In 2018 it takes an effort to keep one's head in the sand and remain oblivious. There is great energy mounting, rallying against these oppressions. Many people are coming together to build networks and connections, to challenge all abuses of power, not just the most recent but also those that have been present and systemic for a long time. Documenting harms, participating in protests, speaking at public rallies, working and reporting from conflict zones, providing facts and writing thought-provoking articles in the mainstream media are just some examples of what people are doing and what we can do. There are so many who work to highlight the ongoing violence and injustice, who critique and analyze the structures of power and seek social justice. Through active involvement in dissent and resistance, through research and action, sociologists can, and need to, reflect on the positive impact our perspectives can have in grappling with the problems of the world.

Populism and Human Rights

There is a direct nexus between the rise of right-wing populist nationalism across the world and the international disregard for human rights violations. A significant aspect of such populism is its insular and divisive character. There is a shift from globalism to narrow narcissistic nationalism. A sense that only one's own nation matters and that's where the lines must be drawn – America first, Hungary First, the Brexit syndrome. As society gets polarized between the narrow framing of citizenry and 'the Other', populist leaders play on the insecurities and fears of the people. They attribute all the blame for their perceived grievances on antagonistic forces, which are variously defined as anti-national, elitist, corrupt or terrorists. The populist constituency is portrayed as the long-suffering victims of domestic or foreign enemies, and the majority is seen as being more equal than the few, which then perpetuates their fear of becoming marginalized. In such a social milieu that scapegoats vulnerable sections of the population, the values of inclusivity, tolerance and respect lose their salience in both interpersonal and larger social interactions.

As a consequence of this rise in populism, there is now an unwillingness on the part of the world's democracies to intervene, even in areas where there have been heinous human rights violations. The world today watches as the most horrendous atrocities occur, in countries such as Syria, Yemen, South Sudan, Myanmar and Venezuela, to name just a few. The exercise of economic and political power, and the use of suffering as a tool for coercion and control, is increasingly justified by the perpetrators of these atrocities. Violence through forced displacement, starvation, rape, burning, chemical attacks and the spectrum of widespread injustices have not been met with an adequate global response. Perhaps facing precariousness at home, nations no longer feel it is their responsibility to intervene to ensure the safety of those considered 'foreigners', particularly the vulnerable and the violated.

The reluctance of the international community to effectively intervene even in the world's hotspots of genocidal conflict has resulted in widespread human suffering and death. One example of an unremitting assault on human rights is the ethnic cleansing offensive against Rohingya Muslims in Myanmar. Over the decades, the Rohingyas, an ethnic minority, have been victims of endemic discrimination and violence in a majority Buddhist nation. But in August 2017, following an attack by Rohingya insurgents using knives, and crude homemade bombs, in which 12 members of the security forces were killed, the full force of the State was mobilized in a targeted 'ethnic cleansing' strategy. This resulted in thousands of deaths, rampant rape and destruction of properties and the exodus of around 700,000 Rohingya Muslims, primarily to Bangladesh. While the scale of violence has since reduced, there seems little hope of the refugees returning to their homes, and as such they join the 68.5 million displaced and dispossessed people across the world (Casali, 2018).

The structural and relational aspects of power, violence and (in) justices, and the corresponding crises of displacement and dispossession are major areas for us sociologists to address.

Violence Against Women and Gender, and Intersectional Violence

Gender equality and justice are fundamental to democracies and indeed must be to all societies. They are necessary for national and global stability, well-being, prosperity and progress. We need to continue to address the position of women and girls in society's complex power matrix. There are numerous interconnections between gender, violence and the State. Feminists, activists and scholars have underscored how gender inequalities intersect with other inequalities such as race, class, citizenship, immigrant or minority status, unequal access to resources, exclusion from participation in decision-making – all of which tend to exacerbate violence against women (Abraham, 2002; Abraham et al., 2010; Abraham and Purkayastha, 2012; Abraham and Tastsoglou, 2016; Bhambra, 2007; Collins, 1990; Connell, 2011; Crenshaw, 1989, 1991; Garita, 2016; Mies, 1986; Minh-Ha, 1989; Mohanty, 2004; Purkayastha, 2012; Rege, 2006; Richie, 2012; Romero and Stewart, 1999; Tastsoglou and Dobrowolsky, 2006; Yuval-Davis and Werbner, 1999). States are intimately connected to the structural violence that perpetuates these gendered oppressions. As an integral part of the power apparatuses in society, through the expression and reproduction of gendered power relations, the State plays a key role in normalizing gender-based and intersectional violence, which then often becomes socially invisible.

International forums like Convention on the Elimination of All Forms of Discrimination Against Women (CEDAW) and international tribunals have provided valuable insights on State complicity in violence against women. The systematic targeting of women for sexual violence is also characteristic of modern-day warfare and conflict (Abraham and Tastsoglou, 2016). Despite the laws and women's movements that have tried to criminalize violence against women, there has not been adequate progress made in ensuring women's safety. We all need to worry that the UN Report of 2015 on the status of Violence against Women has pointed to its persistence 'at alarmingly high levels' in the majority of countries.

The persistence, prevalence and pervasiveness of gender-based and intersectional violence requires continued attention. Time and again, women continue to be denied control over their own bodies and are excluded from decision-making. Millions of women experience violence at the hands of an intimate partner. Violence is used as a political tool and as part of the process of displacement. Violence and discrimination against LGBTQ have also been a part of the propaganda used by States and populist leaders. When those who trivialize, demean and normalize violence against women are elected to the highest offices, we need to examine and illuminate both the subtle and overt causes, contexts and structures that support and recreate the objectification, harm and disregard for the voice and experience of all women. We must do this if we are to have any hope of ending such violence.

Although the term was first created by Tarana Burke in 1997, the recent attention gained through the 'MeToo' movement has been celebrated as a social revolution with millions of like-minded women from more than 85 countries bombarding cyberspace with the hashtag #MeToo, in solidarity with those who have suffered sexual assault and harassment. Although a critical watershed, this movement garnered international attention partly because of the high-profile individuals involved. When *The New York Times* first broke the story, there was surprise that even celebrities, who were powerful and perceived to have broken the glass ceiling, were vulnerable to sexual assault and violence like any ordinary woman. The movement offered a reflection of society's patriarchal structures, the forms of power and control, and its implications for the lives and life chances of survivors. It is a reminder of the formidable but important task we must continue to take on, to combat patriarchy, point out sexism and seek justice.

The transformations and contributions that women's movements have made to our lives, our institutions, and our understanding of the world have been substantial, and they should not be underestimated. Increasingly we can see an increase in awareness of gender inequalities around the world as well as the corresponding struggles that have then been taken up to rectify these issues. Various theoretical frameworks and academic perspectives have contributed to anti-violence and liberation movements in different parts of the world, and have advocated for more grassroots movements, inclusivity, and participatory activism and research. We have made a lot of progress in addressing gender issues, yet this progress is uneven and there is still a long way to go, as we see the persistence of gender inequality intersecting with other forms of discrimination.

The growth of right-wing populism and attempts to set back some hard-won struggles for greater equality and the increased polarization of civil society requires a response. Women and social justice movements, I believe, are attempting to respond by drawing attention to intersecting identities, making women's rights as human rights and human rights as women's rights – this then has implications for gender justice and social justice for all. One of the ways that the women's movement attempts to counter right-wing populism has been to challenge patriarchal structures and relations within societies. They challenge those structures of power and institutions that create and maintain other forms of inequality and oppression, which maintain and exacerbate oppression.

On 21 January 2017, under the auspices of the Women's March on Washington, millions of people took to the streets within the United States and across the globe to protest Trump's election. It was also one example indicative of the need to confront the persistence and prevalence of patriarchal power and its intersections with other axes of oppression, such as race/ethnicity, class, religion, sexual identity, citizenship and more. The Women's March on Washington mobilized and brought to the mainstream the notion of 'intersectionality' to address issues of reproductive rights, gender and intersectional violence, migrant rights, labour rights, citizenship, racial justice, freedom of speech, right to science, environmental justice and more.

The Power of the Media

Globalization, technology and social media have facilitated a more connected world, but it is increasingly coming at the cost of truth. This has been called a post-truth era, and it is an extreme crisis that democracies are facing, as the credibility of the media is both questionable and being challenged. No discussion on power, violence and justice today would be complete without factoring in the enormous influence of the knowledge and information that is disseminated, distorted or dismissed by the media. The insurgency of social media in particular, with its boundless capacity for good, bad and trite, creates a world of reaction and gullibility, where drama and division play out in seconds, often with little regard to human cost or reality. Social media has become the major instrument of political and cultural power, and its psychological and emotional effect is beginning to be looked at and understood. Today bigotry and falsehood can be manufactured and transmitted worldwide instantaneously.

In the 21st century, social media has, to some degree, replaced traditional forms of knowledge and information gathering. Social media has become the prime tool for dissemination of ideas, news and opinions. Social media also carries the danger of misinformation, fake news and false equivalences, but it is also an opportunity to challenge and contest lies, and to foster global connections and collaborations. The press has a particularly important role and responsibility to report accurately and with rigour. The fourth estate is vital to reporting on issues of power, violence and justice, thus preserving and strengthening the pillars of democracy.

Protest Movements

There are social scientists and political thinkers who believe that hope for the future lies in civil society. The difficulty is then the deep divides that polarize us all. In fact, the greatest threat is the burgeoning power of majoritarianism that is sweeping through many countries, using the momentum of polarization and fear. The mobilization of various fundamentalist majorities against ethnic and religious minorities, migrants, the LGBTQ and others is the new terrorism that affects societies around the globe.

Protest movements have been an important part in addressing these issues (Bringel and Domingues, 2015; Porta et al., 2006). Globally, people are mobilizing and challenging oppressive social, political and economic regimes. There are encouraging signs of a growing resistance to systems that have exacerbated inequality and injustice. Protest movements like those led by the 'Indignados' in Spain and Portugal, Indigenous movements around the world, the Black Lives Matter movement in the United States, the Farmers

Movement in India, the Landless People's Movement in South Africa, Time's Up, Say Her Name and #MeToo movements are all at the forefront of the resistance against entrenched exploitative systems. They offer us real hope for the future. What is required, however, is to understand how such movements can translate into structural and systemic change for a better world.

Sociology Matters

Sociologists around the world have a long history of research related to the concepts and meanings embedded in power, violence, and justice. I firmly believe that we have to find ways of combating the growing inequality and injustice, the endless cycle of wars and violence in our world. It is not only the atrocity of war and armed conflict that is the problem, it is also the violence that runs deep in our homes, neighbourhoods, schools, and work places. We are increasingly becoming cognizant of how inundated our world is by violence, around issues of gender, race, religion, class, and many others, even violence against the environment. The challenge for sociology is to find meaning and make sense of these complex and ever changing dynamics, through a greater understanding of structures and relationships.

In these troubled times, the ISA, as the global association of sociologists, has an important role to play. Founded in 1949 against the backdrop of World War II, the ISA mandate was not just to serve purely intellectual and cultural functions, but rather, it was 'for promoting democracy and for serving broad social purposes' (Platt, 1998, p. 3). Its aim has always been to both envisage and work towards a future in which the organization could grapple with the problems in our world and be proactive in pointing out new directions for progressive social change.

It is, in this same vein, towards the goal of increasing the public visibility, accessibility and effectiveness of sociology and sociological knowledge, globally, that ISA initiated the first comprehensive *Global Mapping of Sociologists for Social Inclusion* (GMSSI). Officially released in February 2018, we hope GMSSI will serve as a resource to help identify, connect, and enable global collaborations, and particularly support sociologists who encounter barriers, either economic or political, which impede their participation in global exchanges.

Sociology, together with other disciplines, can help contour a better place and understanding, but this means that we must share our research with the main stakeholders – the public. At this critical time, we sociologists must share our research, reflect and respond to issues, provide clear frameworks for analysis, counter distortions and mis-representations, and substantiate our perspectives on key concepts in terms that are accessible and straightforward. We must use our analysis to intervene and address injustice.

Of course, I am also aware that this can be personally perilous, with swift retribution for some. So many of us, however, have the advan-tage of freedom of expression as scholars and public intellectuals. We therefore also have the responsibility to mobilize through research and action for the greater good of society. We must make an impact, and challenge conventional impulses around how things have been done, because it is now time for change. For some of us this will mean climbing down from the tower of our academia and modifying our channels of communicating, clarifying our findings and insights in a manner that can be heard above the din and clamour.

We will have to harness the power of those very tools that are currently being used to distort and misinform. We will have to go beyond the traditional sources of knowledge dissemination and communicate our sociological perspectives using a wide array of avenues and technologies. In the next few days, let our sociological endeavours forge pathways towards a better present and a hopeful future. We have an intellectual, moral and social responsibility to generate and share knowledge and engage in collective action to build a better and more just world.

Acknowledgements

I want to take this opportunity to acknowledge my parents, especially my mom, Mary Abraham, who is my inspiration. My life partner and soul mate, Pradeep Singh, who has been an important and integral part of my life journey, and our son, Arun Abraham-Singh, who, along with his generation, continue to give me hope for the future. I am grateful to my larger family, many friends, colleagues, academics, activists and students who have supported and helped expand my worldview. Although I cannot individually name all of them here, I would like to acknowledge that they have been a vital, strong and sustaining community for me. I also want to especially thank Mathew John, Amanda Hester, Taisha Abraham, Chandra Sunkara, Annie Mathew, Amrita Mathew, Evangelia Tastsoglou, Vineeta Sinha, Herman Berliner, Michael Burawoy, Bandana Purkayastha, Sharryn Kasmir, Sally Hillsman, Emma Porio, Simon

Mapademing, Tina Uys, Chin Chun Yi, Celi Scalon and Elena Zdravomyslova. A special thanks to members of the ISA Executive Committee for 2014–18 and the ISA editors, and to Marta Soler, Editor of *International Sociology* that first published the presidential address in its journal. My deep gratitude to the National Associations, Regional Associations and various institutions in the fifty-three places that I visited during my tenure as ISA president for their warm hospitality and for sharing their sociological perspectives and realities on the ground. Thanks to the Research Committees especially RC32, Women in Society; to SAGE Publications, especially Robert Rojek; to Kevin O'Neill of The Conference Exchange and the Confex team for their work on conferences and GMSSI. A special thanks to Izabela Barlinksa and ISA Secretariat team for their invaluable support. I am very grateful to Hofstra University for the immense support that I have received over many years.

Author's Note

This presidential address was given on 15 July 2018 at the XIX International Sociological Association World Congress of Sociology, in Toronto, Canada. The Congress theme was 'Power, Violence and Justice: Reflections, Responses and Responsibilities' with a strong programme of over 1,200 sessions organized due to the immense efforts of the Research Committees, Working Groups, National and Regional Associations, ISA Congress Programme Committee and Local Organizing Committee. It was first published in *International Sociology*, 2019.

Funding

This research received no specific grant from any funding agency in the public, commercial or not-for-profit sectors.

Note

1   Bálványos Summer Open University and Student Camp, July 2014: https://freedomhouse.org/report/modern-authoritarianism-illiberal-democracies

References

Abdul Bari, M. (2018). *The crisis: A people facing extinction*. Leicester: Kube Publishing.

Abraham, T. (2002). *Women and the politics of violence*. New Delhi: Har-Anand Publications.

Abraham, M. (2019). *Sociology and social justice. Sage studies in international sociology*. London: SAGE.

Abraham, M., Ngan-ling Chow, E., Maratou-Alipranti, L., & Tastsoglou, E. (Eds.). (2010). *Contours of citizenship: Women, diversity and practices of citizenship*. Farnham: Ashgate.

Abraham, M., & Purkayastha, B. (2012). Making a difference: Linking research and action in practice, pedagogy, and policy for social justice. *Current Sociology*, *60*(2), 123–141.

Abraham, M., & Tastsoglou, E. (2016). Interrogating gender, violence, and the state in national and transnational contexts: Framing the issues. *Current Sociology Monograph, 64*(4), 517–553.

Arena, M. P. (2006). *The terrorist identity: Explaining the terrorist threat.* New York, NY: New York University Press.

Baxter, E. (2017). *Amina: A Kurdish woman's triumph through oppression and genocide.* Scotts Valley, CA: CreateSpace Independent Publishing Platform.

Bhambra, G. (2007). *Rethinking modernity: Postcolonialism and the sociological imagination.* New York, NY: Palgrave Macmillan.

Bringel, B. M., & Domingues, J. M. (Eds.). (2015). *Global modernity and social contestation.* London: SAGE.

Casali, C. (2018, October 12). *No way home for the Rohingya. France 24.*

Collins, P. H. (1990). *Black feminist thought.* New York, NY: Routledge.

Connell, R. (2011). Gender and social justice: Southern perspectives. *South African Review of Sociology, 42*(3), 103–115.

Crenshaw, K. (1989). Demarginalizing the intersection of race and sex: A black feminist critique of antidiscrimination doctrine, feminist theory and antiracist politics. *University of Chicago Legal Forum, 1989*(1), Article 8.

Crenshaw, K. (1991). Mapping the margins: Intersectionality, identity politics, and violence against women of color. *Stanford Law Review, 43*(6), 1241–1299.

Fanon, F. (1963). *The wretched of the Earth.* New York, NY: Grove Press.

Finkelstein, C., & Skerker M. (2018). *Sovereignty and the new executive authority.* Oxford: Oxford University Press.

Fukuyama, F. (1992). *The end of history and the last man.* New York, NY: The Free Press.

Garita, N. (2016). *Pueblos in movement: Feminist and indigenous perspectives.* Retrieved from https://isaconf.confex.com/isaconf/forum2016/webprogram/Paper83737.html

Mies, M. (1986). *Patriarchy and accumulation on a world scale.* London: Zed Books.

Minh-Ha, T. (1989). *Woman, native, other: Writing postcoloniality and feminism.* Washington, DC: Georgetown University Press.

Mohanty, C. T. (2004). *Feminism without borders: Decolonizing theory, practicing solidarity.* Durham, NC: Duke University Press.

Murray, D. (2017). *The strange death of Europe: Immigration, identity, Islam.* London: Bloomsbury.

Orwell, G. (1949). *1984.* London: Harvill Secker.

Platt, J. (1998). *History of ISA: 1948–1987.* Madrid: International Sociological Association 50th Anniversary Publication; ISA.

Porta, D., Andretta, M., Mosca, L., & Reiter, H. (2006). *Globalization from below: Transnational activists and protest networks.* Minneapolis, MN: University of Minnesota Press.

Prabhu, R. K., & Rao, U. R. (Eds.). (1967). *The mind of Mahatma Gandhi.* Ahmedabad: Navajivan Publishing House.

Purkayastha, B. (2012). Human rights, global visions. In A. Omara-Otunnu, S. Mobilia, & B. Purkayastha (Eds.), *Human rights: Voices of world's young activists.* Kolkata: Frontpage Publications, pp. 1–9.

Rege, S. (2006). *Writing caste/writing gender: Reading dalit women's testimonios*. New Delhi: Zubaan.

Richie, B. (2012). *Arrested justice: Black women, violence and America's prison nation*. New York, NY: New York University Press.

Romero, M., & Stewart, A. J. (1999). *Women's untold stories: Breaking silence, talking back, voicing complexity*. New York, NY: Routledge.

Tastsoglou, E., & Dobrowolsky, A. (2006). *Women, migration and citizenship: Making local, national and transnational connections*. Farnham: Ashgate.

Weber, M. (1946). *From Max Weber: Essays in sociology* (H. H. Gerth and C. Wright Mills, Trans. and Eds.). New York, NY: Oxford University Press.

Yuval-Davis, N., & Werbner, P. (1999). *Women, citizenship and difference*. London: Zed Books.

2

Indigenous Land Appropriation and Dispossession in Australia

In Search of Justice

Maggie Walter

Introduction

In June 2017 more than 250 Aboriginal and Torres Strait Islander delegates from around Australia met at Uluru, the traditional lands of the Yankunytjatjara and Pitjantjatjara people, to discuss Indigenous recognition. The result was an open letter to non-Indigenous Australia: *The Uluru Statement from the Heart*. The Statement is essentially the same missive sent by Aboriginal and Torres Strait Islander peoples since colonization began. It pronounces our unbroken possession of the Australian continent even as it articulates our ongoing sense of powerlessness at the embedded inequality of our peoples (Walter, 2018). Like the many communications that went before it, the Statement proposes a way forward, calling for a Makarrata Commission to oversee the development of a fair, just and truthful relationship between Indigenous and non-Indigenous peoples in Australia. The core of the Statement is the Indigenous claim to a sovereignty that has never been ceded, one that is positioned as a spiritual notion, whereby:

> The ancestral tie between the land, or 'mother nature' and the Aboriginal and Torres Strait Islander peoples who were born therefrom, remain attached thereto, and must one day return thither to be united with the ancestors. This link is the basis of the ownership of the soil, or better, of sovereignty. (Uluru Statement from the Heart, 2017)

Thus, the Uluru Statement rearticulates the core Indigenous ontology: that relationship to land is the foundation of both Indigenous social order and a lived embodied reality. As a Palawa (Tasmanian

Aboriginal woman) I reflect this ontology in this article through my use of the term 'we' and 'our' to refer to Aboriginal peoples, rather than the usual 'them' and 'their'.

Inextricably combined in how we be Aboriginal people, our relationship to Country anchors our lifeworld from dual intersubjectivities: as Indigenous peoples, where our everyday reality is shaped by our traditional and ongoing culture, belief systems, practices, identity and ways of experiencing/understanding the world and our place within it; and as dispossessed Indigenous peoples with our everyday realities shaped by our contested historical and ongoing relationship with the colonizing nation state. As the inheritors of over 60,000 years of deep history and cultural knowledges embedded in country; and a colonized minority, deeply socioeconomically, politically and culturally marginalized within our own lands, past and present, Indigenous land justice and societal justice, for us, are co-dependent.

Despite this sacred connection to the land, in 1770, the mere raising of the British flag by a British naval officer at Possession Island in North Queensland claimed the entire Australian continent for the British Crown. This legal trickery deemed the Aboriginal inhabitants as being without sovereignty or a system of land tenure (distinguishable to British eyes), making the country 'un-owned' (Terra Nullius). While officially overturned in 1993, the legacy of Terra Nullius continues across dual lifeworlds and intersubjectivities through continued marginalization and a continual denial of indigenous land rights and territory. This chapter uses community-level data to empirically link Aboriginal and Torres Strait Islander's socioeconomic and political disenfranchisement with historic and contemporary dispossessions. Framed within Australian sociocultural discursive realities, and inclusive of the *Uluru Statement from the Heart*, the strong relationship between land justice and societal justice is established.

The Task of Dispossession

Under Terra Nullius, Aboriginal peoples were made to legally disappear as the owners of our own country. A more tangible disappearance was also enacted through the processes of colonization, which included the violences of greed, deceit, duplicity, corruption, theft, contempt, massacres, tragedy, mistreatment, wilful indifference and rampant dehumanization. The accompanying belief in a naturally occurring racial hierarchy meant that the marginalization of the surviving Aboriginal peoples in the new colonial order, who were deemed inferior, homeless and disposable, was the expected outcome of an evolutionary process.

Over 200 years the concept of Terra Nullius was used to position the Aboriginal peoples as being inconsequential to the colonial project. This premise justified continual land grabs, the removal of populations. The Aboriginal populations that remained were frequently the subject of euphemistically named Aboriginal Protection Acts and Ordinances whereby nearly every aspect of Aboriginal peoples' existence was controlled (Chesterman and Galligan, 1999). The near genocide of my own *Palawa* people from *lutrawita*/Tasmania provides an illustration of this. In the early 1800s, small British colonial outposts were established at either end of the Tasmanian island, ostensibly to keep the prowling French at bay. Aboriginal resistance brought unrestrained violence and military decrees hurtling down upon my forebears, reducing the people of the land to a handful of scarred survivors in just a few short years. Kidnapped to work as slaves and concubines in the sealing trade, driven from traditional homelands and hunting grounds to allow the land to be bestowed upon arriving British settlers, the last survivors of such depredations were forcibly removed from Tasmania and imprisoned on the Bass Strait Islands (Ryan, 2012).

Under this assault fewer than 10 women survived to raise children who then had children of their own. My matriarch *woretemoeteyenner* was a survivor of sealer abduction and one of those 10 women. The death of *Truganina*, the Bruny chief's daughter, in 1876, was deemed by the colonizers as the death of the last of the Tasmanians. The people of *lutrawita* were relegated to a historical footnote; human obstacles to usurpation of country in the name of Empire. The existence of surviving descendants was officially denied until the mid-1980s (Ryan, 2012). Even today it is impolite in Tasmania to raise the topic of the campaign of orchestrated violence, deception, broken promises and captivity, which killed all our old people. The sparse official discourse refers to these events as 'tragic', as if they happened all by themselves, a sort of act of nature.

Such distancing allows Aboriginal people to be rendered as both invisible and non-legitimate in contemporary Tasmania. It allows the beneficiaries of colonization to exculpate themselves from its reality, while continuing to take and assert their ownership of the land. In this way, the narrative of colonial ownership remains dominant. In June 2018, the traditional name for the Hobart area *nipaluna* was gifted by the Aboriginal Community to the Hobart City Council as a dual name. This gift was received with open hostility by significant sections of the political class and the public. The following letter, published in the opinion section of the local newspaper, *The Mercury* (2018), sums up the arguments on why even discussing the reality that Tasmania has an Aboriginal past, or a contemporary reality, is deemed deeply problematic.

> Not only will Tasmanians, but all with connection or plans relating to our city, now have to remember, learn to spell and pronounce this new name. Why must we be subjected to constant reminders of the deeds of our forefathers? Has anyone stopped to realise most early Tasmanians arrived with the compliments of the UK and the continual talk of atrocities are not our fault and we are, I'm sure, all happy to live in harmony with the original occupants so such demands do more harm than good when it really isn't necessary. Let us all live in harmony please. (Name withheld, Austin's Ferry)

Even a surface-level textual analysis reveals the letter's discursive intent: to position the gift as the source of excessive difficulties, untenable divisiveness and non-Indigenous discomfort. Truth modalities are deployed to deem the name *nipaluna* (which is not actually mentioned) as being an unacceptable reminder of the colonizing past, with Aboriginal people labelled as unreasonable in their references to it. Aboriginal people are exhorted to stop 'making demands' (meaning: making references to colonization, including referring to Aboriginal names for the land that was taken). The letter's equating of social 'harmony' with Aboriginal silence around the practices of dispossession makes evident the writer's underlying disease. Claims that they are not responsible for past misdeeds lay bare their concerns about the ongoing legitimacy of the non-Aboriginal occupancy of the lands of the *Palawa* peoples.

Dispossession, Land and Social Injustice Are Structures, Not an Event

This chapter focuses on the Australian experience, but dispossession and its legacy of social injustice are the reality for most British colonized Indigenous peoples. The many similarities between colonizing histories and contemporary marginalization with its socioeconomic and political positioning can be found in places as far flung as Tasmania, Aotearoa, the United States, Canada and Hawaii. These similarities are evidence of the systemic nature of the practices and processes of dispossession. Colonized First World nations, such as Australia, are undergirded by a specific set of narratives, logics and epistemologies. Glenn (2015) argues, settler colonialism is a 'distinct transnational formation whose political and economic projects have shaped and continue to shape race relations' in nation states established through dispossession (54). Similarly, Wolfe (2006) describes invasion as being a structure, not an event.

The structure of invasion is founded upon the dispossession of land. In his 2012 book, *The Inconvenient Indian*, which details how Europeans, settling what would become the United States and Canada, took, and continue to take, the North American continent for themselves. King asks the elemental question, asked by colonized Indigenous peoples everywhere, 'What do Whites want?' His answer, and one that will resonate for Indigenous Australia, is: 'They want the land'. Preparing to write a book review, my margin notes remind me that I wrote in response to this statement: 'No they want everything.' After a moment's contemplation I realized that the land is everything. King (2012) was a step ahead, writing eloquently of the land as containing the 'languages, the stories, and the histories of a people. It provides water, air, shelter, and food. Land participates in the ceremonies. And the land is home' (King, 2012, p. 218).

The central problem is that the land is also everything to the colonizers. Land is power and wealth; it is a commodity that brings riches, prestige, status and influence. To translate land into these outcomes, the land must be owned, exclusively. Land is thus divided and sub-divided into ownable pieces, titles and deeds are drawn up, and fences erected. All these signal ownership and create boundaries, which together manifest power for those who covet the land in this way. This fundamental ontological disjuncture between land as home and land as wealth underpins the murderous terrain of settler colonialism and the contemporary frame of Indigenous/colonial race relations.

The Interdependency of Indigenous Land Justice and Societal Justice

In 1993, the High Court of Australia upheld the traditional land rights of the Merian people from the Murray Islands off North Queensland (the Mabo Case). This ruling officially overturned colonization's justifying doctrine of Terra Nullius, or 'empty land' (Chesterman and Galligan, 1999). Nevertheless, the legal fiction of Terra Nullius continues its dispossessing work over multiple levels. Non-Aboriginal claims to land and its use, for example, still consistently outrank Aboriginal claims. In a recent clash of values around Country, Aboriginal protesters had to camp to prevent further bulldozing of culturally significant trees ostensibly the 'way' of a new Victorian highway (BBC, 2020). More generally, the Native Title Legislation that was supposed to support Aboriginal and Torres Strait Islander peoples access our stolen lands is deliberately slow and cumbersome. High levels of proof are demanded of peoples ancestral connections to our traditional lands and cases take on average, 6 years to completion, with no guarantee of success. The first land claim lodged in 1994 was not resolved until 2010 (Creative Sprits, 2021).

Despite the protracted frontier wars and evidence of massacres and forcible displacements, the comfort myth that Australia was settled, not invaded, remains the dominant discourse of the Australian nation state's genesis. This myth, along with the lingering but unspoken discourse of a racial order, fuels the rationale that the cause of the intergenerational social, economic, political and cultural marginalization of Aboriginal and Torres Strait Islander peoples is about individual and collective deficits, not the legacy of colonization. The dismantling of the last of the 'Aboriginal Protection' laws and the passing of anti-race discrimination legislation during the 1980s are cited as proof of Australian egalitarianism and are used as justification for resistance to the granting of land rights for the Indigenous peoples of this country (Chesterman and Galligan, 1999).

For Aboriginal or Torres Straits Islander peoples a different narrative exists. In this narrative, the data tell the story of continuing inequality, an inequality founded upon a legacy of colonization. The narrative of *our* lives describes the structure of invasion. Evidence to support this includes national statistics on health and socioeconomic inequality, the wide-ranging resistance of white Australians to the concept of Indigenous rights, especially land rights, and the ongoing disregard that permeates the non-Indigenous public and political discourse around Indigenous issues (Watson, 2012). As an example, the 10th annual *Closing the Gap Report*, in 2018, the key Australian Aboriginal and Torres Strait Islander policy-setting framework, stated that no progress had been made in most of the six target areas, and in some cases the gap between Aboriginal and Torres Strait Islander outcomes and non-Indigenous outcomes had widened (Commonwealth of Australia, 2018).

The link between land injustice and social injustice can be demonstrated by looking at the colonial history and the contemporary societal positioning of Aboriginal people. This is best done at the level of place. Using place as the foundation makes clear that Australian Indigenous peoples are not a monolithic group. Rather there are more than 500 different First Nations, all with their own traditional country, culture and history, within the Australian nation state. Using data from the 2016 National Census of Population and Housing, the following section explores this link in three geographically diverse settings: Perth, the capital city of Western Australia; Dubbo, a large region in New South Wales; and Maningrida, a remote largely Indigenous community in the Northern Territory.

Land Justice and Societal Justice Across Three Sites

Dubbo, 400 km northwest of Sydney, is a major regional hub built on Wiradjuri country. The traditional owners are the Tubbagah people who were dispossessed during frontier expansion, occurring from the early 1800s until the 1850s. In 1898, the New South Wales Aborigines Protection Board opened the Talbragar Reserve. This continued under various legalisations and was not fully overturned until 1969. Aboriginal people in the Dubbo area were precluded from being sold alcohol, from voting at the state or federal level, had their wages paid to an official rather than to the worker and could have their children taken from their families by the Board (Hill, 2008). In the early 1970s the last residents of Talbragar were moved into public housing in town, creating the Gordon Estate in west Dubbo, which in turn was later dismantled with former residents spread throughout the town, mostly against their wishes (ABC, 2006). In 1995, the Tubbagah lodged a native title claim to the 16.2 ha Terramungamine Reserve – a traditional gathering area. This claim was immediately contested by local and state authorities who cited the presence of a historic stock trail in the area. An agreement was finally made in 2002, which protected Aboriginal burial grounds and reserves as being part of the preservation of Aboriginal cultural heritage; however, this agreement also guaranteed continuing public access to the riverside and the protection of the non-Indigenous historical sites (Native Title Tribunal, 2002).

Table 2.1 displays the comparative socioeconomic positioning of the Aboriginal and non-Aboriginal population of Dubbo. While the Aboriginal population makes up around 16% of the total, it is only one-third as likely to hold an undergraduate degree or above. Aboriginal people in Dubbo are also less likely to be working full time, nearly three times as likely to be unemployed, are less likely to own their own home and are more likely to be a single-parent household.

With similar experience, the Noongar people are the traditional owners of the land on which Perth, the capital city of Western Australia, sits. From 1829 onwards, the Noongar were progressively dispossessed via European settlement along the Swan River. In 1886 colonial guardianship was imposed with many Noongar forcibly relocated to settlements such as the Carrolup Native Settlement. The Western Australian *Aborigines Act of 1905* legislated that the Aboriginal population were excluded from voting, could be removed to a reserve, could be arrested without warrant for any breach of the Act and required Aboriginal women to seek written permission if they wanted to marry a non-Aboriginal person. The final remnants of the Act were not repealed until 1972.

Table 2.1 Demographic profile Dubbo: aboriginal and non-aboriginal populations, 2016

	2016	2016
Dubbo	**Aboriginal (%)**	**Non-aboriginal (%)**
Indigenous population	15.8	84.2
Hold bachelor degree or above	4.5	15.0
Working full time	50.9	62.6
Unemployed	15.9	5.9
Own home (outright and mortgage	40.0	60.1
Sole-parent household (children <15 years)	32.2	21.4

Source: Table derived from 2016 Census of Population and Housing QuickStats.

In 2006, a land claim made by the 218 Noongar Indigenous family groups was recognized by the Australian Federal Court. The Western Australian and Commonwealth Governments immediately appealed, however, with the original ruling overturned in 2008. Continuing claims and negotiations were undertaken in 2012, and the South West Aboriginal Land and Sea Council signed a heads-of-agreement with the State Government, which included large tracts of Crown land to be taken as full and final settlement of the area around Perth.

As shown in Table 2.2, the Aboriginal people of Perth are socio-economically disadvantaged. Now making up just a tiny portion of the total Perth population, these Aboriginal people remain less than a third as likely to hold an undergraduate degree or above, are less likely to be in full-time work and are 2.5 times as likely to be unemployed. Rates of Aboriginal single-parent households are substantially higher, and rates of Aboriginal home ownership are substantially lower.

Maningrida is in Central Arnhem Land in the Northern Territory, 500 km east of Darwin, with road access limited during the wet season from December to May. The area's traditional owners are the Kun-bidji people. *The Aboriginals Ordinance Act 1918* (NT), which was not repealed until 1971, gave the Northern Territory's Chief Protector of Aborigines control of Aboriginal children, the power to force Aboriginal people to live on designated reserves and the power to regulate employment. Aboriginal people were excluded from voting, could not marry without permission, or conduct business in their own right, and were paid very low wages (Chesterman and Galligan, 1997).

Table 2.2 Demographic profile Perth: Aboriginal and non-Aboriginal populations, 2016

Perth	2016 Aboriginal (%)	2016 Non-Aboriginal (%)
Indigenous population	1.6	98.4
Hold bachelor degree or above	6.8	22.9
Working full time	48.8	56.4
Unemployed	20.2	8.1
Own home (outright and mortgage	44.0	70.0
Sole-parent household	29.5	14.5

Source: Table derived from 2016 Census of Population and Housing QuickStats.

Being a former Aboriginal settlement, many clan groups other than the Kunbidji people also live in the town. Maningrida's current facilities include a community health centre, a school with grades from pre-school to Grade 12 (secondary education only became available in 2003), a Centrelink office, a police station, a Centre that provides basic services such as post, banking and community internet, business facilities, and a women's centre. Maningrida is also a 'dry' town restricted under the NT Liquor Act (West Arnhem Regional Council, 2022).

The Federal *Aboriginal Land Rights (Northern Territory) Act* 1976 granted inalienable freehold title to the Indigenous peoples of the area. This control was disrupted in 2007 when the town was included as one of the 73 Aboriginal towns covered by *The Northern Territory National Emergency Response Act 2007* (Cth of July 2007). Under this Act, the town's lease is compulsorily acquired by the Federal Government for 5 years. Other measures include broad-scale health checks for children, a review of the Aboriginal land permit system and the quarantining of Indigenous resident's welfare payments. Maningrida's traditional owners challenged the validity of the town lease takeover on the basis that the property was not acquired on just terms. This challenge was dismissed in 2009 (SMH, 2009).

Table 2.3 profiles the socioeconomic position of the Aboriginal population in Maningrida. Around 90% of the population are Aboriginal and the non-Aboriginal population are not long-term residents, but mostly made up of government and service provider personnel are non-Aboriginal, bought to the town for work. For this

Table 2.3 Demographic profile Maningrida: Aboriginal population 2016

	2016	2016
Maningrida	**Aboriginal (%)**	**Non-Aboriginal (%)**
Indigenous population	89.2	10.8
Hold Bachelor degree or above	0.8	n.a
Working full time	38.1	n.a
Unemployed	34.2	n.a
Own home (outright and mortgage	1.0	n.a
Sole-parent household	17.2	n.a

Source: Table derived from 2016 Census of Population and Housing QuickStats.

reason, their socioeconomic status is not included in the Table. As shown, only a very few Aboriginal residents have an undergraduate degree, and these people may also be from outside the area. The rate of full-time employment is almost the same at the rate of unemployment, with almost no home ownership and relatively high rates of single-parent households.

Linking Land Justice and Social Justice

These three case studies are from very different areas in Australia. They also have different colonizing histories. Yet despite their geographic diversity, despite the very different conditions in each place, where these very different Aboriginal peoples are living their lives, and despite their different colonial pasts, there are strong similarities on display both in the process of dispossession, now and then, and in the examples of contemporary social injustice. Historically, although each Aboriginal people were dispossessed at different times, in different colonies of Australia, the pattern of that dispossession is remarkably consistent. First, the colonial forces arrive, usually with 'settlers' ready to take up the vacated (or not vacated) land, and colonial violence ensues. Once resistance has been quashed militarily, those remaining are contained and separated from the non-Indigenous population through constraining legislations. For all three populations, despite the narrative of Australian egalitarianism, the last vestiges of these racially oppressive legislations remained in place well into the latter half of the 20th century.

Each traditional owner group has also endeavoured to reclaim some of the stolen lands in recent times. While the outcomes of those claims have varied, what is consistent is the immediate resistance, usually through the courts or the political mechanisms, of the Australian nation state. Thus, the original socioeconomic marginalization, alongside the current marginalization, are linked to the original and continuing dispossession of land. Socioeconomic and political marginalization can be seen here as being an inherent aspect of dispossession, keeping those dispossessed powerless and contained. It is no coincidence that the socioeconomic positioning of these populations is now remarkably similar, despite the very different social and geographical spaces where they live their lives. All three populations experience high levels of socioeconomic disadvantage, and this disadvantage has been instituted alongside dispossession, with little evidence of improvement in recent years. It is therefore impossible to disentangle our lifeworld intersubjectivity as the Indigenous peoples of the land with our intersubjectivity as dispossessed colonial subjects.

The concluding interpretation is that for dispossessed peoples, escaping the confines of intergenerational socioeconomic disadvantage includes addressing land rights. That the nation state of Australia thinks socioeconomic and health disparities can be addressed in isolation of land justice is indicative of a national cognitive dissonance. Yet there is continuing and dedicated effort by the nation state to decouple the dispossession of Australia's First Nations people and the embedded inequalities that frame those peoples' lives. The now admitted failure of 'Close the Gap' policies over the last 10 years (Commonwealth of Australia, 2018) reinforces this point: societal justice and land justice are inextricably linked. As long as one is denied, there is little likelihood of progress on the other.

This brings the discussion back to the *Uluru Statement from the Heart* which after referring to the dire social circumstances of Aboriginal and Torres Strait Islander peoples states:

> These dimensions of our crisis tell plainly the structural nature of our problem. *This the torment of our powerlessness.*

> We seek constitutional reforms to empower our people and to take *a rightful place* in our own country ... we call for the establishment of a First Nations Voice enshrined in the Constitution ... We see a Makarrata Commission to supervise a process of agreement-making between governments and First Nations and truth-telling about our history (italics in original).

Conclusion

Terra Nullius was formally overturned in 1993, however, the quest for Indigenous re-possession has been slow and resisted at every turn. The Australian nation state continues to invalidate or resist with vigour Aboriginal claims or control of lands. Within this terrain of continued dispossession, it is not coincidental that Indigenous people in Australia remain deeply socioeconomically, political and culturally marginalized within our own land. As shown, Aboriginal and Torres

Strait Islander's socioeconomic and political disenfranchisement can be empirically linked to historic and contemporary dispossessions. The *Uluru Statement from the Heart* makes manifest the strong relationship between 'country' and well-being. Past and present, Indigenous land justice and societal justice are co-dependent.

How could land and social justice be moved from aspiration to reality? Treaty and Voice, as advocated by the *Uluru Statement from the Heart* are prerequisites. But there can be no treaty without truth: on the forceful colonization and dispossession of the people of the land origins of the Australian nation state; on how that dispossession was achieved; and on the impact, then and now, of the injustices perpetrated to ensure ongoing dispossession. The *Uluru Statement* also call for truth-telling, but truth-telling is difficult, especially where silence and silencing have been effective and widely used tools of the colonial project.

Yet truth-telling is necessary, achievable and now underway in Australia. A truth-telling commission is a formal body tasked with discovering and revealing past wrongdoings in the hope of resolving conflict and rebuilding new relationships between those who were wronged and perpetrators. In 2021, the Yoo-rrook Justice Commission was tasked with establishing, via hearing the truth of Victorian First Peoples, a formal record of the experience of past and present systemic injustices from colonization to the present. Aboriginal led, with four of its five Commissioners being Indigenous, Yoo-rrook is the first such truth-telling inquiry in Australia. Critically, the Commission has broad powers to hold public hearings, compel evidence and make recommendations as to what should change (Bourke et al., 2021). Due to deliver its final report in June 2024, this Commission and those that follow it in other states may be the precursor needed to underpin, finally, a reckoning on land justice and societal justice in Australia.

References

ABC. (2006). The world today – NSW Govt to move Gordon Estate population. *ABC Online*. Retrieved 10 September 2007, from https://www.abc.net.au/worldtoday/content/2006/s1637124.htm

BBC. (2020). *Djab Wurrung tree: Anger over sacred Aboriginal tree bulldozed for highway*. Retrieved from https://www.bbc.com/news/world-australia-54700074#

Bourke, E., Atkinson, W., Hunter, S., Walter, M., & Bell, K. (2021, November 5). From dispossession to massacres, the Yoo-rrook Justice Commission sets a new standard for truth-telling. *The Conversation*. Retrieved from https://theconversation.com/from-dispossession-to-massacres-the-yoo-rrook-justice-commission-sets-a-new-standard-for-truth-telling-170632

Chesterman, J., & Galligan, B. (1999). *Citizens without rights, Aborigines and Australian citizenship*. Cambridge: Cambridge University Press.

Commonwealth of Australia. (2018). *Closing the gap – Prime Minister's report 2018*. Department of the Prime Minister and Cabinet. Retrieved from https://closingthegap.pmc.gov.au/sites/default/files/ctg-report-2018.pdf

Creative Spirits. (2021). *Native title issues and problems*. Retrieved from https://www.creativespirits.info/aboriginalculture/land/native-title-issues-problems

Glenn, E. N. (2015). Settler colonialism as structure: A framework for comparative ethnicity US race and gender formation. *Sociology of Race and Ethnicity, 1*(1), 54–74.

Uncle John Hill. (2008, April). *Personal communication*.

King, T. (2012). *The inconvenient Indian*. Minneapolis MN: University of Minnesota Press.

Native Title Tribunal. (2002, December 06). *Media release: Strong commitment the key to Terramungamine agreement*. Retrieved 5 September 2007, from http://www.nntt.gov.au/media/1039146342_532.html

Ryan, L. (2012). *Tasmanian aborigines: A history since 1803*. Sydney, NSW: Allen & Unwin.

SMH. (2009, February 2). Protesters storm High Court as case dismissed. *The Sydney Morning Herald*. Retrieved from https://www.smh.com.au/news/national/protesters-storm-high-court-as-case-dismissed/2009/02/02/1233423124774.html

The Mercury. (2018). *Subjected to reminders*. Monday June 4 2018. (Your Voice, Letters to the Editor).

Uluru Statement from the Heart. (2017). Retrieved 1 May 2018, from https://www.referendumcouncil.org.au/sites/default/files/2017-05/Uluru_Statement_From_The_Heart_0.PDF

Walter, M. (2018). The voice of Indigenous data: Beyond the markers of disadvantage. *First Things First - Griffith Review*, 60.

Watson, I. (2012). *The future is our past: We once were sovereign and we still are*. Retrieved from http://www.austlii.edu.au/au/journals/IndigLawB/2012/43.pdf

West Arnhem Regional Council. (2022). *Maningrida*. Retrieved from https://www.westarnhem.nt.gov.au/our-communities/maningrida

Wolfe, P. (2006, December). Settler colonialism and the elimination of the native, *Journal of Genocide Research, 8*(4), 387–409.

3

Surveilling Blackness in the 21st Century USA

Modernity/Coloniality, Objectivity and Contemporary Forms of Injustice

Natalie P. Byfield

First of all, modernity is not an ontological unfolding of history but the hegemonic *narrative* of Western Civilization. Walter Mignolo (2011) (Emphasis mine)

Background

Every feature of our very existence today has been rendered into digital data. For each of us participating in and/or carrying out our lives on the digital platforms of the socioeconomic and political arenas of all modern Western states, a 'data doppelganger'[1] or data double of our physical selves exists on databases that are maintained by state agencies, like the tax collection agencies or the local transit authorities that use metro passes with magnetic strips that track our usage. One can also expect that if they have been in trouble with the law the criminal justice system will or may also maintains a data doppelganger or data double of you. The existence of our digital doubles does not end there. Our data doppelganger exists in databases of public–private partnerships. An example is the Port Authority of New York and New Jersey that manages the bridges and tunnels and previously used an electronic toll collection pass and now uses licence plate readers that record your passage and bills your toll account. Our data doppelganger also exists in databases of private entities such as cell phone companies like Verizon and Telus and social media companies like Facebook and Twitter that record our associations, and retailers like supermarket chains and Amazon that electronically document our preferences through our purchases.

The ascendance of data or information in our world corresponded with the development of 'information capitalism'[2] that occurred in the major Western states because of the technological advancements that created *digital* platforms. These major Western states are also the racial states[3] that rose to prominence as colonial states under another system of capitalism called mercantilism. The mechanisms for their current dominance, which some have referred to as 'coloniality of power' (Quijano, 2007) remains. Today's digital platforms allow these states to continue their global dominance. The platforms represent a revolution in communication technologies because they eliminated the time delay in communications and because the various types of communication (such as still and moving images, text and audio) could be rendered as digital data, all this allowed for convergence onto one platform 'so that the same transmission infrastructure can be used for different services' (Kundnani, 1999). These technological developments led to the rise of information capitalism and allowed data to become one of the most important commodities in the private and public sectors. The platforms underpinning the data doubles of everyone just described above is used and, in many instances, can and will be controlled by the state. With such developments, the state has since found itself in many conflicts with private enterprise over the collection, use and control of people's personal data, particularly in the area of security.[4]

Rise of the Carceral State Under Information Capitalism

As these technological developments in our information society have been underway over the last 40–50 years, there have been another set of societal conversions taking place. Over the last 50 plus years, a transformation in the institutions that by design are supposed to foster social control either through socialization and/or forced conformity has taken place in the United States (and the United Kingdom as well as other major Western societies). Many of the changes in the US institutions that force conformity occurred through the passage of major 'crime-fighting' legislations in consecutive so-called liberal and so-called conservative administrations[5] beginning with the Johnson Administration in 1965 and continuing through to today. These legislations, some of which were assigned titles like the 'War on Crime' and the 'War on Drugs', were supposedly in response to moral panics around drugs, gangs and guns. Many carceral state scholars, e.g. Alexander (2010) view these legislative developments as a 'backlash' against the increasing racial democratization taking place in the United States in the form of the civil rights and other movements for equity. The new laws institutionalized a new attitude about crime, criminality and criminalization under a political agenda referred to as 'law and order'.

Under the law and order agenda, the federal government accomplished a number of very significant changes in the criminal justice system. It financed a great expansion of the federal prison system, instituted mandatory minimum prison sentences, increased the length of sentences, added a plethora of new laws, drastically expanded and/or created new federal bureaucratic regimes to help local communities address a perceived crime problem[6] – which translated into increased local surveillance from the federal level, and it enhanced the federal government's financial support of local police. These transformations have created what many scholars refer to as the carceral state (Alexander, 2010; Camp and Heatherton, 2016; Gottschalk, 2016; Hinton, 2016; Murakawa, 2014; Thompson, 2016).

The judiciary branches of government also played a very significant role in this transformation of the systems of social control through rulings from the bench that greatly expanded local police powers in the communities they are supposed to serve. One of the most significant judicial decisions made by the US Supreme Court during this era is the court's support of the police in the landmark case of *Terry v. Ohio* in which the Court ruled that police do not violate people's constitutional rights against unlawful searches and seizures when they stop and search people on the street in an 'investigatory' manner.

Many carceral state scholars use a 'theory of the backlash' against racial democratization to explain the rise of the carceral state (Forman, 2017). Much of the critique of the political economy made by these scholars focusses on the loss of manufacturing section, a transition to a 'service economy' while eliding the concomitant developments in communication and information technologies and the ascendance of data that accompanied the build-up of the carceral state. This article is most concerned with the contemporaneous developments in these technologies undergirding the so-called Western liberal democracies and the application of these technologies to the new culture of control that emerged in those societies. Parallelling how European expansion into the 'New World' centralized racism and racialization in the development of capitalism, this article centres racism and racialization in its analysis and asks how these phenomena are being transformed under information capitalism. My hope for this work is that by centring racism and racialization in the analysis new nuanced understandings of the evolution of racial states will emerge that can contribute to studies of how racism and racialization operate when information capitalism serves as the foundation of this society and with its technologies created a surveillance society that now maintains the carceral state.

The emergence of a carceral state atop the foundation of information capitalism should encourage scholars and/or those concerned with social justice to assess surveillance practices for the following: (1) the collection, management and mining of these data by policing agencies for social control, specifically racialized social control; (2) the ease with which police are able to bring together data from disparate and discrete sources in our digital lives; (3) the significance of those changes to this latest era of policing that engages strategies like predictive policing and (4) the scientific methodologies and processes underlying those developments and their use in the continued development of policing as a form of racism and repression.[7] The racialized surveillance developed in these liberal democracies/racial states since modernity have been deployed with a 'white gaze' (Browne, 2015).[8] How is that 'white gaze' deployed in the contemporary racial and racial/creole states with the use of digital technologies in information society? How is the 'white gaze' used to manage risk related to behaviours and/or groups of people defined as deviant and/or as a threat. Social theorist, David Garland (2002) argues that the transformation of the criminal justice systems in the United States – for example, the legislations and judicial verdicts that built the carceral state, the politicization of crime policy, the seeming bankruptcy of criminological thought, among other things – the 'culture of control' 'permeate(s) the entire society'. He contends that this is unlike anything ever experienced before (Garland, 2002). Likewise, the ascendance of data and the digital platforms that advance the use of data is unlike anything we have seen before.

Surveillance, Dataveillance and Policing of Blacks in New York City

The centring of racism and racialization in the analysis of the contemporaneous changes in the technologies undergirding Western liberal democracies and the application of those technologies to the new culture of control that emerged in those societies encourages a focus on policing and how police agencies conduct themselves. Policing has historically in a settler state like the United States been one of the first activities to control racial boundaries. The deployment of the policing practice 'stop and frisk' in Black and other racial-minority neighbourhoods in cities in the United States as well as metropolitan areas in other Western nations has existed for the better part of the last 100-plus years.[9] In addition to the United States, police departments in nations with majority white populations like England, Scotland, Wales, Australia, France, Germany and Canada include 'stop and search', as some other nations and/or cities call it, in their crime-fighting arsenals. As in the United States, these practices are directed disproportionately at racial and ethnic minorities in most of those nations. The police departments that use this practice make the argument that stop and frisk represents one of the most effective crime-control measures and that it is beneficial because it provides protection to the people of colour living in these often-hyper-policed communities.

The recent history of the surveillance of Blacks in New York City, where like most urban areas in Western liberal democracies racial profiling is a common and historical concern, reveals the extensive levels at which the state collects biological/descriptive data of African American and Latino individuals not associated with crime. These are data that can be used for the tracking of individuals as well as their associations with other people and places. The recent history of surveillance in New York City also reveals how the historical divisions between the rank-and-file police officers and police management are exploited by management to facilitate the surveillance of Blacks and Latinos in New York City.

The American Civil Liberties Union[10] (ACLU) defines racial profiling as the 'discriminatory practice by law enforcement officials of targeting individuals for suspicion of crime based on the individual's race, ethnicity, religion or national origin'.[11] Using Stop and Frisk, allows police to stop or detain a person if they have 'reasonable suspicion' that an individual committed, is committing or *may* commit a crime.[12] This is a lesser legal standard than 'probable cause', which is required by the Fourth Amendment of the US constitution and which would require that police were fairly certain a crime was committed.

Thus, the Terry case, which was decided by the US Supreme Court during the earlier period in the construction of the carceral state, served as a landmark case because it broadened the discretionary powers of police, particularly the rank and file.

Although there is a long history of more than 100 years of the indiscriminate stopping of Blacks and other people of colour by the New York Police Department (NYPD), contemporarily this type of practice began being deployed more formally as the Stop, Question and Frisk programme under the mayoral administration of Rudolph Giuliani, which ran from January 1994 to December 2001. His administration oversaw a continuation of the decline in crime rates[13] that began under the previous mayoralty of David Dinkins, the first African American elected mayor of the city. Despite the decline in crime rates from the beginning of the Giuliani administration, the police department began using the now-famous Broken Windows theory of policing, which is based on the premise that the heavy policing of minor infractions prohibits more serious violations. Stop and Frisk operated as one of the important practical applications of the Broken Windows theory; and CompStat, a computerized mapping system for tracking crime, supported it by recording and analyzing data collected primarily from the policing activities of the rank and file cops. With the availability of CompStat, the NYPD began tracking police stops and documenting various details about the individuals stopped as a way, according to department claims, of making the policing by rank-and-file officers more efficient and legal.

David Lyon (1994) argues that all modern states and capitalist organizations engage in surveillance, particularly in the development of cities, as a necessary function for their advancement. They developed bureaucratic arms with 'administrators (that) collected and recorded details' about people and all components of the society or business 'in order to enhance their efficiency' (Lyon, 1994, p. 27). However, increasing the efficiency in the policing of communities of colour by placing greater mechanisms of surveillance on the rank-and-file police translated into greater degrees of surveillance of communities of colour that are typically the targets of police surveillance. This drive towards efficiency also serves as an avenue for police management to use a so-called science to legitimize data gathered from the broad discretionary powers the police have been granted.

During the Giuliani Administration in 1996, the police recorded 140 stops by the Street Crime Unit (SCU) by way of a form called UF-250; the next year, that unit alone submitted 18,000 UF-250s due to pressure from police leadership to use the form to document all stops. See Image 3.1 on the next page.[14]

Data collected on New Yorkers stopped by police regardless of their guilt or innocence of a crime include the following: name, age, gender, physical description (like tattoos and birthmarks), race and other information of the person 'stopped'. The UF-250 form also calls for a reporting of the time, place and precinct where the 'stop' occurred, and the physical location of the stop. The form also calls for the 'suspected charge' which gave rise to the stop. Some of the questionable factors which provide an officer with enough reasonable suspicion to detain someone include the following: inappropriate attire (creating the suspicion of a possibly hidden weapon), furtive movements and the suspicious bulge/object. Other questionable circumstances or factors the officer could consider include the following: the person's proximity to crime location, whether or not the person is associating with a person known for their criminal activity, whether or not an area has high incidence of report offence under investigation, and the time of day, day of week, season corresponding to reports of criminal activity. The officers clearly have broad discretion. Under the criteria of the UF-250, just about anyone can be a suspect.

Since the SCU were responsible for approximately 10% of the city's stops and frisks,[15] we can extrapolate that there were about 1,400 in 1996 and 180,000 stops the following year. This steep rise reflects the desire among management to collect data on the people living in the communities they target for hyper-policing. The range in outcomes from such police–civilian interactions initiated with stop-and-frisk/ racial profiling are broad. They vary from release from custody (albeit with the diminishment of police legitimacy within the public, in particular among racial minorities) to verbal and physical abuse from police brutality, to sexual assault, to the death of the stopped individual. By the end of the 20th century, these aggressive surveillance tactics spawned another set of outcry from Black and Latino communities because this surveillance strategy led to more police killings of unarmed Blacks and precipitated widespread protests. There were a number of well-publicized killings including the 4 February 1999 killing of 23-year-old Amadou Diallo by two police officers from the

(COMPLETE ALL CAPTIONS)

STOP, QUESTION AND FRISK REPORT WORKSHEET
PD344-151A (Rev. 11-02)

Pct.Serial No.

Date | Pct. Of Occ.

Time Of Stop | Period Of Observation Prior To Stop | Radio Run/Sprint #

Address/Intersection Or Cross Streets Of Stop

☐ Inside ☐ Transit
☐ Outside ☐ Housing

Type Of Location Describe:

Specify Which Felony/P.L. Misdemeanor Suspected | Duration Of Stop

What Were Circumstances Which Led To Stop?
(MUST CHECK AT LEAST ONE BOX)

☐ Carrying Objects In Plain View Used In Commission Of Crime e.g., Slim Jim/Pry Bar, etc.
☐ Fits Description.
☐ Actions Indicative Of "Casing" Victim Or Location
☐ Actions Indicative of Acting As A Lookout.
☐ Suspicious Bulge/Object (Describe)
☐ Other Reasonable Suspicion Of Criminal Activity (Specify)

☐ Actions Indicative Of Engaging In Drug Transaction.
☐ Furtive Movements.
☐ Actions Indicative Of Engaging In Violent Crimes.
☐ Wearing Clothes/Disguises Commonly Used In Commission Of Crime.

Name Of Person Stopped | Nickname/ Street Name | Date Of Birth

Address | Apt. No. | Tel. No.

Identification: ☐ Verbal ☐ Photo I.D. ☐ Refused
☐ Other (Specify) _____

Sex:☐ Male Race: ☐ White ☐ Black ☐ White Hispanic ☐ Black Hispanic
☐ Female ☐ Asian/Pacific Islander ☐ American Indian/Alaskan Native

Age | Height | Weight | Hair | Eyes | Build

Other (Scars, Tattoos, Etc.)

Did Officer Explain Reason For Stop ☐ Yes ☐ No | If No, Explain:

Were Other Persons Stopped/ Questioned/Frisked? ☐ Yes ☐ No | If Yes, List Pct. Serial Nos.

If Physical Force Was Used, Indicate Type:
☐ Hands On Suspect
☐ Suspect On Ground
☐ Pointing Firearm At Suspect
☐ Handcuffing Suspect
☐ Suspect Against Wall/Car

☐ Drawing Firearm
☐ Baton
☐ Pepper Spray
☐ Other (Describe)

Was Suspect Arrested? ☐ Yes ☐ No | Offense | Arrest No.

Was Summons Issued? ☐ Yes ☐ No | Offense | Summons No.

Officer In Uniform? ☐ Yes ☐ No | If No, How Identified? ☐ Shield ☐ I.D. Card ☐ Verbal

Image 3.1 UF-250 form used in terry stops

Was Person Frisked? ☐ Yes ☐ No **IF YES, MUST CHECK AT LEAST ONE BOX**

☐ Inappropriate Attire – Possibly Concealing Weapon
☐ Verbal Threats Of Violence By Suspect
☐ Knowledge Of Suspects Prior Criminal Violent Behavior/Use Of Force/Use Weapon
☐ Other Reasonable Suspicion of Weapons (Specify)
☐ Furtive Movements
☐ Actions Indicative Of Engaging In Violent Crimes
☐ Refusal To Comply With Officer's Direction(s)
☐ Leading To Reasonable Fear For Safety
☐ Violent Crime Suspected
☐ Suspicious Bulge/Object (Describe)

Was Person Searched? ☐ Yes ☐ No **IF YES, MUST CHECK AT LEAST ONE BOX** ☐ Hard Object ☐ Admission Of Weapons Possession
☐ Outline Of Weapon ☐ Other Reasonable Suspicion of Weapons (Specify)

Was Weapon Found? ☐ Yes ☐ No If Yes, Describe: ☐ Pistol/Revolver ☐ Rifle/Shotgun ☐ Assault Weapon ☐ Knife/Cutting Instrument
☐ Machine Gun ☐ Other (Describe)

Was other Contraband Found? ☐ Yes ☐ No If Yes, Describe Contraband And Location
Demeanor Of Person After Being Stopped
Remarks Made By Person Stopped

Additional Circumstances/Factors: (Check All That Apply)

☐ Report From Victim/Witness
☐ Area Has High Incidence Of Reported Offense Of Type Under Investigation
☐ Time Of Day, Of Week, Season Corresponding To Reports Of Criminal Activity
☐ Suspect Is Associating With Persons Known For Their Criminal Activity
☐ Proximity To Crime Location
☐ Other (Describe)
☐ Evasive, False Or Inconsistent Response To Officer's Questions
☐ Changing Direction At Sight Of Officer/Flight
☐ Ongoing Investigations, e.g., Robbery Pattern
☐ Sights And Sounds Of Criminal Activity, e.g., Bloodstains, Ringing Alarms

Pct. Serial No. _____ Additional Reports Prepared: Complaint Rpt.No._____ Juvenile Rpt. No._____ Aided Rpt. No._____ Other Rpt. (Specify)_____

REPORTED BY: Rank, Name (Last, First, M.I)   REVIEWED BY: Rank, Name (Last, First, M.I)
Print_____ Tax#_____   Print_____ Tax#_____
Signature_____ Command_____   Signature_____ Command_____

Image 3.1 UF–250 form used in terry stops *(Continued).*

Street Crime Unit, who fired 41 shots at Diallo claiming they mistook the Guinean immigrant's wallet for a gun. The officers were acquitted by a jury in Albany, New York.

Giuliani left office at the end of 2001. Statistics indicated that crime rates continued to decline. Yet during the next Mayoral Administration of Michael Bloomberg in New York City, which ran from 1 January 2002 to 31 December 2013, the NYPD led by Commission Raymond Kelly engaged in close to five million police stops of New Yorkers. As part of its Stop-and-Frisk programme under Bloomberg, the NYPD stopped 5,081,689 people walking in the city between the years 2003 and 2013 (see Image 3.2 below). The overwhelming majority of the people stopped were African American males and Latinos. The overwhelming majority of the people stopped – 88 percent – were innocent of any crime. With crime on the decline, this continuation of the aggressive use of Stop and Frisk for the policing of Black and Latino or minority communities appeared to be for the purpose of gathering and analyzing data about the members of the community. In the first study of stop and frisk, New York State Attorney General Elliott Spitzer (1999) noted the following:

From this perspective, the Terry decision was born of and perpetuated deep conflicts in values. On the one hand, the Terry Court clearly

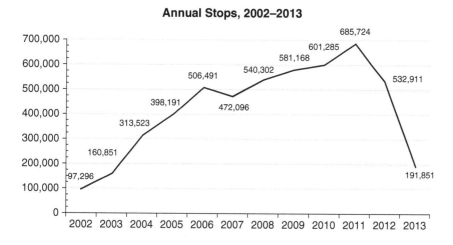

Image 3.2 Illustration of stops under Bloomberg administration
Source: Dunn et al., New York Civil Liberties Union (2014).

recognized the importance of "stop & frisk" to the tasks of crime detection and prevention and the goal of officer safety.[25] From the point of view of law enforcement, a "stop & frisk" encounter that yields a lawful arrest or *useful information*, or deters a would-be violent criminal from going forward is a success. (p. 21)[16]

Given our digitized platform and our economic foundation in information capitalism, this 'useful information' and the desire to collect it should be an urgent concern.

This type of racial discrimination has historically been a deep concern in Black communities across the United States The unwarranted targeting has been at the root of many police killings of Blacks in New York City and across this nation. It has also been the cause of violent and non-violent protests in our communities. There is a strong historical record going back over a century of NYPD violence against Blacks and other racial minorities. Over the years, various individuals and groups, both community leaders and elected officials, have advocated for justice on behalf of the Black communities in the city with no consistent relief occurring from this type of state repression, and in the context of information capitalism there is little information about how their data (which excluded names and addresses after new state law enacted in 2010) are being used and have been used in future policing.

Police, Racialization and the Social Sciences

During the Bloomberg Administration, three law suits filed against the NYPD for the unconstitutional use of Stop and Frisk were collapsed into one case, *Floyd v. The City of New York* (Floyd, 2013), and the New York Civil Liberties Union and the Center for Constitutional Rights argued on behalf of the plaintiffs. On 12 August 2013, federal Judge Shira Sheindlin ruled in favour of the plaintiffs arguing that the police acted with 'indifference' to the constitutional rights of Black and Latino residents.

Plaintiffs do not seek to end the use of stop and frisk. Rather, they argue that it must be reformed to comply with constitutional limits. Two such limits are paramount here: first, that all stops be based on "reasonable suspicion" as defined by the Supreme Court of the United States; and second, that stops be ... conducted in a racially neutral manner. (p. 2)

Many mainstream scholars of policing tend to frame stop-and-frisk analysis through the narrow lens of the activity of a racially unbiased state agency conducting its routinized affairs that happen to be crime fighting, public safety, public service and order maintenance. Through this lens, at best they assume a racially neutral posture can exist. At worst, they contend that the racial profiling and the outcomes that this practice precipitates are viewed as a necessary evil. Flacks (2018) notes the state's response:

> (M)inority victimization by the police tends to be framed, particularly—as might be expected—by organs of the state, as an accidental or necessary consequence of effective police tactics, or a failure of governance, rather than as a potentially central characteristic of the racial state. (p. 5)

Can a society in which the 'white gaze' has been central to policing, because of the history of the role of policing activities and agencies in the United States as institutions created to maintain racial boundaries, conduct themselves in a racially neutral manner?

In addition to revealing patterns of racism, the stop-and-frisk data have revealed patterns of racialization in policing. Of those near five million pedestrian stops in New York City during the Bloomberg Administration, there were tens of thousands stops in the predominantly Black neighbourhoods of Central Brooklyn, a borough in New York City, that also has large Black immigrant populations. I am particularly concerned with the neighbourhoods of East Flatbush, Flatbush, Bushwick, Brownsville and East New York. The boundaries of East Flatbush correspond with the boundaries of the 67 Precinct. The boundaries of Flatbush correspond with the boundaries of the 70 Precinct. The boundaries of Bushwick correspond with the boundaries of the 83 Precinct. The boundaries of Brownsville correspond with the boundaries of the 73 Precinct. The boundaries of East New York correspond with the boundaries of the 75 Precinct.

More than 50% of the people in East Flatbush are foreign born. About 50% of the people in Flatbush are foreign born. In Bushwick, 37% of the people are foreign born but that neighbourhood has experienced the fastest rate of increase of foreign born when the data were collected in 2011. In Brownsville, 24.9% of the people are foreign born. And, in East New York about 30% of the people are foreign born. With the exception of Bushwick which is experiencing this spurt of growth in its foreign-born population, a pattern seems to emerge in the policing of predominantly native-born Black communities as compared to predominantly Black-immigrant communities. See Chart 3.1.

When Bushwick is added to the mix as I have done in Chart 3.2, Bushwick follows the pattern of the predominantly Black immigrant communities. What does it mean that there is a disparity between the policing of neighbourhoods with large numbers of immigrants from Caribbean and African nations and a preponderance of traditionally native-born Black communities? Could coloniality of power be responsible for this? The mother countries of Black immigrants had a different colonial relationship to the United States. (I have excluded Bedford–Stuyvesant, which is in the 70 Precinct, which has one of the lowest foreign-born populations because it is less contiguous.)

Predictive Policing

In the *Floyd* case, the plaintiff's argument, the ruling and the statistical analysis on which the case is based did not reference the significance of

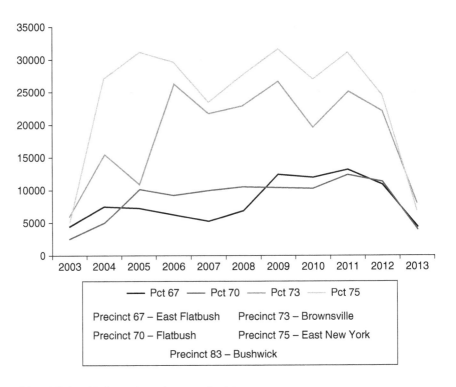

Chart 3.1   Police stops by precinct by year

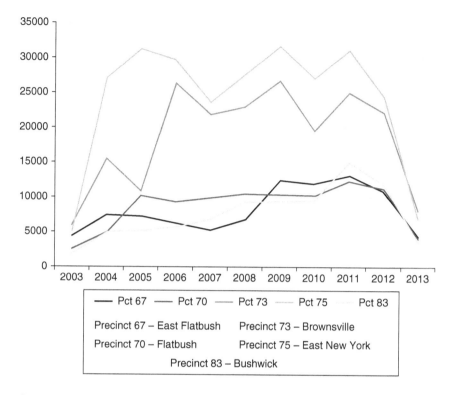

Chart 3.2 Police stops by precinct by year

Stop-and-Frisk data in future policing practices. They treated it as a thing of the past; there is no past for data. Under information capitalism, with the collection and analysis of data – particularly data about people of colour – police operate as a type of knowledge producing institution about race. In this case, many policing agencies have used data from past policing patterns to turn to predictive policing as a way to manage the discretionary powers of the police rank and file, to address community-based challenges of racism, comply with court-ordered race neutrality and manage risk. While the current reform of Stop-and-Frisk practice may cut down immediately on the frequency of such police stops, it does not address how these data patterns in past police stops affect future policing decisions given the role of technologies, like algorithms in those decisions. This information-based society that we live in merges the social and technological concerns. Information technology gives opportunities to those who previously did not have the capability, the opportunity to create knowledge producing systems. But, the idea that this digital revolution would democratize society is a fallacy because of the limited access people have to control it. What we can expect to see is a reproduction of old patterns of power, i.e. coloniality of power.

In the new 'information society' coloniality of power exists in the ways in which the analysis of the data collected in policing continue to tie people to geographic locations, particularly stigmatized territories. The powerless, particularly those who cannot afford to participate in any way, are rendered even more powerless or invisible. Decisions-making about the categories used to analyse the data will not or rarely will include them in any way.

As McQuillan (2015) argues, once these data are categorized for use in the data mining process, their legibility is determined by the algorithms in use and the other elements of the 'material-political apparatus that connects data to decision-making and governance' (p. 565), e.g. a surveillance apparatus rooted in state security/threat assessment and/or surveillance driven by commercial/profit-making imperatives. The data's human originator does not have control over the subject categories they are being placed in, but any results from the analysis would become new content/data for future data fields of future analyses. Even if we make the argument that the original data belongs to the human originator, who does that new data belong to? New subjects are continuously being created that take the shape of data doppelgangers. This new digital world is being built by algorithmic assessments that exist outside the laws and regulations that previously guided us, such as due process and rights to privacy; they exist in 'algorithmic states of exception' (McQuillan, 2015).

We see that people and the data they leave behind, like shedded skin, after online incursions are vulnerable to being categorized based on how the government or private entity wants to structure the data. Often the data's structure is based on risk management and not legal criteria, such as, presumption of innocence or due process (McQuillan, 2015). It is problematic to assume that the ideals of 18th century revolutions on which American democracy is based will suffice to manage ownership of data given the way predictive analytics and the ways in which the software that accomplish this operates. Who controls our data doppelganger? How are these data doppelgangers being racialized? And, for what purposes? Could the control over our data doppelganger represent a new form of slavery in which the individuals are complicit unless the individual has access to systems that allow for them to control the pieces of data/themselves that have been left behind like shed skin.

David Lyon (1994) noted that another element of surveillance existed for the purpose of discipline. Lyon made this assessment based on his analysis of Michel Foucault who interpreted surveillance in modern societies as a 'technique and strategy' for amassing power (1994, p. 26). Lyon is somewhat critical of Foucault's approach disapproving of a 'perspective (that) seems to revolve around the concept of power in a way that almost excludes other proper sociological considerations; Power, expressed as domination or violence, is all there is' (Lyon, 1994, p. 26). Like Lyon, Simone Browne (2015), who also builds on Foucault's work, critiques analyses of surveillance that limit our understanding of 'how people actually interact in surveillance situations' (Lyon, 1994, p. 26).[17] However, understanding surveillance as a tool for discipline and the amassing of power is important given the totalizing surveillance of Africans that existed under slavery and the ways in which this allowed for the surveillance of racial boundaries to creep into all areas of white life and shape an important feature of white supremacy – the protection of the boundaries of whiteness. Surveillance of blackness for the protection of the boundaries of whiteness restricts Blacks from of housing, educational and financial opportunities.

Policing today in the United States is less locally practised and more driven by institutional strategies that reflect larger state/ governmental (and even international) goals about presumed threats to security – e.g. terrorists – and threats to order maintenance. While today the strategies focus on presumed threats to security and order maintenance, in prior periods, the foci were different. This view into racialized surveillance in the context of information capitalism provides a view of new areas of not only racialized state repression but also state repression of everyone in general. Blacks, Indigenous people and other people of colour have served in the past as the miners' canary.

Notes

1   *In Exposed: Desire and Disobedience in the Digital Age*, Bernard Harcourt (2015) uses the term 'doppelganger' to signify the process or logic used for making

predictions that he interprets is taking place in the analysis of big data, that is, data mining is performed for the purposes of finding *another* person that represents a 'doppelganger' or double of the individual that is the object of enquiry in order to make predictions about the individual who is the object of enquiry. I use the term 'data doppelganger', and I use it differently from Harcourt. I treat 'data doppel-ganger' as *the* data representation of the flesh-and-blood object of enquiry. Harcourt's use of the term incorporates the understanding that the scientific enterprise is legiti-mate. I challenge its legitimacy because predictions are based on categories that are specious. The scientific enterprise would be legitimate if the categories were not specious. Treating the categories as 'real' or legitimate places that work in the cate-gory of race science. My work places race at the centre of analysis.

2   This terminology is derived from the work of Arun Kundnani (1999) in which he describes the significance of the computer and information technology revolutions on the system of capitalism and the culture it spawned.

3   Using David Theo Goldberg (2002) I define all modern states in Europe, North America, South America as racial states. Goldberg (2002) notes, '(R)ace and nation are defined in terms of each other in the interests of producing the picture of a coherent populace in the face of potentially divisive heterogeneity' (p. 10). This research is particularly concerned with the racial states or settler colonies in the so-called New World – like the United States – that are defined as 'creole states' by Benedict Anderson (2006) who essentially argued that the nationalism we see have seen in those states should not be 'align(ed) ... with ... self-consciously held political ideologies but with the large cultural systems ... out of which – as well as against which – (they) came in being' (p. 12). The cultural system that gave birth to these states made congruous the boundaries of the racial group and the nation state.

4   Most recently the US Supreme Court Case *Carpenter v. United States* in which the conviction of an armed robber was challenged because Carpenter's conviction was, in part, based on the police use of surveillance technology in a warrantless collection of data from his personal phone that places him near the scene of nine armed robberies for which he was convicted. The Court ruled in favour of Carpenter.

5   See Murakawa (2014) and Hinton (2016).

6   Stats, even those from the FBI Uniform Crime Report, have been very unreliable.

7   The latter is where these 'new hegemonic' narratives about modernity are being created. See Mignolo (2011).

8   In the case of the US racial state, 'blackness (functions) as a key site through which surveillance is practiced, narrated, and enacted' (Browne, 2015, p. 9). In other words, racialized surveillance takes the form of a panoptic 'white gaze' that is con-structed in the techniques and social policies and processes used for surveillance that divide the society into racial groupings of those with access to the power and benefits of full state membership and those excluded (Browne, 2015).

9   See Simon Flacks (2018). Law, necropolitics and the stop and search of young people." *Theoretical Criminology*. Article first published online: May 31, 2018 https:// doi.org/10.1177/1362480618774036. Also see, Jacques de Maillard, Daniela Hunold, Sebastian Roché & Dietrich Oberwittler. (2018). Different styles of policing: discre-tionary power in street controls by the public police in France and Germany. *Policing*

and *Society* 28, 2, 175–188, DOI: 10.1080/10439463.2016.1194837. Also see, Khalil Gibran Muhammad (2010). *The condemnation of blackness: race, crime, and the making of modern urban America.*

10   I use the American Civil Liberties definition because their work has brought some of the most important court decisions in these cases in New York City. See https://www.aclu.org/other/racial-profiling-definition.

11   See: https://www.aclu.org/other/racial-profiling-definition.

12   Floyd v. The City of New York. S.D.N.Y. United States District Court in the Southern District of New York, August 12, 2013, p. 15. (Judge Shira Sheindlin's decision)

13   Crime data either from the FBI Uniform Crime Reports or even within the NYPD are historically unreliable. But, they are typically used as justification for policy.

14   The UF-250 forms have been in use since 1986, but in 1997, the police commission at the time Howard Safir declared the use of the forms a priority. 'In 1986, the Department implemented a policy requiring officers, in certain specified circumstances, to document "stop & frisk" street encounters on the UF-250 form. See Patrol Guide – Police Department City of New York, Procedure No. 116-33, effective 11/14/86 ('Patrol Guide "Stop and Frisk" procedure'). The number of UF-250 forms filed in a particular period is available at COMPSTAT meetings and precinct commanders may be questioned about them'.See New York State Attorney General Report on Stop and Frisk by Elliott Spitzer, pp. 57 and 59, respectively.

15   Ibid., p. 59.

16   Emphasis on 'useful information' is mine.

17   Lyon (1994) sees electronic surveillance as bringing us closer to exerting this type of power. Browne (2015) uses an eight-point model of surveillance to account for the agency of people who are being surveilled.

References

Alexander, M. (2010). *The new Jim Crow: Mass incarceration in the age of color-blindness.* New York, NY: The New Press.

Anderson, B. (2006). *Imagined communities: Reflections on the origin and spread of nationalism.* Brooklyn, NY: Verso.

Browne, S. (2015). *Dark matters: On the surveillance of blackness.* Durham, NC: Duke University Press.

Camp, J. T., & Heatherton, C. (Eds.). (2016). *Policing the planet: Why the policing crisis led to Black Lives Matter.* London; New York, NY: Verso Press.

Dunn, C., LaPlante, S., & Carnig, J. (2014). *Stop and frisk during the Bloomberg administration 2002–2013.* New York, NY: New York Civil Liberties Union. Retrieved 8 August 2015, from https://www.nyclu.org/en/publications/stop-and-frisk-during-bloomberg-administration-2002-2013-2014

Flacks, S. (2018, May 31). Law, necropolitics and the stop and search of young people. *Theoretical Criminology*, *24*, 387. https://doi.org/10.1177/13624 80618774036

Floyd v. The City of New York. S.D.N.Y. United States District Court in the Southern District of New York, 12 August 2013.

Forman, J., Jr. (2017). *Locking up our own: Crime and punishment in black America*. New York, NY: Farrar, Straus and Giroux.

Garland, D. (2002). *The culture of control: Crime and social order in contemporary society*. Chicago, IL: The University of Chicago Press.

Goldberg, D. (2002). *The racial state*. Maiden, MA: Blackwell Publishers Inc.

Gottschalk, M. (2016). Razing the carceral state. *Social Justice*, *42*, 31–51.

Harcourt, B. (2015). *Exposed: Desire and disobedience in the digital age*. Cambridge, MA: Harvard University Press.

Hinton, E. (2016). *From the war on poverty to the war on crime: The making of mass incarceration in America*. Cambridge, MA: Harvard University Press.

Kundnani, A. (1999). Where do you want to go today? The rise of information capital. *Race & Class*, *40*, 49–71.

Lyon, D. (1994). *The electronic eye: The rise of surveillance society*. Minneapolis, MN: University of Minnesota Press.

McQuillan, D. (2015). Algorithmic states of exception. *European Journal of Cultural Studies*, *18*, 564–576.

Mignolo, W. (2011). Geopolitics of sensing and knowing: on (de)coloniality, border thinking, and epistemic disobedience. *Transversal Texts*. Retrieved 19 May 2015, from http://eipcp.net/transversal/0112/mignolo/en

Muhammad, K. G. (2010). *The condemnation of blackness: Race, crime, and the making of modern urban America*. Cambridge, MA: Harvard University Press.

Murakawa, N. (2014). *The first civil right: How liberals built prison America*. Oxford: Oxford University Press.

New York State Office of the Attorney General. (1999). *The New York police department's 'stop and frisk' practices*.

Quijano, A. (2007). Coloniality and modernity/rationality. *Cultural Studies*, *21*, 168–178.

Thompson, H. (2016). *Blood in the water: The Attica prison uprising of 1971 and its legacy*. New York, NY: Vintage Books.

4

Socio-Ecological Violence, Resistance and Democratization Processes[1]

J. E. Castro

Introduction

On 24 February 2019, Francisco Lopez, a 28-year-old leader from the Ava Guarani Tacuara'i Indigenous community was assassinated in front of Paraguay's National Congress in the capital city of Asuncion. He represented the plight of peasant families that were violently expelled from their lands in October 2018, by paramilitary forces acting on behalf of powerful interest groups linked to the expansion of extractivist activities in South America (ACI, 2019). The event has a powerful symbolism that recalls the turbulent relationship between the formal institutions of Western democracy and the actual democratization processes that are present in the peripheries of the present world order. I use this example from Paraguay not because of any claims to originality or because it adds any exceptional new empirical evidence to a long-standing academic and political debate. Far from it. Indeed, large-scale displacement of populations and criminal violence exercised against local Indigenous and Afro-descendant communities has been common currency in the formally democratic countries of the American continent, and elsewhere, for centuries. Bringing this example forward into the light, however, helps to make observable the social struggles that continue against the violence, silencing and invisibilization that affects marginalized populations in the forgotten regions like Paraguay, which is one of the territories affected by an aggressive expansion of accumulation strategies promoted primarily by governments, international organizations and transnational corporations (Areco and Palau, 2016; Ortega, 2013).

This chapter discusses the relationship between violence and social change focusing on processes pertaining to the socio-ecological dimension. Social struggles connected with different forms of socio-ecological violence have a long history, including struggles against the impacts of soil, air or water pollution on human well-beings; struggles against the mass displacements of populations or against the appropriation of land, water and other natural goods, including life itself (i.e. through biopiracy, commodification of the human body or similar tactics). In recent decades, however, these forms of violence have been exacerbated through the unrelenting global expansion of capitalist commodification and related processes and mechanisms of neoliberal capitalism. The horrific effects of these practices, processes and policies are now prompting widespread and multiple forms of social resistance.

The aim of this chapter is to discuss, from a sociology-grounded political ecological approach, the interplay between socio-ecological violence and resistances both, as being structuring forces, driving the destruction, transformation and emergence of socio-ecological orders. The focus relates to forms of violence affecting local communities and other actors who are at the forefront of social struggles connected with the defence of the basic conditions of life. These include struggles against the negative impacts of poorly regulated, unregulated and often illegal extractivist activities, the commodification and privatization of common and public goods, and the unequally distributed impacts of extreme geophysical or weather-related events, among other processes.

The chapter's reflections are grounded on research carried out within the framework of an ongoing project looking at the relationship between socio-ecological inequalities and injustices and democratization processes (DESDEMO, 2019). Although the project addresses examples from Latin America, the discussion has a wider relevance given the global scope of the problem. The first part of the chapter briefly discusses the concept of violence and its role in social processes. The second part explores war and conflict as being specific forms of violence, and their relationship with socio-ecological processes. The third part examines examples of how despite the accumulation of knowledge and mounting evidence to the contrary, there is a persistent approach that plays down and denies the role of anthropogenic drivers in environmental processes and events, such as weather-related disasters. The conclusion summarizes the main arguments and highlights some of the challenges that are faced in relation to the production of knowledge on socio-ecological orders and their relationship with democratization processes.

Violence and Social Processes

A systematic theorization of violence can probably be traced back to the 16th century (Joas and Knöbl, 2013); social thinking about violence, and the regulation of violence among social relations, is as old as recorded human history. Thus, what Johan Galtung defined long ago as being an 'extended concept of violence' (1969, p. 168) includes forms of violence that inspired the first laws ever developed by humans. For example, ancient Middle Eastern societies enshrined the principle that water, essential for human and animal consumption, could not be denied to anyone, a principle known as the 'Right of Thirst' (Caponera, 1954; Civic, 1998; Hirsch, 1959). Clearly, the need to introduce legislation on the matter was raised by frequent occurrence of what Galtung termed 'personal somatic violence', which could include harmful actions like water poisoning and denial of air, water or food (1969, p. 174). This form of violence has yet to be eradicated, even though relevant regulations and legislation have existed for millennia.

A recent example of this kind of violence, is what Paul Mohai (2018b) termed 'the most egregious example of environmental injustice', referring to the series of conscious decisions by the municipal government of Flint, Michigan, in the United States, leading to the 'poisoning of the city's water'. Governments and other powerful stakeholders in so-called civilized societies often normalize and justify the denial of these essential goods to sectors of the population, typically the poorest and most socially marginalized, actions that include criminalizing the activities of anyone who dares to defend the 'Right of Thirst', or, by extension, the 'Right of Hunger', the 'Right to Sleep' or even the 'Right of Breathing' (Andrews, 2017; FAO, 2019; Fernandez Evangelista and Jones, 2013; National Coalition for the Homeless, 2019).

The quest for developing an 'extended concept of violence', as suggested by Galtung decades ago, has the objective of moving beyond the conventional definition of violence as being just the use of physical force to cause injury, harm, damage or destruction. A sample from the specialized literature shows a wide array of terms connected to the concept that bring out multidimensional and multi-scale aspects of violence beyond the conventional notions (Figure 4.1).

These various terms have been grouped to reflect common attributes, including some specifically connected to the topic of this chapter, such as: natural, nature's, or environmental violence, which are considered later in more detail. Most terms in Figure No 1 interlink and are connected to closely related concepts, for example: 'slow violence, necropolitics, and petrochemical pollution' (Davies, 2018), 'environmental military violence and weaponized landscapes' (Hall, 2017, p. 4), 'judicialized violence' (Areco and Palau, 2016) or 'environmental violence and genocide' (Zimmerer, 2014). The wide range of terms, adjectives and their mutual interconnections illustrate the centrality of violence, in its multiple forms and scales, in the development of social processes, orders and disorders.

The fact that violence is a structuring factor for social processes was a central concern for Nobert Elias (1994) and is a crucial component of his theorization of the 'civilizing process'. Drawing on Max Weber, Elias (1994) gave centrality to what he termed 'the monopoly mechanism', that is, a blind, unplanned socio-historical process that over the course of several centuries led to the transformation of the feudal order in Europe and the emergence of a new social order structured around nation states (pp. 338–355). The monopoly mechanism referred particularly to what Weber had termed the 'monopoly of the legitimate use of physical force within a given territory', characteristic of the nation state, and it included not only the monopoly of the means of violence but also of the powers of taxation (Weber, 1978, p. 909; Mennell, 1992, pp. 66–79; Elias, 1994, pp. 338–355).

The reception of Elias's theory has been mixed, not least concerning the relation between violence and the 'civilizing process' and its applicability to societies outside the small group that provided the main empirical evidence for his study, namely France, Germany and Great Britain (Fletcher, 1997; Goudsblom, 1994; Landini and Depelteau, 2017; Linklater and Mennell, 2010; Pepperell, 2016). However, Elias' work provides important clues for the study of the role of violence in the dynamics of ever-changing social configurations, including the emergence and transformation of social orders. Elaborating on Elias work, Dutch sociologist Johan Goudsblom (2001) highlighted what he termed 'the paradox of pacification', the permanent tension between 'peace' and 'war', the fact that pacification

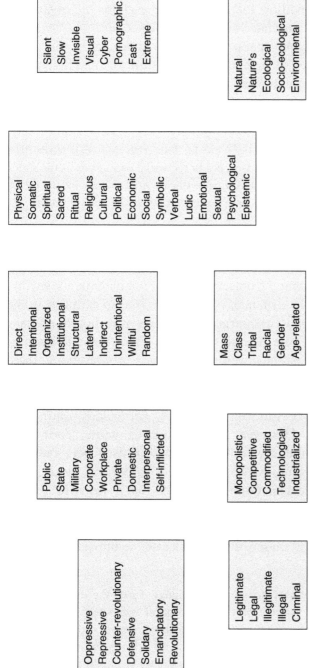

Figure 4.1 Extended conceptualization and adjectivation of violence

is often achieved through much violence, and that the internal pacification of territories through the monopolization of the means of
violence is a precondition for the effective exercise of 'organized'
inter-state violence, particularly wars (pp. 5–8).

Despite its changing character, war continues to be the most
extreme manifestation of violence, at least historically and in terms of
the scale of destruction involved. Yet, as Carl von Clausewitz put it, at
least 'in theory', 'war is an act of violence meant to force the enemy to
do our will' (Clausewitz, 1989, p. 90). Clausewitz also wrote:

> If wars between civilized nations are far less cruel and destructive than
> wars between savages, the reason lies in the social conditions of the states
> themselves and in their relationships to one another. These are the forces
> that give rise to war; the same forces circumscribe and moderate it.
> (Clausewitz, 1989, p. 90)

Clausewitz's analysis provided a systemic explanation of war, and
insisted that the use of violence in war was a mean to force the enemy
to accept one's will, that the objective was not to obliterate the enemy.
Even if in practice the dynamics of war often lead to extremes in the
use of violence, Clausewitz argued that this was not a primary
objective, and that the 'social conditions' and the relationships
between 'civilized' nations were key factors in preventing these
extreme situations. In a way not dissimilar from certain aspects of
Elias' approach, Clausewitz based his reflections on the experience of
war among 'civilized' European countries, particularly during the
Napoleonic period. However, after Clausewitz wrote, during the
mid-19th century, military violence, and war itself was radically
transformed. In a lecture on what he called 'barbarism', given in the
aftermath of the Persian Gulf War (1990–1991), Eric Hobsbawm
(1994) argued that civilized nations have been experiencing a serious
regression of the social conditions and moral conventions that historically helped to circumscribe and moderate the impacts of war. In
Hobsbawm's words,

> I understand 'barbarism' to mean two things. First, the disruption and
> breakdown of the systems of rules and moral behaviour by which all
> societies regulate the relations among their members and, to a lesser
> extent, between their members and those of other societies. Second, I
> mean, more specifically, the reversal of what we may call the project of
> the eighteenth-century Enlightenment, namely the establishment of a

universal system of such rules and standards of moral behaviour, embodied in the institutions of states dedicated to the rational progress of humanity: to Life, Liberty and the Pursuit of Happiness, to Equality, Liberty and Fraternity or whatever. Both are now taking place and reinforce each other's negative effects on our lives. (Hobsbawm, 1994, p. 45)

Hobsbawm suggests that Clausewitz took for granted that the rules of war would be accepted and followed by both sides, included respecting the lives of war prisoners and civilian populations, something that rebels and revolutionaries have not always followed. These rules of moral behaviour can no longer be taken for granted, as showed by the uncivilized and criminal behaviour characterizing contemporary wars.

Citing Hobsbawm's powerful defence of the Enlightenment, the institutions of national states, and the idea of 'rational progress', may not just raise some eyebrows but also prompt disagreements among many of those involved in the struggles against socio-ecological inequality and injustice worldwide. This is understandable given the prominent role played by nation states in the 'betrayal' of the promises of universal development and progress (Merchant, 2006; Noorgard, 1994). Yet, the betrayal of civilization by the very institutions that were supposed to uphold its principles and secure its advancement is an essential feature of the barbarism denounced by Hobsbawm, an issue that will be discussed later in the chapter.

War, Conflicts and Socio-Ecological Violences

The previous reference to war has direct implications for the consideration of the interconnection between socio-ecological violence and social order. The following examples illustrate this:

In August 1995, the Vice President for Environmentally Sustainable Development of the World Bank, Ismail Serageldin, famously stated that while many wars of the 20th century were about oil, in the 21st century wars would be over water (Crossette, 1995). This was an important statement, though not an original idea, as the notion of wars connected with natural resources and the environment more generally were prominent at the time and were becoming part of the international security agenda (Gleick, 1993). In June 1999, the United Nations Environment Programme (UNEP) published a special report on the links between environment and conflict, including wars

(Schwartz and Singh, 1999). In the Foreword to the report, the Executive Director of UNEP, Klaus Toepfer, stated, 'It is clear that the opportunity for humankind to combat international and intranational conflict must be seen in light of the connections between environmental conditions and resources, and conflict' (Toepfer, 1999, p. 4). Toepfer's comments were widely reported by the global media. In the year 2000, the US National Intelligence Council announced that focusing on the period 2000–2015, 'US foreign priorities will be more transnational' to deal with growing problems including 'competition for scarce natural resources such as water ... and environmental crises' (NIC, 2000, p. 18). In 2002, a group of organizations concerned with the conservation of natural resources published a report titled *Conserving the Peace: Resources, Livelihoods and Security*, arguing that traditional sources of human conflict were exacerbated by environmental problems, which was 'placing massive pressure on societies and especially on their poorest members', and that improved management and planned conservation of natural resources and biodiversity could 'contribute to peace and stability' and, by extension, to 'development and social justice' (Matthew et al., 2002, pp. 4–5). In February 2006, the former British Defence Secretary, John Reid, announced that the country's armed forces would be placed on standby to intervene anywhere worldwide to face the increasing threat of violence and political conflict connected with global warming and its impact on natural resources, particularly water (Russell and Morris, 2006). Less prominent in the international media was the decision announced in April 2008, by the US government of President George W. Bush, to re-establish the 4th Fleet that had patrolled the seas in the Caribbean and in Central and South America since the end of World War II but had been decommissioned in 1950 (United States of America Department of the Navy, 2008). This decision 'provoked reactions of indignation and anger' in Latin America, and a few weeks later, when South American governments signed the Constitutive Treaty of the Union of South American Nations (UNASUR), on 23 May 2008, they created a working group on military questions (Dabène, 2014, p. 85). Several countries in the region, notoriously Argentina, Brazil and Venezuela, redefined the objectives of their military forces to focus on the defence against potential attempts by foreign powers to gain control over their natural resources, notoriously oil and water (de Paula, 2009). Recent developments in the region suggest that these concerns were not overstated.

These examples leave little space for doubt about the strong relationship between conflict and violence, and socio-ecological processes and orders (Downey et al., 2010; Hall, 2017; Hsiang et al., 2013; Kuletz, 2001). Focusing on war as the foremost expression of 'extreme violence' provides a signpost for the analysis. Nevertheless, despite their enormous impacts, wars and other large-scale human conflicts only account for a small share of the violence associated with socio-ecological orders. Although there have yet to be any open wars, in the conventional sense, explicitly declared over the control of natural resources, widespread violence enacted against local communities, primarily Indigenous and Afro-descendants, are quite common. An ensuing social struggle to defend territories and livelihoods has become endemic to Latin America and other regions because of this.

Along these lines, it is important to consider the issue of Internally Displaced People (IDPs), which has been chronicled since the year 2008 by the Internal Displacement Monitoring Centre (IDCM). The IDCM has produced annual global estimates of IDPs resulting from 'conflicts and violence' and 'disasters', which include geophysical events like earthquakes and volcanic eruptions, and 'weather related' events such as storms, floods, droughts, etc. The IDCM figures must be read with discernment, given the fact that they are estimates, and because 'disasters' can be the cause of conflict and violence, and therefore the difference between the two categories are somewhat blurred. The results, however, provide a useful perspective, as seen in Table 4.1, which presents information from the latest IDCM report collected from over 140 countries for the period of 2008–2017.

The table shows that, although the numbers of IDPs have decreased from the peaks recorded in 2008 and 2010, with an estimated 41.1 and 45.3 million IDPs respectively for each year, large-scale population displacement has become a permanent feature worldwide. Moreover, every single year the estimated number of IDPs produced by 'disasters' greatly exceeded the numbers resulting from 'conflict and violence', reaching a peak in 2010 when 93.6% of IDPs were caused by disasters. Table 4.2 complements this information from a different angle, focusing on the specific types of events included under the label of 'disasters'.

Table 4.2 shows that most people displaced by 'disasters' recorded in 2017, around 96% of the total 18.8 million IDPs, were affected by 'weather-related' events, among which the majority corresponded to floods (46%) and storms, including cyclones, hurricanes and typhoons

Table 4.1 Estimates of internally displaced people by conflict and violence and disasters between 2008 and 2017, in percentages and absolute numbers

Year	Conflicts and violence	Disasters	Total
2008	11.19% (4.6)	88.81% (36.5)	100% (41.1)
2009	28.02% (6.5)	71.98% (16.7)	100% (23.2)
2010	6.4% (2.9)	93.6% (42.4)	100% (45.3)
2011	18.92% (3.5)	81.08% (15)	100% (18.5)
2012	16.92% (6.6)	83.08% (32.4)	100% (39)
2013	27.06% (8.2)	72.94% (22.1)	100% (30.3)
2014	36.54% (11)	63.46% (19.1)	100% (30.1)
2015	30.94% (8.6)	69.06% (19.2)	100% (27.8)
2016	22.19% (6.9)	77.81% (24.2)	100% (31.1)
2017	38.56% (11.8)	61.44% (18.8)	100% (30.6)

Source: Elaborated from IDCM (2018, p. 2).

Table 4.2 Estimates of internally displaced people by disasters in 2017, in millions of people

			Subtotal 1	Subtotal 2	Total
Geophysical	Earthquakes		0.59		0.8
	Volcanic eruptions		0.17		18
Weather-related	Floods		8.6		
	Storms	Cyclones, hurricanes, typhons	6.9	7.5	
		Other storms	0.6		
	Droughts		1.3	1.87	
	Wildfires		0.52		
	Landslides		0.04		
	Extreme temperatures		0.005		
Total			18.8		

Source: IDCM (2018, p. 7).

(40%). The report highlights the facts that the Americas accounted for 24% of disaster-related IDPs recorded globally, and that in the region the number of people displaced by disasters was 10 times higher than those who were displaced by 'conflict and violence' (IDCM, 2018, p. 38). However, evidence from the ground prompts us to query to what extent occurring violences remain hidden when we put the label of 'disasters' to these events. Moreover, statistical significance should not lead us to dismiss the importance of events directly connected with conflict and violence. For example, another report focusing on environmental conflicts in Latin America, also recorded in 2017, concluded that the region 'remains at the top of the scale for global killings of land and environment defenders', adding that 'agribusiness has overtaken mining as the industry most linked to the murder of activists – together these industries make up over 60% of known links' (Global Witness, 2018). The report also addressed the situation of Honduras, a country that sadly became singled out as a prime example of extreme violence against 'environmental defenders' worldwide, although the figures of IDPs recorded in Honduras are not high. The Global Witness report provides a damning picture of the complex transnational interests behind the torture and murder of local people opposing the extractivist activities in their territories:

> Our investigation sheds light on the back-door deals, bribes and law-breaking used to impose [infrastructure] projects and silence opposition. We also scrutinise how the US is bankrolling Honduran state forces, which are behind some of the worst attacks. ... We have documented countless chilling attacks and threats, including the savage beating by soldiers of pregnant women, children held at gunpoint by police, arson attacks on villagers' homes, whilst hired assassins still wander free among their victims' communities ... the US ... contributed US$100 million in bilateral aid .... But tens of millions of aid dollars were directed to the police and military, both of which are heavily implicated in violence against land and environmental activists. ... The US embassy has been promoting ramped-up investment in Honduras' extractive industries, for instance, with US mining giant Electrum already planning a US $1 billion investment. (See Global Witness, 2017; Lakhani, 2017, 2018 on the famous case of the murdered Indigenous leader Berta Caceres.)

The involvement of governments and local and transnational actors in different forms of extreme violence against defenceless communities struggling to defend their territories and livelihoods has been recorded in many other countries of the region as well, notably Brazil (CPT, 2019; Valencio, 2010, 2012; Zhouri and Laschefski, 2010), Colombia (Vélez Galeano, 2017) and Mexico (Kloster, 2018; Poma, 2017) but also across the Americas, and in other continents (Bettini, 2013; Black, 2001; Downey et al., 2010; Environmental Justice, 2019; Lyons, 2019; Nixon, 2011; Peluso and Watts, 2001; Sridhar, 2006; WoMin, 2014; Zimmerer, 2014). In this regard, although it is obvious for the specialists, it must be said that the reference to violence and disasters included in the previous paragraphs as illustration of the main arguments cannot pretend to provide even a synthesis of the available empirical evidence to substantiate the 'extended concept of violence', as discussed earlier and represented in Table 4.1.

Naturalizing 'Disasters' and Anthropomorphizing Nature

There has been a long-standing debate among social scientists about the relative significance of social factors in the explanation of environmental processes, with contributions from a wide array of theoretical traditions, whereby the intertwined character of social and 'natural' processes has been well established. That notwithstanding, it can be argued that in the wider world, outside such specialized discussions, it is not widely understood that disasters are almost universally connected with violence and conflict in different ways. There is, instead, a tendency to 'naturalize' disasters in ways that hide the role that humans play in their production, as well as their impacts, and to deny human responsibility altogether. Conversely, there is also a tendency to anthropomorphise Nature and natural processes, which often contributes to an occlusion of the social dimension to disasters and their consequences. In addition, 'naturalizing' disasters and anthropomorphizing Nature makes invisible the structural violence and social inequalities that are a root cause of the enormously unequal impacts of socio-ecological occurrences. To be fair, in the case of the IDCM report on population displacements, any attempt to analyse the occurrence and impacts of disasters as being primarily the result of 'natural', geophysical or weather-related causes is dispelled from the start in the report itself, which states:

> Complex and interdependent risk drivers, including poverty and inequality, political instability and state fragility, water stress and food

insecurity, climate change and environmental degradation, unsustainable development and poor urban planning combine in different ways in different countries to increase people's exposure and vulnerability to displacement. (IDCM, 2018, p. 2)

Any recognition of how environment-related events are interwoven with socio-economic and political drivers must be welcome. Despite the accumulated knowledge and mounting empirical evidence about the spatial and temporal interconnectedness of socio-ecological processes, there is a persistent tendency to 'naturalise' disasters, including the militant denial of responsibility around their causes and consequences, by governments, multinational companies and other powerful actors. A recent example of this was provided by the media coverage of Brazil's 'largest environmental disaster', in the words of former President Dilma Rousseff, caused by the rupture of a tailing dam of the SAMARCO mining complex in Mariana, state of Minas Gerais, Brazil, on 5 November 2015 (OGlobo, 2016). The disaster was enormous, it had far-reaching and long-term consequences that are yet to be fully understood, and, more importantly, the human communities affected are still waiting for adequate compensation and solutions to their urgent needs. It has been established that SAMARCO's multinational owners are responsible for the accident that caused the disaster, and that the lack of proper regulation contributed to this (Hatje et al., 2017; Losekann et al., 2015; Tuncak, 2017). Yet, the mainstream national media widely reported the event as 'Brazil's largest *natural* disaster' (Azevedo, 2016, emphasis added). The discussion continues, exacerbated by the recent occurrence of a very similar accident-turned-disaster involving some of the same multinational companies, which took place in Brumadinho, also in Minas Gerais, Brazil, on 28 February 2019 (Darlington et al., 2019). The 'naturalization' of disasters is so deeply embedded that even institutions like the United Nations find it difficult to move into a more advanced terminology, as suggested by reports such as: 'one in three children misses school in countries affected by conflicts or *natural* disasters [19 September 2018]' or 'a new report from the United Nations alerts about the link between climate change and the increasing recurrence of *natural* disasters [10 October 2018]' (UN, 2019, emphasis added). Unfortunately, these examples of essentialist and reductionist conceptualizations of complex socio-ecological events, like disasters, are not isolated and are, rather, part of a well-documented global pattern.

The naturalization of disasters has the effect of limiting if not altogether denying the significance of human actions and responsibility in the occurrence and in the impacts of disasters. However, as stated in the early 1970s by scientists working on complexity theory and the sociogenesis of 'natural' disasters, 'Nature pleads not guilty' (García and Smagorinsky, 1981). From another angle, in addition to naturalizing disasters, hiding the hand of humans in their making is often done by anthropomorphizing Nature. There is a persistent treatment of disasters as 'natural' forms of violence, the 'violence of Nature', which has become a topical and convenient anthropomorphism. As an example, in an article listing a series of extreme environmental events recorded worldwide in 2017, a reporter stated that '*Natural* disasters set records around the world in 2017 ... look at some of the deadly power *Mother Nature wielded* in 2017' (Brueck, 2017, emphasis added). In another example, the American Museum of Natural History posted an educational video titled '*Nature's Fury*: The Science of *Natural Disasters*' and explained that 'earthquakes, volcanoes, tornadoes, hurricanes ... are *natural events* [that] remind us that we are small and vulnerable—and that living on this dynamic planet will always entail risk' (American Museum of Natural History, 2014, emphasis added). More pragmatic approaches also take advantage of the anthropomorphism, as illustrated by an advert selling insurance policies, which exhorted the readers to 'Act now, before there's an *act of God*', referring to what insurance companies describe as a 'major catastrophe', 'acts of nature' caused by a 'superior force', such as lightning, fires, windstorms, volcanic eruptions, floods, etc (Cavaglieri, 2014, my emphasis added). 'Nature's fury' has become a suitable target for commodification, a process marked by the production and reproduction of material, epistemic and cultural forms of violence.

Conclusion: Socio-Ecological Violence, Resistance and Order

During the last few decades there has been an increasing agreement about the centrality of anthropogenic factors among the causes of large-scale environmental transformations. This includes an ongoing campaign coordinated by scientists for the official recognition of the existence of a 'defined geological unit within the Geological Time Scale' termed Anthropocene, which would have started in the early 19th century 'around the beginning of the Industrial Revolution in Europe', as originally proposed by Nobel Prize winner Paul Crutzen (Anthropocene Working Group, 2019; Steffen et al., 2004). There is an important debate among geologists and others about the scientific strength of the proposal, but also about the appropriateness of the term, given that social scientists who are weary about the potentially apolitical reductionism that would be implicit in the term 'Anthropocene' have proposed alternatives like 'Capitalocene' (Anthropocene Working Group, 2019). This ambitious debate highlights an interconnectedness between geological and human time scales, and the diverse pace and scale of change and transformation characterizing them. The bewildering complexity of such problems should not take the focus away from the essential tasks required to enhance our understanding of 'the vital network of interdependencies in which human lives evolve', including the development and transformation of socio-ecological regimes and orders (De Vries and Goudsblom, 2002, p. 414).

In this regard, the study of socio-ecological violence, in its different manifestations, can contribute to a better understanding of the emergence, consolidation, expansion and destruction of social orders. The recognition that very-long-term processes of social transformation result from the largely blind, unplanned and uncontrolled interweaving of socio-natural events does not necessarily keep us from discerning the overall direction of these processes. Therefore, it could be argued that another manifestation of what Goudsblom (2001) termed the 'paradox of pacification' is the internal contradictions of a capitalist world order discursively committed to the pursuit of freedom, peace and democracy, however, in practice relentlessly driven towards the monopolization of economic power and private wealth by means of extreme violence and an escalation of structural inequalities and injustices. As Galtung (1990) put it, 'I see violence as avoidable insults to basic human needs, and more generally to life, lowering the real level of needs satisfaction below what is potentially possible' (p. 292). These avoidable insults seem to reach ever higher levels when the struggles of resistance against the advance of renewed forms of criminal accumulation organized and promoted by nation states and multinational companies, supported by international institutions once created to promote enduring peace and development,

are criminalized as terrorist activities, and denied the status of legitimate defence.

Sadly, this can be illustrated by the plight of peasant, Indigenous
and Afro-descendant communities in Brazil, which have been the
target of recurrent massacres owing to their resistance to the expansion of extractivist activities leading to the unlawful appropriation of
their territories. As the Pastoral Land Commission that provides
support to the movement of landless workers in Brazil put it, 'to
struggle is not a crime, we will not forget [the massacres]' (CPT,
2019). However, in October 2018, millions of Brazilians voted for a
President that campaigned for the criminalization of those defending
their right to land, and to a safe environment more generally, under
charges of terrorism, leading the critical press to denounce that the
new President 'promotes rural carnage and ecological holocaust', not
to say the demise of an already fragile, incipient democracy (Balloussier, 2018; Carta Capital, 2018). It would be entirely wrong to
dismiss the Brazilian case as an outlier in the chart of democratic
progress; rather it should be examined as a pilot experiment, along
with the processes of rapid dismantling of the basic and frail democratic structures and processes underway in most countries of the
Latin American and Caribbean region. As reported by the UN
Economic Commission for Latin America and the Caribbean
(ECLAC), Latin America had fared better than the countries of the
Organization for Economic Cooperation and Development (OECD)
in response to the 2008 financial crisis and had made significant
advances in reducing extreme poverty, but there has been a rapid
reversal since 2015 (ECLAC, 2016, pp. 47–56; ECLAC, 2017, pp.
24–30). The return of neoliberal market extremism, which in certain
cases, like Brazil, are married to explicit neo-fascist political projects,
cast serious doubts about the possibilities of advancing substantive
democratization processes in the foreseeable future. This barbaric
reversal of the moral standards and commitments to universal civilized well-being, borrowing from Hobsbawm (1994), is an expression
of a moment in the long-term process of development and emergence
of a potentially new socio-ecological order, or orders, which we
should probably not rush to name, not yet.

A fundamental task in the production of knowledge about violence
and socio-ecological orders lies in the primacy of the formulation of
questions and problems over pre-empted answers and prescriptions.

Scientific knowledge is the answer to problems formulated as research questions. In relation to socio-ecological violence and orders, what research problems are given primacy? What questions are being formulated? What questions should be formulated? Why these questions and no others? Who is formulating the questions? Whose interests are addressed in these questions? What violence? Whose violence? Prevailing reductionism and determinism, especially techno-centric, but also social-science-isms continue to be major obstacles in our quest to advance knowledge that may contribute towards progressive transformations in society.

The dominance of reductionist and deterministic understandings of 'development' processes and of their interrelation with, say, democratization and commodification processes, including among progressive social scientists and political actors, continues to be a formidable challenge in our search for more advanced and complex understandings and explanations of socio-ecological orders and disorders. This kind of knowledge, however, is essential for contesting and defeating the regrettable but highly successful neoliberal and neofascist erosion of principles, values and practices. The destruction of these social orders is required for the construction of more humane and universalistic socio-ecological orders to replace them, ones grounded upon a defence of the common good, the public good, emancipatory freedom, equality, inclusion and human rights.

Note

1   The chapter is partly based on the presentation of the same title given at the semi-plenary session 'Globalization, Structures of Violence in Everyday Life', XIX ISA World Congress of Sociology *Power, Violence and Justice: Reflections, Responses and Responsibilities*, Toronto, 15–21 July 2018.

References

ACI - Agencia Católica de Informaciones. (2019). Obispos de Paraguay condenan asesinato de indígena frente a Congreso Nacional. *ACI Prensa*. Asuncion: ACI. Retrieved March 2019, from https://www.aciprensa.com/noticias/obispos-de-paraguay-condenan-asesinato-de-indigena-frente-a-congreso-nacional-78888

American Museum of Natural History. (2014). *Nature's fury: The science of natural disasters*. New York, NY. Retrieved February 2019, from https://www.youtube.com/embed/oRiLLd2hX0E

Andrews, A. (2017). The right to breathe clean air. *United Nations Environment Programme (UNEP)*. Retrieved February 2019, from https://www.unenvironment.org/news-and-stories/story/right-breathe-clean-air

Anthropocene Working Group. (2019). What is the 'Anthropocene'? – Current definition and status. Retrieved March 2019, from http://quaternary.stratigraphy.org/working-groups/anthropocene/

Areco, A., & Palau, M. (2016). *Judicialización y violencia contra la lucha campesina. Casos de criminalización en el período 2013-2015*. Asuncion: Base Investigaciones Sociales.

Azevedo, A. L. (2016, November 6). Desastre de Mariana ainda esta vivo. *O Globo*. Retrieved February 2019, from https://oglobo.globo.com/brasil/desastre-de-mariana-ainda-esta-vivo-20416385

Balloussier, A. V. (2018, December 6). Movimentos temem que até 'like' baste para virarem terroristas no governo Bolsonaro. *Folha de Sao Paulo*. Retrieved February 2019, from https://www1.folha.uol.com.br/poder/2018/12/movimentos-temem-que-ate-like-baste-para-virarem-terroristas-no-governo-bolsonaro.shtml

Bettini, G. (2013). Climate Barbarians at the gate? A critique of apocalyptic narratives on 'climate refugees'. *Geoforum, 26*(1), 63–72.

Black, R. (2001). Environmental refugees: Myth or reality? *Working Papers, New Issues in Refugee Research*. Brighton, University of Sussex.

Brueck, H. (2017). *Natural disasters set records around the world in 2017—these were the worst*. Retrieved March 2019, from https://www.businessinsider.com/worst-natural-disasters-hurricane-flood-wildfire-2017-12

Caponera, D. A. (1954). *Water laws in Moslem countries*. Rome: Food and Agriculture Organization (FAO).

Carta Capital. (2018, October 13). Bolsonaro insufla carnificina no campo e holocausto ecológico. *Carta Capital*. Retrieved March 2019, from https://www.cartacapital.com.br/politica/bolsonaro-insufla-carnificina-no-campo-e-holocausto-ecologico

Cavaglieri, C. (2014, February 8). Act now, before there's an act of God. *The Independent*. Retrieved March 2019, from https://www.independent.co.uk/money/insurance/act-now-before-theres-an-act-of-god-9116945.html

Civic, M. A. (1998). A comparative analysis of the Israeli and Arab water law traditions and insights for modern water sharing agreement, *Denver Journal of International Law and Policy, 26*(3), 437–452.

von Clausewitz, C. (1989). *On war*. Princeton: Princeton University Press.

CPT – Pastoral Land Commission. (2019). *Massacres no campo*. Retrieved March 2019, from https://www.cptnacional.org.br/mnc/

Crossette, B. (1995). Severe water crisis ahead for poorest nations in next 2 decades. *The New York Times*. Retrieved March 2019, from https://www.nytimes.com/1995/08/10/world/severe-water-crisis-ahead-for-poorest-nations-in-next-2-decades.html

Dabène, O. (2014). La cuarta ola de regionalismo. en E. Jourcin (Ed.), *Los Desafíos del Desarrollo en América Latina. Dinámicas Socioeconómicas y Políticas Públicas*. Paris: Agence Française de Développement (AFD), p. 64–95.

DESDEMO. (2019). *Socio-ecological inequality and injustice as obstacles to the democratization process in Latin America and the Caribbean. A theoretical and empirical study*. Research Project, J. E. Castro Coordinator. Retrieved from http://www.desdemo.org

Darlington, S., Glanz, J., Andreoni, M., Bloch, M., Peçanha, S., Singhvi, A., & Griggs, T. (2019, February 29). A tidal wave of mud. *The New York Times*. Retrieved from https://www.nytimes.com/interactive/2019/02/09/world/americas/brazil-dam-collapse.html. Consulted in March 2019.

Davies, T. (2018). Toxic space and time: Slow violence, necropolitics, and petrochemical pollution. *Annals of the American Association of Geographers, 108*(6), 1537–1553.

De Vries, B., & Goudsblom, J. (2002). Mappae Mundi. Humans and their habitats in a long-term socio-ecological perspective. *Myths, maps, and models*. Amsterdam: Amsterdam University Press.

Downey, L., Bonds, E., & Clark, K. (2010). Natural resource extraction, armed violence, and environmental degradation. *Organization & Environment, 23*(4), 417–445.

ECLAC – United Nations Economic Comission for Latin America and the Caribbean. (2016). *Horizons 2030: Equality at the centre of sustainable development*. Santiago de Chile: ECLAC.

ECLAC – United Nations Economic Comission for Latin America and the Caribbean. (2017). *Annual report on regional progress and challenges in relation to the 2030 Agenda for Sustainable Development in Latin America and the Caribbean*. Santiago de Chile: ECLAC.

Elias, N. (1994). *The civilizing process. The history of manners, and state formation and civilization*. Oxford; Cambridge, MA: Basil Blackwell.

Environmental Justice. (2019). *Environmental justice, a research project to study and contribute to the global environmental justice movement*. Retrieved March 2019, from http://www.envjustice.org/section/resources/scientific-papers/

FAO – Food and Agriculture Organization. (2019). *The right to food*. Retrieved March 2019, from http://www.fao.org/right-to-food/en/

Fernandez Evangelista, G. C., & Jones, S. E. (2013). *Mean streets. A report on the criminalisation of homelessness in Europe*. Brussels: Fédération Européenne d'Associations Nationales Travaillant avec les Sans-Abris (FEANTSA).

Fletcher, J. (1997). *Violence & civilization. An introduction to the work of Norbert Elias*. Cambridge: Polity Press.

Galtung, J. (1969). Violence, peace, and peace research, *Journal of Peace Research, 6*(3), 167–191.

Galtung, J. (1990). Cultural violence, *Journal of Peace Research, 27*(3), 291–305.

García, R., & Smagorinsky, J. (1981). *Nature pleads not guilty*. Oxford: Pergamon Press.

Gleick, P. (1993). Water and conflict: Fresh water resources and international security. *International Security, 18*(1), 79–112.

Global Witness. (2017). *Honduras. The deadliest place to defend the planet*. Retrieved March 2019, from https://www.globalwitness.org/documents/18798/Defenders_Honduras_full_report_single_v5_AH12dtf.pdf

Global Witness. (2018). *New data reveals 197 land and environmental defenders murdered in 2017*. Retrieved March 2019, from https://www.globalwitness.org/en-gb/blog/new-data-reveals-197-land-and-environmental-defenders-murdered-2017/

Goudsblom, J. (1994). *The theory of the civilising process and its discontents.* Amsterdam: Amsterdam School for Social Research.

Goudsblom, J. (2001). *The paradox of pacification.* Amsterdam: Norbert Elias Foundation. Retrieved March 2019, from http://archive.norbert-elias.com/docs/pdf/Figs/ParadoxofPacification.pdf

Hall, S. D. (2017). *War by other means: Environmental violence in the 21st century.* Doctoral Thesis, Environmental Studies Program. Eugene, OR: University of Oregon.

Hatje, V., Pedreira, R. M. A., de Rezende, C. E., Schettini, R., de Souza, C. A., Cotrim, G., . . . Hackspacher, P. C. (2017). *The environmental impacts of one of the largest tailing dam failures worldwide*, Scientific Reports, *7*, 10706, 1–13.

Hirsch, A. M. (1959). Water legislation in the Middle East, *American Journal of Comparative Law, 8*, 168–186.

Hobsbawm, E. (1994). Barbarism: A user's guide, *New Left Review, 206*, 44–54.

Hsiang, S. M., Burke, M., & Miguel, E. (2013). Quantifying the influence of climate on human conflict, *Science, 341*, 1235367.

IDCM - Internal Displacement Monitoring Centre. (2018). *Global report on internal displacement 2018*. Geneva: IDCM.

Joas, H., & Knöbl, W. (2013). *War in social thought: Hobbes to the present.* Princeton, NJ; Woodstock: Princeton University Press.

Kloster, K. (Ed.). (2018). Water conflicts, violence, and capitalist territorialisation in Latin America. WATERLAT-GOBACIT Network Working Papers, 4(4). Retrieved March 2019, from http://waterlat.org/publications/working-papers-series/vol4/vol4no4/

Kuletz, V. (2001). Invisible spaces, violent places: Cold War nuclear and militarized landscapes. In N. L. Peluso, & M. Watts (Eds.), *Violent environments*. Ithaca, NY: Cornell University Press, p. 237–260.

Lakhani, N. (2017, January 31). Honduras elites blamed for violence against environmental activists. *The Guardian*. Retrieved March 2019, from https://www.theguardian.com/world/2017/jan/31/honduras-environmental-activists-global-witness-violence-berta-caceres

Lakhani, N. (2018, November 29). Berta Cáceres murder trial plagued by allegations of cover-ups set to end. *The Guardian*. Retrieved March 2019, from https://www.theguardian.com/global-development/2018/nov/29/berta-caceres-trial-plagued-by-allegations-of-cover-ups-set-to-end

Landini, T. S., & Depelteau, F. (Eds.). (2017). *Norbert Elias and violence*. New York, NY: Palgrave Macmillan.

Linklater, A., & Mennell, S. (2010). Norbert Elias, the civilizing process: Sociogenetic and psychogenetic investigations—an overview and assessment, *History and Theory, 49*(3), 384–411.

Losekann, C., de Oliveira Sá, A. C., Santos, A. A., Jesus, B., Castro, J., Lima, L., . . . Galvão, W. (2015). Sem-Terra, Sem-Água e Sem-Peixe – Impactos socioambientais da ruptura da barragem de rejeitos da Samarco no Espírito Santo. *WATERLAT-GOBACIT Network Working Papers, 2*(17), 8–35. Retrieved March 2019, from http://waterlat.org/WPapers/WPSATAD217.pdf

Lyons, K. (2019). Securing territory for mining when Traditional Owners say 'No': The exceptional case of Wangan and Jagalingou in Australia, *The Extractive Industries and Society, 6*, 756. https://doi.org/10.1016/j.exis.2018.11.007

Matthew, R., Halle, M., & Switzer, J. (Eds.). (2002). *Conserving the peace: Resources, livelihoods and security.* Winnipeg, MB: International Institute for Sustainable Development and IUCN – The World Conservation Union.

Mennell, S. (1992). *Norbert Elias. An introduction.* Oxford; Cambridge, MA: Blackwell.

Merchant, C. (2006). The scientific revolution and the death of nature, *Isis, 97*(3), 513–533.

Mohai, P. (2018a). Environmental justice and the flint water crisis, *Michigan Sociological Review, 32*, 1–41.

Mohai, P. (2018b, October 19). Flint water crisis: Most egregious example of environmental injustice, says U-M researcher. Retrieved March 2019, from https://news.umich.edu/flint-water-crisis-most-egregious-example-of-environmental-injustice-says-u-m-researcher/

National Coalition for the Homeless. (2019). Criminalization of homelessness. Retrieved March 2019, from https://nationalhomeless.org/issues/civil-rights/

NIC – National Intelligence Council. (2000). *Global Trends 2015: A dialogue about the future with nongovernment experts.* Washington, DC: NIC.

Nixon, R. (2011). *Slow violence and the environmentalism of the poor.* Cambridge, MA; London: Harvard University Press.

Noorgard, R. B. (1994). *Development betrayed. The end of progress and a coevolutionary revisioning of the future.* London: Routledge.

OGlobo. (2016, October 17). O maior desastre ambiental de Brasil, Rio de Janeiro. Retrieved March 2019, from https://acervo.oglobo.globo.com/em-destaque/maior-desastre-ambiental-do-brasil-tragedia-de-mariana-deixou-19-mortos-20208009

Ortega, G. (2013). *Extractivismo en el Chaco Paraguayo. Un Estudio Exploratorio.* Asuncion: Base Investigaciones Sociales.

de Paula, G. (2009). Diseño de políticas de defensa para el control y defensa de recursos naturales estratégicos. *Revista Política y Estrategia, 114*, 243–270.

Peluso, N. L., & Watts, M. (Eds.). (2001). *Violent environments.* Ithaca, NY: Cornell University Press.

Pepperell, N. (2016). The unease with civilization: Norbert Elias and the violence of the civilizing process, *Thesis Eleven, 137*(1), 3–21.

Poma, A. (2017). *Defending territory and dignity. Emotions and cultural change in the struggles against dams in Spain and Mexico [in Spanish].* Campina Grande; Seville; Guadalajara: WATERLAT-GOBACIT Network, State University of Paraiba Press (EDUEPB), School of Hispanic-American Studies (EEHA), Higher Council of Scientific Research (CSIC), and Western Institute of Technology and Higher Education (ITESO). Retrieved March 2019, from http://waterlat.org/publications/books/defending/

Russell, B., & Morris, N. (2006, February 28). Armed forces are put on standby to tackle threat of wars over water. *The Independent.*

Schwartz, D., & Singh, A. (1999). *Environmental conditions, resources, and conflicts: An introductory overview and data collection.* Nairobi: United Nations Environment Programme (UNEP).

Sridhar, V. (2006). Why do farmers commit suicide? The case of Andhra Pradesh, *Economic and Political Weekly, 41*(16), 1559–1565.

Steffen, W., Sanderson, A., Tyson, P. D., Jäger, J., Matson, P. A., Moore III, B., . . . Wasson, R. J. (2004). *Global change and the earth system: A planet under pressure.* Berlin; Heidelberg; New York: Springer-Verlag, p. 4.

Toepfer, K. (1999). Foreword. In D. Schwartz & A. Singh (Eds.), *Environmental conditions, resources, and conflicts: An introductory overview and data collection.* Nairobi: United Nations Environment Programme (UNEP).

Tuncak, B. (2017). Lessons from the Samarco disaster. *Bussiness and Human Rights Journal, 2*(1), 157–162.

UN – United Nations. (2019). *Desastres Naturales.* Retrieved March 2019, from https://news.un.org/es/tags/desastres-naturales

United States of America Department of the Navy. (2008). *Navy reestablishes U.S. 4th fleet.* Mayport, FL: United States of America Department of the Navy. Retrieved March 2019, from https://www.navy.mil/submit/display.asp?story_id=36606

Valencio, N. (2010). Desastres, ordem social e planejamento em defesa civil: o contexto brasileiro, *Saúde e Sociedade, 19*(4), 748–762.

Valencio, N. (Ed.). (2012). *Sociologia dos Desastres. Construção, interfaces e perspectivas no Brasil.* Sao Carlos, SP: RiMa Editora.

Vélez Galeano, H. (2017). *Gobernanza del agua en Territorios Ancestrales de Comunidades Negras en el Alto Cauca, Colombia.* Doctoral Thesis, Doctorado Interinstitucional en Ciencias Ambientales. Santiago de Cali: Universidad del Valle (UNIVALLE).

Weber, M. (1978). *Economy and society.* Berkeley, CA; Los Angeles, CA; London: University of California Press.

WoMin - African Women Unite Against Destructive Resource Extraction. (2014). *Women, gender and extractivism in Africa.* A collection of papers. Johannesbourg: International Alliance on Natural Resources in Africa (IANRA). Retrieved March 2019, from https://womin.org.za/images/papers/Full-collection-Women-gender-and-extractivism-in-Africa.pdf

Zhouri, A., & Laschefski, K. (Eds.). (2010). *Desenvolvimento e Conflitos Ambientais.* Belo Horizonte: Editora UFMG.

Zimmerer, J. (2014). Climate change, environmental violence and genocide, *The International Journal of Human Rights, 18*(3), 265–280.

5

The Moral Crusade on 'Gender Ideology'

Alliances Against Sexual and Reproductive Rights in Latin America

Richard Miskolci

Nearly a century ago, in *A Room of One's Own* (1929), Virginia Woolf observed: 'The history of men's opposition to women's emancipation is more interesting perhaps than the story of that emancipation itself'. A similar sentiment can be applied to Latin America's recent history. In the decade of 2010, strong reactions emerged in response to advances made in the areas of sexual and reproductive rights in several countries, mainly after the approval of civil unions or marriage between people of the same sex in Argentina, Brazil, Colombia and Mexico. In the case of the last three countries, the legal recognition of homosexual unions was made by the highest courts and the subsequent mobilization against feminist and LGBTI+ demands targeted educational materials created from a gender perspective that opposed sexual discrimination.

In this brief chapter, I synthesize a broad and complex situation that touches on many elements of the Latin American context. I recognize the importance of being as specific as possible to avoid rushing to extreme conclusions like those that can be found in recent activist work that posits the existence of a conspiratorial orchestration against sexual and reproductive rights, referred to as an 'anti-gender movement'.

The fact is that we all live in a globalized society and diverse types of interest groups – pros and cons on any agenda – participate in international exchanges. A sociological and historical perspective on the ongoing battles over gender and sexuality demands situated analysis, as well as greater attention to local contexts and how they interact with other national realities. Mechanically connecting local cases and diagnosing them as a unified international movement results in a kind of progressive 'conspiracy theory' that simply mirrors conservatives' own conspiracy theory on 'gender ideology'.

That said, the reactions to the advance of sexual and reproductive rights in Latin America, and their connections to gender studies, share several common characteristics, especially in their use of a vocabulary that labels such rights as 'gender ideology'. This is a term originally created in the late 1990s by Catholic and secular activists to oppose the reforms that involved equality between men and women, same-sex marriage, access to new reproductive technologies, contraception and the interruption of pregnancy, sexual education and the criminalization of homophobia.

The origin of the term 'gender ideology' has been documented by scholars in various countries (Corrêa, 2018; Lopéz, 2018; Miskolci, 2018; Patternote & Kuhar, 2017; Rondón, 2017). In the late 1990s a reaction was forged against the use of the concept of gender in international human rights agreements. Most scholars agree that it was after the IV World Conference on Women held by the United Nations in Beijing, in 1995, that secular intellectuals and Catholic religious leaders coined the term 'gender ideology' to synthesize what they understand as a divergence between feminist thinking and their own interests.

Examples of such reactions include the pro-life militant Dale O'Leary, who participated in the UN's conferences, and published the book *Gender Agenda* (1996) in which she accuses the United Nations of adopting a gender perspective in public policies (Junqueira, 2017). Sônia Corrêa (2018) observes that O'Leary does not use the term gender ideology, but, rather, 'radical feminist ideology'. In 1997, then Cardinal Joseph Ratzinger – now Pope Emeritus Benedict XVI – warned that the concept of gender contradicted Catholicism and introduced what he defined as being a new anthropology, that is, a new definition of the human that '*dissimulates an insurrection against the limits man carry within him as a biological being*' (1997, p. 142). In 1998, the Episcopal Conference of the Catholic Church of Peru began to use the term, which it expressed in its theme: 'Dangers and Scope of Gender Ideology'.

The Catholic opposition to human rights activists and to feminist thinking based on the concept of gender unified two different social groups against a single target; in doing so it also associated them, in a mechanical way, with a specific (leftist) branch of politics. 'Gender ideology' was officially defined in the Vatican Index of 2003, and took a leading role in the Document of Aparecida (2007), which resulted from the Fifth General Conference of the Episcopate of Latin America and the Caribbean. This conference expressed concerns about gender theory and its applications for gay people who demanded full citizenship rights.

What triggered the panic about 'gender ideology' on the subcontinent was the legal recognition that same-sex couples had and were receiving in the decade of 2010, suggesting that they have the same legal rights as married heterosexual couples. In the aftermath of the global economic crisis of 2008, with the popularization of online social networks, religious groups began to initiate online campaigns against LGBTI+ rights in a variety of different national contexts. These groups stoked social concerns over gay marriage and its possible consequences for childhood, family and society as a whole (cf. Scala, 2010). Making strategic use of social and mass media, political actors tried to attract popular support by spreading fear and anxiety in relation to advances in sexual and reproductive rights. The ensuing moral panic that was created stimulated reactionary activity at many levels. Eventually, these actors were able to cause panic with their newly created phantom of 'gender ideology'.[1]

LGBTI+ Rights in Latin America

	Partnership/Marriage	Adoption	Gender identity
Argentina	2010	2010	2010
Brazil	2011/2013	2010	2018
Chile	2015		2018
Colombia	2015	2015	2015
Ecuador	2014	2008	
Mexico	2007–16		
Peru			2016*
Uruguay	2013	2009	2009*

* with restrictions.

Conservative 'lay' intellectuals and politicians have contributed to spreading and encouraging the fear of this phantom menace, the so-called 'gender ideology', which has now taken shape and is no longer a mere creation of the Vatican. The term 'ideology' is used to associate feminism, gender studies and the demands for recognition of sexual diversity, with the threat of a return to communism, which creates even greater anxiety in the former-socialist countries of Europe and Latin America. This is also the case among social sectors opposed to leftist governments in the regimes of Cuba and Venezuela.

Contrary to the statements made by groups opposed to sexual and reproductive rights, there is no evidence that leftist governments have defended these movements, not even in countries led by leftist female presidents, such as: Argentina (2007–2015), Brazil (2011–2016), Chile (2006–2010 and 2014–2018) and Costa Rica (2010–2014). The hegemony of a political narrative involving the notion of 'gender ideology', however, has coincided with the arrival of women politicians to the presidencies of these countries, indicating that social fears about the break-up of traditional gender roles and hierarchies may have been amplified by the presence of women in presidency, positions traditionally held by men.

Historically, there has been a well-documented resistance in Latin America's political left to the incorporation of feminist and LGBTI + demands (Alvarez, 2014; Bimbi, 2010; Pinto, 2003). Conservative rhetoric, however, tends to associate the left, communism and liberal ideas with the political agendas of these demands. The use of sexuality and gender politics has been used as a way of defining the left as an enemy, threatening the moral construction of their nations.

Evidence from various countries in the region suggests that there is a growing separation of the anti-gender ideology agenda from its Catholic and religious origins. Politicians and interest groups, in the form of opportunistic moral entrepreneurs, have adopted it as their own. It has become an electoral strategy that turns a political dispute into a moral conflict between 'good citizens' and 'bad', with the 'bad' typically identified as feminists, homosexuals, trans people and their allies (Messenberg, 2017). This tactic is typically adopted by politicians, political parties and organizations who are connected to a conservative, right-wing, populist agenda.

The alliance between Catholic activists, those in Brazil known as Neopentecostal evangelicals, and civil society organizations with a right-wing profile, frequently takes on characteristics of a moral crusade. The creation of a moral panic that identifies a threat to children has been a common expedient in various countries for fighting educational materials or reforms that include content about gender and anti-homophobia. This occurred in Brazil in 2011, and later in 2014–2015, during debates in congress over the National Education Plan and related state and municipal measures (Balieiro, 2018). In 2016, something similar took place in Colombia (Rondón, 2017), Mexico (Lopéz, 2018) and Peru, reaching Paraguay in 2017. In Brazil, this led to persecution of teachers, artists and intellectuals. The most emblematic case was the reaction to a visit by Judith Butler in November 2017, who was seen by these groups as the 'mother of gender ideology' (Miskolci & Pereira, 2018).

These campaigns that take the shape of a moral crusade often spark alliances among heterogeneous social sectors interested in attracting followers on social networks and mobilizing people to attend public demonstrations. In legislative arenas the aim has been to stop the approval of laws, plans or programmes that could include a perspective supportive of sexual and reproductive rights. In 2016, it was perceived that they joined to take advantage of opportunities to disseminate their ideology by tying it in Brazil to a campaign against corruption that called for the impeachment of President Dilma Rousseff (Workers Party), and also in Colombia, in the drafting of a peace agreement with the Revolutionary Armed Forces of Colombia (FARC). In each country, different interest groups created political campaigns in the form of moral crusades. In the new public sphere created by the hegemony of social networks platforms, to present a political issue as a moral one became strategic to forge alliances and gain followers and supporters (Miskolci, 2021).

Anchored in the influence of the Catholic Church and Pentecostal evangelical churches, but increasingly in the way that their secular arms act in online networks, they succeeded – with support at times from the mainstream media – in presenting themselves to public opinion as having expressive popular support even if only isolated studies have come to measure their actual social base. In several Latin American countries, there are civil society organizations that function as 'empty shells', that is, they are led by a small group of people with economic and symbolic capital, which allows them to create the false public image that they are a social movement with many supporters.

The relative success of the campaign against sexual and reproductive rights can be explained based on the alliance that unites at least three actors with separate yet converging objectives. The first of these actors is the Catholic Church with its moral recognition and historic influence in Latin America, seeking to shape the human rights agenda according to its interests. The second is the evangelicals – especially the neopentecostals – who are striving to conquer greater moral and political ground and influence in countries like Brazil, Colombia, Costa Rica and Venezuela. The third are right-wing interest groups and politicians who make strategic use of these moral agendas to create or broaden their base of popular support.

The alliance between these three groups has proven to be beneficial to both the religious and secular components of their agendas. The religious and political actors have become allies in their efforts to bar the expansion of gender equality rights that they argue contradict their principles, and/or limit their influence.[2] The alliance benefits the secular interest groups – and politicians who represent them – by helping them promote an agenda that often includes an unpopular neoliberal economic perspective regarding state involvement and public policies (Miskolci & Pereira, 2019).

The moral platform has been defended within a repertoire of action that involves the creation of moral panics to disseminate fear as a strategy of mobilization to stop legal and cultural change. This then also creates a polarization between feminist and LGBTI + movements, and religious actors and their supporters. It is possible that this polarization would not be created without the use of social media in the configuration of the campaign as a moral crusade. The social media networks help to disseminate slogans and strong images, but above all – because they allow individual access – they tend to convert political discussions into moral ones, spreading forms of behavioural vigilance.

Instead of making the personal political (as in the 1960s feminist slogan), social media tends to make politics a matter of personal opinion or belief. On the internet, posts and information circulate inside a culture of popularity that tends to favour content that can attract the most attention and the highest number of followers. Usually, such content is sensationalistic and based on common sense (Pasquale, 2017) since the dynamics of digital social networks tend to reinforce established ideas and even prejudices instead of promoting critical thinking. Therefore, the online moral crusade against 'gender ideology' has functioned by connecting and creating conservative activist networks wherein the main actors and leaders belonged to right-wing political interest groups, especially populist and neoliberal ones.

The crusade's discursive trope involves hyperbolic language that presents gender studies and sexual and reproductive rights as a potential catastrophe for collective life (cf. Scala, 2010). In their public manifestations they defend the 'natural' family and children as if they were threatened by a homosexual conspiracy. The moral entrepreneurs who mounted these crusades define the family as being inseparable from heterosexuality and from the control by men of women and children, and thus defend the absolute authority of the father and the patriarchy (Miguel, 2016).

In some countries it is possible to recognize in these ideas the coordination of conservative local organizations and international movements (both religious and secular ones).[3] In some national contexts, such as Colombia, Peru, Mexico and Argentina, religious activists have been able to mobilize large street demonstrations in support of the family and/or in supposed defense of children, in others, like Brazil, their action has mainly focused on smaller protests aimed at legislative chambers, or in legal persecution of teachers who they believe are indoctrinating (from the left) students, and artists whose work or performances threaten childhood development.

The creation of a moral panic aimed at triggering a campaign in the form of a moral crusade tends to make its origins in secular groups invisible. These panics suggest a righteousness that hides its political interests and its frequent use as a strategy to attract voters and win elections. In the Brazilian context, secular groups tend to be the most powerful players involved in the alliance.

Patternote and Kuhar (2017) emphasize the fact that we are witnessing the emergence of a new generation of activists with traditional values, questioning, therefore, their classification as conservative because they effectively act to construct a future society. The evidence collected by researchers in Europe and Latin America indicate that we are facing a movement that cannot be accurately classified as religious fundamentalism or conservatism.[4] The doubt about what is retrograde, conservative or a new activism tends to take place among analysts who do not presuppose an inexorable historic route towards the conquest of rights and recognition. It is important to be careful to recognize that nothing guarantees that we are heading in this direction. Many researchers show the dispute about human rights in international forums continues to be conflictual and there is no historical sign of a progressive disappearance of adversaries of sexual and reproductive rights (Corrêa, 2018; Junqueira, 2017). Considering the Brazilian case, sociologist Berenice Bento (2017, 2018) affirms that we are witnessing the beginning of an intensification of disputes in this field in which traditionalist segments have expressed themselves since the 1960s.

The Catholic Church, for example, remains a powerful actor that has recognized the change in its battlefield from Europe to Latin America. It helps to contextualize the political significance of the abdication of Benedict XVI followed by the election of Francis. The first visit made by the Latin American Pope was to Rio de Janeiro, to attend World Youth Day. In one of his talks, the supreme pontiff called on Catholic youth to be 'revolutionaries', strengthening a new generation that, we now know, can struggle with the Vatican against the concept of gender in favour not of equality between men and women, but of their complementarity, and of the family understood in naturalized terms, with sexuality being portrayed as inseparable from reproduction.

Young Catholics, Neopentecostal evangelicals and secularists linked to right-wing groups and politicians that adhere to this moral agenda form a new generation of activists who have only begun to show their influence. Their actions against gender studies in universities, and sexual education in schools, are inseparable from their interests in maintaining the criminalization of abortion and refusing full citizenship rights for LGBTI+ people. Those who suffer the worst repercussions from these activities and agendas are non-white people, as well as the poorest and youngest portions of Latin America's population. Studies indicate that the non-existence of sexual education, access to contraceptives and official services to interrupt pregnancy, expose poor, Black, mestizo or indigenous women to greater risk of death, and that the non-recognition of sexual diversity relegates homosexuals, trans and transvestite people to constant physical and legal insecurity as they suffer continuous forms of discrimination, harassment and violence.

The moral crusade against 'gender ideology' in Latin America is a multifaceted phenomenon with a consistent repertoire of action and a common discursive trope. It always develops from local issues and has involved agents who go beyond religious actors, like conservative politicians and parties that need a popular agenda to attract voters and win elections. Sociologically speaking, it is necessary to overcome interpretations that simply highlight the religious origins of this phenomenon, so as to also identify the secular interest groups that, in every national context, have not simply joined but also backed these moral crusades. A second step would be to analyse how and why these groups participate in such campaigns, given that secular groups tend to be opportunistic moral entrepreneurs with their own political and economic agendas.

Of foremost importance is answering the classic question about moral panics: cui bono? Who benefits from the collective fear and persecution that these crusades engender? The only provisional answer I can provide is based on the situation in Brazil, in which an alliance of religious and agnostic groups succeeded in creating a moral panic that paved the way for the victory of the populist extreme-right in 2018's presidential elections. In Latin America's largest and most populous country, this alliance brought together political actors and interest groups who had once been obscure, but united under an unpopular neoliberal economic agenda.

The alliance seemingly began in May 2011, when the former military officer and little-known congressman Jair Messias Bolsonaro took the first step towards initiating a moral crusade after Brazil's Supreme Court conferred legal recognition on same-sex unions. A Catholic politician with strong ties to Brazil's evangelical caucus, Bolsonaro called media attention to anti-homophobia educational materials; he presented these as components of a supposedly dangerous 'gay kit' that threatened to change children into homosexuals. Thus, Brazil's moral panic originated as a (homo)sexual panic that initially drew most of its support from an authoritarian segment of Brazilian society prone to believing that social cohesion was inseparable from sexual repression.

Later, between 2014 and 2016, discussions of a new federal educational plan – and its state and municipal versions – created an alliance among Catholics, neopentecostal evangelicals and secular right-wing interest groups disseminating panic about what they had begun to call 'gender ideology'. These right-wing interest groups were also concerned with what they described as leftist political indoctrination in schools. Therefore, groups that were primarily opposed to feminism, LGBTI+ rights, and gender studies, joined others opposed to purported Marxist indoctrination, thereby forming a marriage of convenience that quickly opened to yet another partner.

The campaign and massive demonstrations in favour of the impeachment of leftist female president Dilma Rousseff in 2016 associated the political actors described above with an even more popular cause: namely, corruption. In a snowball effect, what had begun as (homo)sexual panic gained support as a moral crusade against leftist political indoctrination. This grew still larger when it embraced the mass disgust towards corruption scandals associated with the Worker's Party government. Soon, feminists, LGBTI+ people, communism and corrupt politicians were associated together as a bigger and more threatening phantom that attracted mass support to a growing extreme right-wing movement.

In the context of changing social hierarchies, economic crises and political turmoil, the appeal of a moral platform embodied by an authoritarian extreme-right politician like Bolsonaro proved to be a recipe for success. Not by chance, his government was composed of a heterogeneous set of four interest groups: (1) ideological/religious interests in charge of education, human rights and foreign relations; (2) military interests that provide institutional structure; (3) neoliberal interests that coordinate economic matters and (4) a moralizing branch charged with maintaining public security and investigating corruption schemes. In all likelihood, none of these groups could have won elections alone, especially on a platform that so exposed its individual interests. Instead, these groups joined forces to present themselves as saviours of the people against enemies like LGBTI+ people, feminists, communism and corrupt (leftist) politicians.

What was the fear that fed the successful Brazilian moral crusade against the emancipation of women and LGBTI+ people, culmi-nating in the election of an ex-army officer known for his homopho-bia, sexism, hate of Communism? It is possible that the fear was around women and homosexuals breaking the bounds of established traditional hierarchies, which would be an infraction of divine law or of the social order, as a large part of Bolsonaro's supporters under-stand it – in an authoritarian manner. In their vision, homosexuals, women, indigenous people, Blacks and others should be named and defined, their rights restricted by religious, psychological and political authorities. It is not mere chance that many among them also perse-cute Afro-Brazilian religions, defend the 'gay cure' or are apologists for dictatorship and torture.

The Latin American crusade against 'gender ideology' in its different national manifestations has had various consequences and results; common ones include the impediment of adoption of a gender perspective in educational policies (cf. Deslandes, 2015). This form of educational censorship contributes to the maintenance of inequalities between men and women and above all to discrimination and violence against gays, lesbians, trans people and others. Appreciating the wisdom of Virginia Woolf who wrote in a European context, observing the opposition of certain Latin American men and women to gender and sexual emancipation, may be more interesting than observing this emancipation itself. Doing so allows us to identify social anxieties and fears that are often involved – but rarely taken into account – in our analyses of conflicts aroused by changing power relations, particularly those concerning gender and sexual hierarchies.

Notes

1   Stanley Cohen has coined the classical sociological analysis of moral panics in the 1960s. According to Kenneth Thompson (2005), different analytical approaches about the phenomenon developed in the United Kingdom – where there is an emphasis on the consequences of economic crisis – while in the United States sociologists tend to focus on collective anxieties. On moral panics, see Cohen (2011); Goode and Ben-Yehuda (2009); Thompson (2005). For a classical reference on sexual panics, see also Rubin (1993).

2   In the Brazilian case, studies such as those by Prandi and Santos (2017) indicate a gap between the conservative agenda of Neopentecostal evangelical politicians and the opinions of their potential voters in their respective churches. Thus, it is possible that the voters who support them in the moral agenda are secular, but only new studies can evaluate if this agenda results less in an adherence to their religious electorate than in an expansion of it.

3   The associations between national and international organizations were observed in the European context by the studies of Cornejo-Valle and Pichardo (2017) and Patternote and Kuhar (2017). In Latin America, most of the studies available only identify the ties among Catholic associations. In the Brazilian case, there is evidence that interest groups such as the Movimento Brasil Livre (MBL) are tied to the Atlas Network.

4   Those thinkers who consider them only as a reaction to conquests of feminist and LGBTI + rights extend an analytical model created in the US context to different realities, giving little attention to their local particularities.

References

Alvarez, S. E. (2014). Para além da sociedade civil: Reflexões sobre o campo feminista. *Cadernos Pagu, 43*, 13–56.

Balieiro, F. (2018). *'Don't mess with my kids': Building the moral panic of the child under threat.* Cadernos Pagu, Campinas: Núcleo de Estudos de Gênero Pagu – UNICAMP, n.53. Retrieved 15 June 2018, from http://www.scielo.br/scielo.php?script=sci_arttext&pid=S0104-83332018000200406&lng=en&nrm=iso&tlng=en

Bento, B. (30 October 2017). Afeto, Butler e os TFPistas. *Cult.* Retrieved 21 May 2018, from https://revistacult.uol.com.br/home/afeto-judith-butler-neotfpistas/

Bento, B. (09 May 2018). Quando o medo se transforma em ação política. *Justificando.* Retrieved 20 May 2018, from http://justificando.cartacapital.com.br/2018/05/09/quando-o-medo-se-transforma-em-acao-politica/

Bimbi, B. (2010). *Matrimonio igualitario: Intrigas, tensiones y secretos en el camino hacia la ley.* Buenos Aires: Planeta.

Cohen, S. (2011). *Folk devils and moral panics: The creation of the mods and rockers.* London/New York, NY: Routledge.

Cornejo-Valle, M., & Pichardo, J. I. (2017). *La 'ideología de género' frente a los derechos sexuales y reproductivos. El escenario español.* Cadernos Pagu, Campinas: Núcleo de Estudos de Gênero Pagu-UNICAMP, n.50. Retrieved 20 May 2018, from http://www.scielo.br/scielo.php?script=sci_arttext&pid=S0104-83332017000200501&lng=en&nrm=iso&tlng=es

Corrêa, S. (2018). *A política do gênero: Um comentário genealógico.* Cadernos Pagu, Campinas: Núcleo de Estudos de Gênero Pagu-UNICAMP, n.53. Retrieved 12 June 2018, from http://www.scielo.br/scielo.php?script=sci_arttext&pid=S0104-83332018000200401&lng=en&nrm=iso&tlng=pt

Deslandes, K. (2015). *Formação de professors e direitos humanos: Construindo escolas promotoras da igualdade.* Belo Horizonte: Autêntica.

Goode, E., & Ben-Yehuda, N. (2009). *Moral panics: The social construction of deviance.* Malden: Blachwell Publishers.

Junqueira, R. D. (2017). 'Ideologia de gênero': A gênese de uma categoria política reacionária – ou a promoção dos direitos humanos se tornou uma ameaça à 'família natural'? In P. R. C. Ribeiro, & J. C. Magalhães (Eds.), *Debates contemporâneas sobre a educação para a sexualidade.* Rio Grande: Editora da FURG. pp. 25–52.

Lopéz, J. A. (2018). Movilización y contramovilización frente a los derechos LGBTI. Respuestas conservadoras al reconocimiento de los derechos humanos. *Estudios Sociológicos XXXVI, 106*, 165–191.

Messenberg, D. (2017). A direita que saiu do armário: A cosmovisão dos formadores de opinião dos manifestantes de direita brasileiros. *Sociedade e Estado, 32*(3), 621–647.

Miguel, L. F. (2016). Da 'doutrinação marxista' à 'ideologia de gênero' – Escola sem Partido e as leis da mordaça no parlamento brasileiro. *Direito & Práxis, 7*(15), 590–621.

Miskolci, R. (2018). Exorcizing a ghost: The interests behind the war on 'gender ideology'. *Cadernos Pagu, 53.* Retrieved 14 June 2018, from http://www.scielo.br/scielo.php?script=sci_arttext&pid=S0104-83332018000200402&lng=en&nrm=iso&tlng=en

Miskolci, R. (2021). *Batalhas morais: Política identitária na esfera pública técnico-midiatizada.* Belo Horizonte: Autêntica.

Miskolci, R., & Pereira, P. P. G. (2018). Who's afraid of Judith Butler? The moral crusade against human rights in Brazil. *Cadernos Pagu*. Retrieved 11 June 2018, from http://www.scielo.br/scielo.php?script=sci_arttext&pid=S0104-83332018 000200400&lng=en&nrm=iso&tlng=en

Miskolci, R., & Pereira, P. P. G. (2019). Education and health in dispute: Anti-egalitarian movements and public policies. *Interface - Comunicação, Saúde e Educação, 23*, 2019.

Pasquale, F. (2017). *The automated public sphere*. New York, NY: Rosa Luxemburg Stiftung.

Patternote, D., & Kuhar, R. (Eds) (2017). *Anti-gender campaigns in Europe: Mobilizing against equality*. London; New York, NY: Rowman & Littlefield.

Pinto, C. R. J. (2003). *Uma história do feminismo no Brasil*. São Paulo: Editora Fundação Perseu Abramo.

Prandi, R., & Santos, R. W. (2017). Quem tem medo da bancada evangélica? Posições sobre moralidade e política no eleitorado brasileiro, no Congresso Nacional e na Frente Parlamentar Evangélica. *Tempo Social – Revista de Sociologia da USP, 29*(2), 187–214.

Ratzinger, J. A. (1997). *La sal de la tierra*. Madrid: Libros Palabra.

Rondón, M. A. R. (2017). La ideología de género como excesso: Pánico moral y decisión ética en la política colombiana, *Sexualidad, Salud y Sociedad – Revista Latinoamericana, 27*, 128–148.

Rubin, G. (1993). Thinking sex: Notes for a radical theory of the politics of sexuality. In H. Abelove, M Barale, and D Halperin (Eds.) *The lesbian and gay studies reader* (pp. 3–44). New York, NY: Routledge.

Scala, J. (2010). *La ideología de género: El género como herramienta de poder*. Rosário: Ediciones Logos.

Thompson, K. (2005). *Moral panics*. London; New York, NY: Routledge.

Woolf, V. (2001). *A room of one's own + Three guineas*. Oxford's World Classics, e-book, 2001.

Document

CONSEJO EPISCOPAL LATINOAMERICANO (Celam) (2007). *Documento conclusivo (Documento da Aparecida)*. Bogotá: Centro de Publicaciones del Celam.

6

The Arc of Justice in the Era of Routinized Violence*

Bandana Purkayastha

The design and institutionalization of the Universal Declaration of Human Rights (UDHR) in 1948 stands as an important moment in the history of human efforts to ensure justice for all. Since that time, a series of conventions have further expanded the scope of who is included within the arc of justice, as defined by human rights. A core component of these human rights conventions is to ensure that justice, as it is defined and enacted within nation-states, is complemented (or even supplemented) by an international tapestry of justice. In an ideal world these multiple levels of justice should ensure better lives of human dignity for all people, including those who have moved or are on the move across borders. Instead of this ideal, however, the case of migrants provides a lens through which we can examine the gaps in the terrains of justice within and across nation-states.

Despite the promise of human rights, the events unfolding in the 21st century, particularly in the United States where I am located, reflect a rapidly expanding chasm between the rhetoric of democracy, freedom and justice, and the practices that routinize violence and lead to injustices. Technologies of surveillance and control have become increasingly sophisticated, as has the weaponry that has expanded the range and scope of State violence far beyond the conventional fields of battle. Along with the traditional weapons wielded by States and non-State entities such as terrorists and vigilante groups, new entities, like special interest groups and corporations, are now also involved in the powerful struggles to enshrine ever new configurations of power and control. Violence is routinized, so that many types appear to be normal everyday practices (Pandey, 2006; Purkayastha and Ratcliff, 2014). New technologies, including the weaponized discourse through social media, have been used to spread and instil fear in the public and erode the traditional paths to justice (Pascale, 2019).

Reflecting on the ideal of justice – by which I mean the creation and maintenance of institutions and social conditions that ensure people can build lives of dignity, free want and fear and other human insecurities – offers us an opportunity to focus on a world where new technologies of injustice and violence are being routinized. This chapter focuses on the issues of routinized violence and justice by focussing on migrants, the group that includes citizens and stateless people, refugees, asylum seekers and trafficked persons, who are supposed to be able to access rights and justice according to UDHR. In practice, within States, a series of shifting assumptions about who exactly is a migrant, and to what extent migrants are constructed, politically, as objects of fear or sympathy, shape the terrain of laws, policies and interactions that construct and/or impede forces of justice.

Migrants, Violence and Justice

There is a persistent popular assumption that democratic States, especially democratic States in the Global North, ensure justice for citizens as well as migrants, i.e. those who are not citizens, but are living within their borders. However, a vast body of critical scholarship demonstrates that the reality is different (for a review, see Purkayastha, 2018). Racialized citizens, including those who are persistently perceived as foreigners, are rarely able to access all the levels of justice, while people who are not citizens, are even further distanced from accessing the institutions and social conditions that might enable them to build lives with human security. To discuss routine violence and justice, I first present different groups of migrants, using United Nations' statistics; I use these categories to show why we should use a migrant continuum instead of discrete categories if we want to reflect on justice. I turn to selected critical scholarship on migrants from the Global North and South to explain some of the less visible assumptions that undergird discrete migrant categories (e.g. Glenn, 2015; Choudhury and Samaddar, 2015; Samaddar, 2018; Simpson, 2017) as well as the ways in which the fragmented foci on migrants – e.g. international vs internal, refugees vs trafficked persons – lead to gaps in tracing the larger processes, such as violence, that shape the lives of migrants, denying them justice (see Purkayastha, 2018). Following a discussion on migrants, I turn to a reflection on violence and current perpetrators. In this section,

I focus on routine violence – the kind of violence that gets normalized everyday by a variety of State and non-State actors – that affect migrants' (and citizens) access to rights and freedoms which are key to understanding justice. The third section is on the question of justice in the contemporary world. Adding discussions on routine violence and structural barriers to justice that affect migrants offers a glimpse of the ways that citizens, especially those marginalized by other structures, are also affected as these structures encroach on their lives.

Migrants

Migrants, or people on the move, make up a significant number of the world's population. According to the World Migration Report (UN-IOM, 2022),

'The number of international migrants worldwide has continued to grow rapidly in recent years, reaching 281 million by 2022, up from 220 million in 2010.'[1] Migrants constitute 1 in 30 of the world's population. According to the United Nations High Commission on Refugees (UNHCR), people who were forced to migrate – refugees, asylum seekers and internally displaced persons – now total 84.7 million people, with 48 million internally displaced people, 26.6 million refugees and 4.4 million asylum seekers; most of the latter live in the countries nearest to them (UNHCR, 2021). These numbers are important because the conditions that encourage or force people to move are related to the larger questions of justice. The rising number of migrants indicates an inverse correlation with socially just conditions in societies.

The key assumption about migrants is they intend to get away from one place and settle in another, though there is some research about multiple moves. A vast global North literature has examined the end point; for instance, in the United States, the century-long focus on assimilation and incorporation examines the efforts of migrants to fit into the United States structurally and culturally (e.g. Portes and Zhou, 1993). Once they reach their destination, some migrants are, with time, able to achieve citizenships that, theoretically, allows them to both access the justice systems of their new home nations and have the ability (right) to challenge injustices. Other migrants, including guest workers, are subject to the laws, policies and controls of the destination country like the citizens, but they are also subject to additional controls that allow only partial access, at best, to the edifices of justice that allow them to challenge their marginalization. In general, a migrant's location within particular prisms of space and time affects them, i.e. in which country they are located during different points of their migration history and how they are viewed by the State at each point in time are relevant. For instance, Chowdhury Lahiri (2021) describes how recent citizenship legislation in India rendered long-term refugees from Bangladesh, stateless and ineligible to stay in the country. Migrants may be affected by geographic configurations of national boundaries, where it is located, how strictly it is enforced, during any historical period, since rivers shifts, islands appear and disappear in riverine areas, etc. (see Chakraborty and Pathan, 2021).

Critics now point out that research that focuses on what migrants do – or should be doing – to fit into the host society is a way to perpetuate dominant groups' supremacy. The dominant approach erases ways in which race/gender/class/sexuality and related structures restrict different groups of migrants' life chances. In order to break away from the research for the powerful, we need to focus on the marginalizing structures that are key to understand the location of migrant and citizen groups within a terrain of justice. Several aspects are important. Critical scholars are documenting the global reach of countries such as the United States through wars and other military engagements that create the structural conditions which lead to the migration of people (Makki et al., 2020); hence, at one level, the structures that affect all migrants – the reasons why people are moving in larger numbers – are linked to these wars, conflicts, construction of scarcity and precarity. Along with an understanding of nested global to local structural contexts, the links between individuals and structural opportunities and barriers *longitudinally* are important for understanding the circumstances through which different migrants attempt to rebuild lives of dignity, are erased. For instance, scholars argue that the designation of 'foreign born', 'migrant' and 'native' are contingent upon the deification of national boundaries that have often been imposed as part of colonial expansion and have changed historically. This last point about changing national boundaries has been the subject of challenge by scholars such as Samaddar (1999), who proposed the term cross-border migration to highlight that the recency of many national boundaries upon which the political status of citizens vs migrants is based. Recent Indigenous scholarship also points to the same problem of assuming national territories are unchangeable because dominant groups are able to erase the histories of territorial expansions and land grabs (*cf:* Simpson, 2017).

There may be methodological reasons to focus on one or another specific group – for instance, on economic migrants or temporary migrants or refugees – to understand a particular aspect of their lives and the structures that shape them, but framing questions about justice amidst routine violence – requires moving beyond the fragmented scholarship that studies migrants, or refugees or trafficked persons or stateless people separately. In fact, I consider migrants, and the structures and processes in which they are enmeshed, are arrayed on a continuum: from international migrants, at one end, through to internal migrants, refugees, internally displaced persons and trafficked persons at the other (Purkayastha, 2018).

Figure 6.1 illustrates broad distinctions between these classifications of migrants; the diagram emphasizes that these descriptors are dynamic at the level of human beings: with a change in structural circumstances, migrants might end up in different categories during their lifetime. This continuum also carries the potential to help us understand the conditions prior to, during and after migration. Who is a migrant, and at what point are they considered a migrant, a refugee, an asylum seeker, or a trafficked person, and which type of migration, to where, best describes their journey at any point? This emphasis on a continuum reflects dynamic worlds of formal policies and laws that

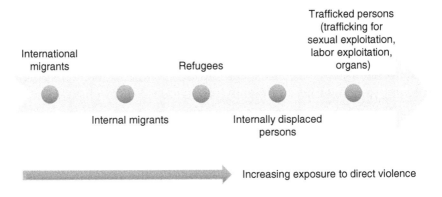

Figure 6.1   A continuum of migrants

govern the movement of people across borders (national or internal borders) that influence people's ability to settle and their access to critical resources that are needed for an individual or group's survival and health. Many layers of complexities, reflecting national and regional histories, further complicate how people are classified in different parts of the world.

While separate bureaucracies continue to manage each type of migrant group, accounts of contemporary migrants, drawn from the United States, European Union (EU) and India, show that the distinction between refugees, asylum seekers and migrants in general are rapidly being weakened politically; at the same time political processes continue to render people stateless (*cf:* Choudhury and Samaddar, 2015; Settalwaad, 2019). The United States provides a good example of the political efforts to describe asylum seekers as 'illegal' migrants and then, based on this political rhetoric, to initiate procedures to justify and enable holding these migrants in camps (Goldbaum, 2019; Goldberg, 2019; Kanno-Young and Dickerson, 2019), despite international criticism (Paul and Miroff, 2019). Similarly, the standards and paperwork to prove citizenship is undergoing rapid transformation in India; as a result people are being thrown into liminal statuses while others are rendered stateless (Chowdhury Lahiri, 2021). In each country where such changes are underway, there is also a corresponding development of a migrant detention industry, including the development of private corporations that profit from detention. These industries are part of routinized violence, as I discuss in the next section.

Violence

A vast body of scholarly work has described a range of violence within intimate spheres, to violence within and between communities, and between and across States (Abraham, 2000; Abraham and Tastsoglou, 2016; Erturk and Purkayastha, 2012; Lalitha and Dhanraj, 2016; Parish, 2017; Pascale, 2019; Sutton, 2010; Walby, 2012). These different types of violence – and the forms in which violence emerges through underlying structural and symbolic processes – affect migrants and citizens constantly. Walby (2012) argues that sociologists have to move beyond the older ideas that violence decreases with modernity and understand 'the important and varied interconnections between violence in the interpersonal sphere, in governance and resistance and in warfare' (p. 97). Kannabiran (2016) points out that 'A historiography of violence would entail unravelling the complex and layered ways in which narratives of violence – as fact, experience, affections, afflictions, trauma, memory, rhetoric, philosophy, law and governmentality – have shifted, changed course, or boomeranged into an imagined past' (p. 2). von Holdt (2013) has discussed both Bourdieu's version of symbolic violence, and also Fanon's colonial violence, as being processes through which violence is normalized or routinized.

Gyanendra Pandey (2006) has argued that routine violence, associated with modern-states, is not episodic in nature; it is almost continual, in that it is so much a part of our everyday lives that we often no longer even recognize it as violence. Pandey emphasizes that routine violence occurs at international, national and community levels. Pandey describes three indicators of routine violence. Firstly, the larger the organization that engages in the violence, such as a State, and the more widespread its scale, the more it is likely to be legitimated and routinized. Secondly, the more technologically sophisticated the scale of the violence, for instance, the use of remotely controlled drones, the more likely these technologies will be presented as routine practices for maintaining security and thus accepted. Lastly, routine violence is often directed towards groups marked by their race/class/gender with associated interactions with age, culture, religion, sexualities.

In order to explain the nexus of routinized violence within States, as it affects migrants, it is instructive to unpack the interrelated forms of violence (illustrated in Figure 6.2). States typically reserve the right to use violence for social control and wars. The top box of Figure 6.2, notes the violence of wars and conflicts which kill, maim and create long-term insecurities. Abraham and Tastsoglou (2016) among others have discussed that the total number of wars and conflicts in the world have increased over the last decades, and the range of their effects have increased through the increased capacity of weapons (UN, n.d.). The weapons used in 21st century conflicts continue to be a rapidly growing business, generating large profits for States as well as corporations. As a result, arms production companies, with United States as a leading location for these companies, seek newer customers leading to the expansion of areas where such

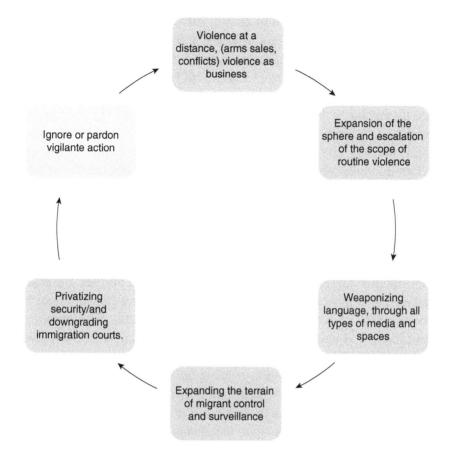

Figure 6.2   Interlinked violence

weapons can be used (Shah, 2013). Moving clockwise in Figure 6.2, the second box indicates the expansion of the sphere of routine violence. On the one hand, it represents the expanding global spaces where modern weaponry is used. On the other, it indicates the sphere of these escalated forms of violence have expanded beyond the spaces of wars into domestic engagements. It emphasizes that some of the weapons that have previously been used as weapons of war are now being brought into domestic use by the police as well as within-State actors including vigilante groups (Beoku-Betts, 2016; Fritz et al., 2011; SIPRI, 2013). In the United States, following the #Black-LivesMatter movement, scrutiny of weapons US police use shows that military equipment is distributed routinely by the US Department of

Defense to the police (Radil et al., 2017; see also Armaline et al., 2011). Even a casual reading of violence by 'ordinary people' against members of groups such as against Asian Americans involves the use of military grade weaponry (Avashia, 2021; Chowdhury-Lahiri et al., 2020). As political terrain shift in countries and authoritarian politics are ascendant, it is not unusual to find weaponized vigilante groups operate with impunity or be pardoned (for examples, see the Bosman, 2021; Dhillon, 2019). These types of violence affect people in situ and target migrants (especially those seen as foreigners irrespective of their citizenship).

Pascale (2019) has pointed to the role of weaponized language in constructing targets of violence. This is the point of the next box in Figure 6.2. Pascale argues that through the weaponization of language, authoritarian governments weaponize language to amplify resentments, target scapegoats, legitimize injustice and lay the essential cornerstones of material violence. She identifies four interlocking components of weaponized language: propaganda, disinformation, censorship and mundane discourse. Weaponized language is deployed through political channels, and increasingly, circulated via WhatsApp and other platforms where the growing business of fabricated 'news' is used to foment violence (Mclaughlin, 2018). The redistribution of this language via social media is then often done by people who do not necessarily believe in far-right ideologies, but get drawn into the process, through seemingly neutral, but increasingly weaponized discourses. Language has the power to cause harm, induce trauma and fear, and has been used for centuries in erasing people and whole civilizations from history. Language is also often a precursor to vigilante violence and direct State violence (in the guise of introducing social order). States in which there is widespread use of these forms of violence also tend to fail to prosecute such violence aggressively and consistently and are, consequently, complicit in vigilante violence against those suspected of being 'foreign' (e.g. for two recent examples, see Dhillon, 2019 on India & Bosman, 2021, or Davidson, 2019, on the United States).

Migrants are especially vulnerable to all these forms of violence, especially when they are distanced from institutions set up to ensure justice. Many of today's conflicts generate conditions that are direct and indirect causes for people to flee their country (Hanafi, 2008) or move to another part of the country where they may not be welcome

(Njiru and Purkayastha, 2015), becoming a part of the internal or international migrant population. These conditions include direct violence, the erosion of social order, which then erodes social protections for the vulnerable and opens the terrain for vigilante violence; the indirect effects include interruptions of normal processes of social life and access to resources such as food, healthcare, education and the destruction of land and water resources (Marc, n.d.). Fleeing is not a whole solution because migrant pathways are fraught with further violence, migrants are vulnerable to traffickers, vigilante groups as well as the organized efforts of States to push them away (Choudhury and Samaddar, 2015).

Other forms of State-facilitated violence further contribute to the routinization of violence. For instance, people who are trafficked for labour – sexual or otherwise – are recognized as being in situations of abuse and violence. Yet, they typically have little recourse to justice, despite significant campaigns to eradicate various types of human trafficking (*cf:* Purkayastha and Yousaf, 2019). The terrain of temporary labour to labour trafficking also weakens access and withholds rights from these migrants so that they are left at the mercy of abuse by their employers (Burnett, 2017; Purkayastha and Yousaf, 2019; Yea, 2014).

As I have illustrated in Figure 6.2, migrants are now encountering additional expanded migrant control and surveillance regimes. States have exhibited an escalation of repressive measures and, at the same time, have expanded the definition and scope of what is considered a crime. In the United States, for instance, the principles and practices of the criminal justice system have been merged with the immigration system (Chacón, 2009; Hartry, 2012; Legomsky, 2007). On the one hand, there is increasing prosecution of immigration violations as criminal acts, workplace raids, harsh sentencing and detention have become a norm (Golash-Boza, 2015).

While these actions could be interpreted as a form of force and violence themselves, their intersection with other more explicit practices further enhances the level of routinized violence evident in societies around the world. As people flee conflict zones – whether these conflicts are related to wars, drug wars or local persecution – countries are working hard to contain and, in many instances, imprison asylum seekers in camps. Since the end of the 20th century, managing migrant flows has become big business: the trade in human beings is part of legal and illicit global commerce (Purkayastha and Yousaf, 2019). Violence pervades all stages of this process. Menjivar and Abrago (2012) point out the normalized and legal violence that has an injurious effect on the life of migrants from Central America coming to the United States (see also Musalo and Lee, 2017). Seeking asylum in the United States, especially through its Southern border, was deemed a crime by the Trump administration (Frelick et al., 2016). The 45th President of the United States, introduced a protracted process to re-classify all refugees and asylum seekers as illegal criminals, and, in a move reminiscent of EU and Australia – who have set up migrant holding centres away from their political borders – is attempting to get countries such as Guatemala to hold the migrants far away from the United States (Fisher and Taub, 2019; New York Times, 2019).

The last box in Figure 6.2 shows records of the association of violence with private security companies that detain and hold migrants. Despite being signatories to a number of migrant and refugee protocols, countries in the Americas, EU and Asia are engaged in creating bounded spaces for stopping and holding men, women and children, and containing them in camps and privatized prisons (Purkayastha, 2021). While the separation and detention of families and children has made headline news in the United States, less attention has been paid to the rapid spread of for-profit detention centres (Barker et al., 2018; Barnett, 2017; Migration Policy Institute, 2017). According to Luan (2018), while the Obama administration intended to wind down these detention centres, the Trump administration further enhanced privatized centres of detention. Luan wrote, 'During 2016, approximately 353,000 immigrants were identified for detention or removal by U.S. Immigration and Customs Enforcement (ICE)....[b]y August 2016, nearly three-quarters of the average daily immigration detainee population was held in facilities operated by private prison companies - a sharp contrast from a decade ago, when the majority were held in immigration-contracted bed-space in local jails and state prisons' (Luan, 2018, no page). Haberman (2018) and López and Park (2018), among others have described the violence in these centres; migrants remain in a zone of political liminality, with little recourse to protest their life conditions. These patterns of profiting from migrants are not new, but their scope and range has increased with the access States have to efficient technologies of violence and control.

Thus refugees, asylum seekers and other desperate migrants often experience conditions that we would associate with human trafficking – forced detention, no human rights and subnormal living conditions (*cf:* Barker et al., 2018; Edwards, 2013; Forced Migration Special Issue, 2013; Luan, 2018; New York Times, 2019; Purkayastha, forthcoming, Yuhas, 2019). There is a growing literature on refugees and efforts of humanitarian groups to alleviate life conditions; however, as Hanafi (2008) and Njiru and Purkayastha (2015) have pointed out, these efforts do not meet the needs of refugees over the long term.

In sum, despite ongoing conventions to protect their human rights, routinized violence envelopes migrants (and marginalized citizens) in ways that appear to overwhelm the existing justice systems. In July 2018, the UN reached several agreements about the human rights of migrants, yet powerful countries ignore their responsibilities with impunity. This point was emphasized by the Commissioner of Human Rights as she condemned the conditions of detention of migrant children and its abrogation of human rights responsibilities (Cummings-Bruce, 2019). Equally important, despite the formal record that 142 nation-states have signed the 1951 Refugee Convention and 1967 Protocol, many governments in the Global North, and some in the South, are actively involved in rebuffing migrants, refugees and asylum seekers, and, in many cases, holding them in distant places. Governance has become about managing flows, creating bounded spaces for stopping and holding men, women and children, and containing them, including in camps and privatized prisons. Powerful nation-states are also involved in changing the discourse about rights of migrants to make these actions palatable for their political constituencies. These practices are part of the contemporary social, legal and political structures that migrants encounter in their quest to seek more secure lives.

The Arc of Justice[2] and Human Insecurities

Based on the complexities of injustices that have been normalized, how can justice be imagined in this era of routine violence? The critical question about the arc of justice begins with the question of access to justice amidst routinized violence. Restorative justice, which occurs after large-scale injustice, addresses one component of this question (*cf:* Hayner, 1994; Wallis, 2014; Zia, 2013). Scholars who have written about peace making also emphasize the larger point that a greater effort needs to be made at the state level to counter and control routinized violence, across institutions, contexts and on a daily basis (e.g. Galtung, 1969; Purkayastha, 2005).

Since the growth of nation-states, the institutions and processes of justice have traditionally resided with States. Since the 1950s, a vast edifice of the United Nations' conventions, compacts and offices to oversee international justice systems has added a layer of international justice. Conventions on human rights, with the objective of recognizing and addressing various types of injustice, offices to monitor these (including the Special Rapporteurs on Violence and other rights violations, and the High Commissioner for Refugees) and institutions such as the International Criminal Court create a robust tapestry of international justice system. Other international actors including powerful NGOs further contribute to this system. The UDHR, which begins with a recognition of the 'inherent dignity' and rights (political, civil, social, economic, cultural rights) of all, is intended to address the variations of what people might claim as justice under different systems.[3]

However, for migrants, despite the international conventions on their rights, there appears to be a morass of insecurities. As the UN data quoted earlier shows, 1 in 30 persons in the world is a migrant, so this group is already bereft of justice. Adding marginalized groups who are not deemed migrants further increases this number. If we think about human security as human lives that are free from constant threats of violence, lives that are secure from threats 'derived from economic, food, health or environmental security, and threats to personal, community, and political security' (Tripp et al., 2013, p. 6), then justice has to be conceptualized in ways that focus on multiple levels and direction of action, as illustrated in Figure 6.3.

Can the justice infrastructure set up through human rights charters and mechanisms work? Specifically, to what extent are States that sign and ratify binding human rights instruments bound to *respect* (not directly violate the treaty), *protect* (prevent others, such as private corporations, from violating the rights defined in the treaty through the rule of law) and *fulfil* (create an environment in which people can

Figure 6.3 Interlocking practices to secure justice

reasonably enjoy their rights) the rights defined in the instrument (Donnelly, 2007). These instruments ultimately codify human rights as legal obligations of member states, subject to the ability, will, and resources of States and State actors (governments) to fulfil these international legal obligations.

The discussion of migrants and their experiences of routine violence show the extent to which States and profit-making private companies are entwined in the process of constructing and using violence. Violence is profitable; managing migrants is profitable. Can the institutions of justice address this nexus?

In her book, *Justice Cascade*, Kathryn Sikkink argues that the work of human rights and the setting up of international courts have also legitimated the norm of individual criminal accountability for human rights violations and an increase in criminal prosecutions on behalf of the norm (p. 5). She views these emergent norms as being nested within human rights regimes. If States cause harm, individuals should be able to bring cases against State officials. If State courts do not respond, individuals should then bring their cases in front of foreign courts. Reflecting on the case of different types of migrants as well as the processes of weaponization of language and profit-making through the escalation of violence should give us pause. While the human rights community has talked about transitional justice, i.e.

justice that is sought through public efforts, after authoritarian governments give way to democracies, that is a long process that may not work during the lifetime of some migrants (e.g. Palestinian refugees in Lebanon, Syrian refugees in Turkey or the Rohingyas).

Looking at the condition of migrants and refugees within the context of human rights, the sad reality is that despite vast edifices of rights statements and attempts to implement them, migrants of all types continue to be vulnerable to severe injustice. There are many accounts documenting migrants' vulnerability to trafficking, which has become one of the largest illegal global businesses. At the same time, the nearly indentured labour conditions that hold thousands of 'temporary' economic migrants in conditions of insecurity, surveillance, and harassment, and distanced from institutions of justice constitutes yet another lens through which to understand the challenges of accessing rights and justice. Those who are detained, or in camps, are yet further removed from accessing justice systems. With an emphasis on humanitarian aid, often through NGOs, the question of rights becomes removed from reality by the layers of action and policy most often carried out by States.

Yet the promise of human rights remains, and groups that continue to fight for conventions and compacts are other sides of the justice coin. The Global Compact on Migration points to the need for upholding human rights of all persons – including migrants – as well as mitigating the circumstances that force them to flee. It calls for ensuring legal identities (i.e. not rendering them stateless), fair and ethical conditions of work, safe passage when needed, and aims to reduce vulnerabilities of people on the move by using integrated and consistent policies to secure borders, only using temporary detention as a last report (Global Migration Group, 2018). In a critical move, scholars and activists from the Global South have issued the Kolkata Compact, which pointed out the extent of overgeneralizations about refugees and migrants, without explicit linking to the action of States to create migrants, practice protectionism (distance migrants from their intended destination and from institutions of justice), and States' failure to deeply address existing discrimination based on race, religion, caste, ability, sexuality, gender and class affect the dignity of all human beings. If justice has to be imagined, it needs to be imagined across the migrant/citizen divide and hold all perpetrators of violence to account (Calcutta Research Group, 2018).

Since migrants fall within and beyond the jurisdiction of nation-states, it is important to emphasize that the intersection between international institutions and practices, and national systems and practices must harmonize in a just way. National justice continues to be important since much of the everyday conditions are still governed by national governments. The specific national context within which a migrant finds themselves will determine the terrain of that individual's struggle with justice. The human rights enterprise at the international level acts merely as a lever. Critical sociologists of human rights point to the need to look at both specific court systems and policies and organize at the societal level to demand just conditions for migrants.

To imagine a terrain of justice beyond its current state, we can turn to the idea of human rights enterprise which includes both legal and statist approaches to defining and achieving human rights through agreements among duty bearing States, but, importantly, this approach includes social movements that manifest as social struggles over power, resources and political voice (Armaline et al., 2015). Justice systems that serve elites – powerful States, groups, entities – are most often forced to practice justice through the struggles of grassroots organizations and non-elites from below. Rarely are they enacted via the compassionate motivations of States, or even out of respect for international agreements. Justice is claimed within a terrain of social struggles, where substantive human rights and human securities are developed and forced into practice, through the struggles of organizations and non-elites from below – from the civil rights movement to modern anti-globalization, anti-war, environmental and anti-capitalist movements. These struggles form against or in spite of the States who are (and often partnered private interests) charged with rights protection (*cf*: Carol Andersen, or Flexnor and Fitzgerald, 1994).

Contrary to thinking about the fulcrum of justice as though it is located in the institutionalized justice system, as scholars we ought to bring those edifices and activists struggles into our conversations together. The reality of justice must be understood as an ever-dynamic movement between the powerful who would deny it and the marginalized who would claim it. Justice is not often obtained from the compassionate actions of States or through their respect for international agreements. Instead, both the laws at hand and the results that come from organizing and direct action, including forms of open resistance and disobedience, keep open those spaces of justice that powerful interests seek to repress.

Conclusion

Routinization of violence poses a particular challenge to the human rights enterprise as a route to ensure justice. At the core of routine and normalized violence is an attempt to entrench or create new configurations of power over others, often those who are already vulnerable and marginalized. These sorts of violence are often an adjustment to realities of transnational political-economic systems and the consequent anxieties about maintaining privilege or creating boundaries between 'us and them'. As groups with constellations of power and privilege within nation-states' attempt to hold onto that power, many societies appear to be in a new phase of guarding their current borders and rejecting whomever they consider to be other, outsider, stranger and migrant. This chapter has reflected upon this era of normalized violence and questions whether our organization of justice has remained effective amidst these new configurations of power, privilege, rhetoric and distancing.

The arc of the moral universe is long, but it bends towards justice. If we imbue our sociologies with histories of struggles – through all of our deliberations and thinking and not simply as a separate unit on social movements and activism – we would recognize routine violence as it continues to expand in our lives, and we would look into migrants' struggles to understand the directions in which State power to control human beings is expanding, and the weapons – including language – that is being used to erode our rights and freedoms. We would know that justice is a dynamic *State*, requiring legal action, protests, documentation of oral histories, keeping memories of injustices as well as celebrating human dignity whenever and wherever it is evident in every sphere of our lives. Our sociologies would have to decolonize, delink from our 'normalized' ways of thinking because it does not equip us to see and protest the harms being done to people. I have been an inheritor of a legacy of many strands of activism – all those who fought for India's independence from the British, and for a constitution that envisioned political, civil, economic, social and cultural rights should be available to all Indians, and all those who continue to fight for these rights on the face of powerful forces dismantling these rights, all those who fought the racist laws that prevented Asian origin people from migrating to the United States, all those who fought for civil rights and opening up access to resources for people who are not white, and all those who fight today against violence, hate and economic and social injustice. From them comes a vision of justice, borne through struggle and sustained through care and humane interaction. These struggles construct the horizon of justice, within which we can continue to envision a less violence prone future.

Notes

*   A version of this chapter was first presented at the XIX ISA World Congress of Sociology, 2018.

1   UN report on International Migration, 2017. Over 60% of all international migrants live in Asia (80 million) or Europe (78 million). Northern America hosted the third largest number of international migrants (58 million), followed by Africa (25 million), Latin America and the Caribbean (10 million) and Oceania (8 million). In 2017, two-thirds (67%) of all international migrants were living in just 20 countries. The largest number of international migrants (50 million) resided in the United States. Saudi Arabia, Germany and the Russian Federation hosted the second, third and fourth largest numbers of migrants worldwide (around 12 million each), followed by the United Kingdom of Great Britain and Northern Ireland (nearly 9 million). In 2016, the total number of refugee asylum seekers in the world was estimated at 25.9 million. Turkey hosted the largest refugee population worldwide, with 3.1 million refugees and asylum seekers, followed by Jordan (2.9 million), the State of Palestine (2.2 million), Lebanon (1.6 million) and Pakistan (1.4 million).

2   Civil rights champion Martin Luther King, Jr. once delivered a powerful speech with this resonant line: The arc of the moral universe is long, but it bends towards justice. Also, Theodore Parker was a Unitarian minister and prominent American Transcendentalist born in 1810 who called for the abolition of slavery. In 1853 a collection of *Ten Sermons of Religion* by Parker was published and the third sermon titled 'Of Justice and the Conscience' included figurative language about the arc of the moral universe[1]: Look at the facts of the world. You see a continual and progressive triumph of the right. I do not pretend to understand the moral universe, the arc is a long one, and my eye reaches but little ways. I cannot calculate the curve and complete the figure by the experience of sight; I can divine it by conscience. But from what I see I am sure it bends towards justice.

3   The Universal Declaration of Human Rights begins with a recognition of the 'inherent dignity and of the equal and inalienable rights of all members of the human family'. Human rights law thus provides that in general, all persons, without discrimination, must have access to all fundamental human rights with narrow limitations related to political rights and freedom of movement. States are further obliged

to ensure that any differential treatment, between citizens and non-citizens or among different groups of non-citizens, is undertaken in a non-discriminatory manner, that is, for a legitimate objective, and that the course of action taken to achieve this objective is proportionate and reasonable. A human rights approach to migration places the migrant at the centre of migration policies and management, and pays particular attention to the situation of marginalized and disadvantaged groups of migrants. Such an approach will also ensure that migrants are included in relevant national action plans and strategies, such as plans on the provision of public housing or national strategies to combat racism and xenophobia.

References

Abraham, M. (2000). *Speaking the unspeakable: Marital violence among South Asians in the US*. New Brunswick, NJ: Rutgers University Press.

Abraham, M., & Tastsoglou, E. (Eds.). (2016). Interrogating gender, violence and the state in national and transnational contexts. *Current Sociology*, 64, 517–534.

Armaline, W., Glasberg, D., & Purkayastha, B. (Eds.). (2011). *Human rights in our backyard: Injustice and resistance in the US*. Philadelphia, PA: University of Pennsylvania Press.

Armaline, W., Glasberg, D., & Purkayastha, B. (2015). *The human rights enterprise: The state, resistance, and human rights*. London: Polity Press.

Avashia, N. (2021). *Unlearning the rules of what a leader looks like*. Retrieved from https://www.wbur.org/cognoscenti/2021/11/02/historic-boston-mayoral-election-michelle-wu-neema-avashia

Barker, L., Kulish, N., & Ruiz, R. (2018, December 2). *He's built an empire, with detained migrant children as the bricks*. Retrieved from https://www.nytimes.com/2018/12/02/us/southwest-key-migrant-children.html

Beoku Betts, J. (2016). Holding African states to violence: Domesticating UNSCR 1325 in Sierra Leone national action plan. *Current Sociology Monograph*, 44, 654–670.

Bosman, J. (2021). Kyle Rittenhouse acquitted on all charges. *The New York Times*. Retrieved from https://www.nytimes.com/live/2021/11/19/us/kyle-rittenhouse-trial

Brancaccio, D., Conlon, R., & Wrenn, C. (2020). How police departments got billions of dollars of tactical military equipment. *Marketplace*. Retrieved from https://www.marketplace.org/2020/06/12/police-departments-1033-military-equipment-weapons/

Burnett, J. (2017). *NPR: Big money as private immigrant jails boom*. Retrieved from https://www.npr.org/2017/11/21/565318778/big-money-as-private-immigrant-jails-boom

Calcutta Research Group. (2018). *Kolkata declaration 2018: Protection of refugees and migrants*. Retrieved from http://www.mcrg.ac.in/RLS_Migration/Kolkata_Declaration_2018.pdf

Chacón, J. M. (2009, December 12). Managing migration through crime, *Columbia Law Review*, 109, 135–148.

Chakraborty, G., & Pathan, S. (2021). Producing the migrant myth. *The India Forum*. Retreived 28 October 2021, from https://www.theindiaforum.in/article/producing-migrant-myth

Choudhury Lahiri, S. (2021). Women's struggles over religion and citizenship in contemporary India, *Contemporary South Asia*, 29(2), 281–287.

Chowdhury-Lahiri, S., Iwata, M., & Purkayastha, B. (2020). The role of religion in building terrains of peace. *Journal of Transdisciplinary Peace Praxis*, 2, 119–142.

Choudhury, B. R., & Samaddar, R. (Eds.). (2015). *The Rohingyas in south Asia: Birth of a stateless community*. London: Routledge.

Cummings-Bruce, N. (2019, July 8). U.N. rights chief 'shocked' by treatment of migrant children at US border. *The New York Times*. Retrieved from https://www.nytimes.com/2019/07/08/world/americas/michelle-bachelet-unhcr-migrants-border.html

Davidson, N. (2019, April 5). Domestic terrorism story renews fears over Trump's coddling of white nationalists. *The Washington Post*. Retrieved from https://www.washingtonpost.com/politics/2019/04/05/domestic-terrorism-story-renews-fears-over-trumps-coddling-white-nationalists/?utm_term=.f88d87885425

Donnelly, J. (2007). The relative universality of human rights. *Human Rights Quarterly*, 29, 281–306.

Dhillon, A. S. (2019). 'Free pass for mobs': India urged to stem vigilante violence against minorities. *The Guardian*. Retrieved from https://www.theguardian.com/world/2019/feb/19/a-free-pass-for-mobs-to-kill-india-urged-to-stem-cow-vigilante-violence

Edwards, A. (2013). Detention under scrutiny. *Forced Migration Review*, 44, 4–6.

Erturk, Y., & Purkayastha, B. (2012). Linking research, policy and action: A look at the work of the special rapporteur on violence against women. *Current Sociology*, 60, 20–39.

Fisher, M., & Taub, A. (2019, July 18). Trump's immigration approach isn't new: Europe and Australia went first. *The New York Times*. Retrieved from https://www.nytimes.com/2019/07/18/world/immigration-trump.html

Flexnor, E., & Fitzgerald, E. (1994). *Century of struggle: The woman's rights movement in the United States*. Boston, MA: Belknap Press.

Forced Migration Review. (2013, September). *Detention and alternatives to detention (44)*. Retrieved from www.fmreview.org/detention

Frelick, B., Kysel, I., & Podkul, J. (2016). The impact of externalization of migrant controls on the rights of asylum seekers and other migrants. *Journal on Migration and Human Security*, 4(4), 190–220.

Fritz, J., Doering, S., & Belgin Gumru, F. (2011). Women, peace, security and the national action plans, *Journal of Applied Social Science*, 5, 1–23.

Galtung, J. (1969). Violence, peace, and peace research. *Journal of Peace Research*, 6, 167–191.

Glenn, E. N. (2015). Settler colonialism as structure: A framework for comparative studies of U.S. race and gender formation. *Sociology of Race and Ethnicity*, 1, 54–74.

Lalita, L., & Dhanraj, D. (Eds.). (2016). *Rupture, loss and living minority women speak about post-conflict life*. Hyderabad: Orient Blackswan,

Global Migration Compact. (2018). Retrieved from https://refugeesmigrants.un.org/sites/default/files/180713_agreed_outcome_global_compact_for_migration.pdf

Golash-Boza. (2015). *Deported: Immigrant policiong, disposible labor and global capitalism.* New York, NY: New York University Press.

Goldbaum, C. (2019, April 21). 'I don't want to die' asylum seekers, once in limbo, face deportation under Trump. *The New York Times.* Retrieved from https://www.nytimes.com/2019/04/21/nyregion/asylum-seekers-deportation.html

Goldberg, M. (2019, June 21). The terrible things Trump is doing in our name. *The New York Times.* Retrieved from https://www.nytimes.com/2019/06/21/opinion/family-separation-trump-migrants.html

Haberman, C. (2018, October 1). For private prisons, detaining immigrants is big business. *The New York Times.* Retrieved from https://www.nytimes.com/2018/10/01/us/prisons-immigration-detention.html

Hanafi, S. (2008). Palestinian refugee camps in Lebanon laboratories of state-in-making, of discipline and of Islamist radicalism. In L. Ronit (Ed.), *Thinking Palestine* (pp. 123–140). London: Zed Books.

Hartry, A. (2012). Gendering crimmigration: The intersection of gender, immigration, and the criminal justice system. *Berkeley Journal of Gender and Law*, 27, 1–27.

Hayner P. (1994, November). Fifteen truth commissions – 1974 to 1994: A comparative study. *Human Rights Quarterly*, 16(4), 597–655.

Kannabiran, K. (Ed.). (2016). *Violence studies.* New Delhi: Oxford University Press.

Kanno-Young, Z., & Dickerson, C. (2019, April 29). Asylum seekers face new restraints under latest Trump orders. *The New York Times.* Retrieved from https://www.nytimes.com/2019/04/29/us/politics/trump-asylum.html

Legomsky, S. H. (2007). The new path of immigration law: Asymmetric incorporation of criminal justice Norms, *Washington and Lee Law Review*, 64, 469–472.

López, V., & Park, S. (2018, November). *ICE detention center says it's not responsible for staff's sexual abuse of detainees.* ACLU.

Luan, L. (2018, May 2). *Profiting from enforcement: The role of private prisons in U.S. Immigration detention.* Retrieved from https://www.migrationpolicy.org/article/profiting-enforcement-role-private-prisons-us-immigration-detention

Majumdar, S., Velath, M. P., Chopra, K., & Chakraborty, M. (2015). *Rohingyas in India: Birth of a stateless community.* Kolkata: Calcutta Research Group.

Makki, M., Azam, A., Akash, S. A., & Khan, F. (Eds.). (2020). *Forced migration and conflict induced displacement: Impacts and prospective responses.* Islamabad: National University of Science and Technology.

Marc, A. (n.d.). *Conflicts and violence in the 21st century.* Retrieved from https://www.un.org/pga/70/wp-content/uploads/sites/10/2016/01/Conflict-and-violence-in-the-21st-century-Current-trends-as-observed-in-empirical-research-and-statistics-Mr.-Alexandre-Marc-Chief-Specialist-Fragility-Conflict-and-Violence-World-Bank-Group.pdf

Mclaughlin, T. (2018). *How WhatsApp fuels fake news and violence in India.* Retrieved from https://www.wired.com/story/how-whatsapp-fuels-fake-news-and-violence-in-india/

Menjivar, C., & Abrago, L. (2012, March). Legal violence: Immigration law and the lives of Central American immigrants. *American Journal of Sociology*, 117(5), 1380–1421.

Migration Policy Institute. (2017). *Profiting from enforcement: The role of private prisons in U.S. immigration detention.* Retrieved from https://www.migrationpolicy. org/article/profiting-enforcement-role-private-prisons-us-immigration-detention

Musalo, K., & Lee, E. (2017). Seeking a rational approach to a regional refugee crisis: Lessons from the summer 2014 "surge" of central American women and children at the US-Mexico border, *Journal on Migration and Human Security*, 5(1), 137–179.

New York Times. (2019). On immigration detention. Retrieved from https://www. nytimes.com/topic/subject/immigration-detention

Njiru, R., & Purkayastha, B. (2015). *Voices of internally displaced persons in Kenya: A human rights perspective.* Kolkata; London: Frontpage Publications.

Pandey, G. (2006). *Routine violence: Nations, fragments, histories.* New Delhi: Permanent Black.

Parish, A. (2017). *Gender based violence against women: Both cause for migration and risk along the journey.* Migration Policy Institute. Retrieved from http://www. migrationpolicy.org/article/gender-based-violence-against-women-both-cause-migration-and-risk-along-journey

Pascale, C. M. (2019). The weaponization of language: Discourses of rising right-wing authoritarianism. *Critical Sociology Review*, 67(6), 898–917.

Paul, D., & Miroff, P. (2019, July 8). U.N. human rights chief 'deeply shocked' by migrant detention center conditions in Texas. Retrieved from https://www. washingtonpost.com/immigration/2019/07/08/un-human-rights-chief-deeply-shocked-by-migrant-detention-center-conditions-texas/?utm_term=.e45723d11521

Portes, A., & Zhou, M. (1993). The new second genderation: Segmented assimilation and its variants. *The Annals of American Academy of Political and Social Science*, 530, 74–96.

Purkayastha, B. (2005). Through 'little steps: Informal networks as a resource for peaceful conflict resolution. In G. Caforio, & G. Kuemmel (Eds.), *Military missions and their implications reconsidered: The aftermath of September 11th, volume 2* (pp. 63–79). Amsterdam: Elsevier Press.

Purkayastha, B. (2018). Migration, migrants, and human security. *Current Sociology Monograph*, 66(2), 167–191.

Purkayastha, B. (2021). Distancing as governance. In P. Banerjee (Ed.), *On the margins of protection.* Kolkata: Orient BlackSwan.

Purkayastha, B. (forthcoming). *Distancing as governance. On the margins of protection*, edited by Paula Banerjee. Kolkata: Orient Black Swan.

Purkayastha, B., & Ratcliff, K. (2014). Routine violence: Intersectionality at the interstices. In M. Segal, & V. Demos (Eds.), *Advances in gender research* (Vol. 18B). London: Emerald Publications.

Purkayastha, B., & Yousaf, F. N. (2019). *Human trafficking: Trade in sex, labor, organs.* London: Polity Press.

Radil, S., Dezzani, R., & McAden, L. (2017). Geographies of U.S. Police militarization and the role of the 1033 program. *The Professional Geographer*, 69(2), 203–213.

Roy Choudhury, S., & Samaddar, R. (Eds.). (2015). *Rohingyas: The emergence of a stateless community*. Retrieved from http://www.mcrg.ac.in/Rohingyas/Report_Final.pdf

Samaddar, R. (1999). *Marginal nation: Transborder migration from Bangladesh to West Bengal*. New Delhi: SAGE.

Samaddar, R. (2018). Histories of the late nineteenth to early twentieth century immigration and our time. *Current Sociology Monograph*, 66(2), 192–208.

Setalwaad, T. (2019). How a government and bureaucracy betrayed its people. *The Telegraph*. Retrieved from https://www.telegraphindia.com/opinion/nrc-how-a-government-and-bureaucracy-betrayed-its-people/cid/1694949

Shah, A. (2013). The arms trade is big business. Retrieved from https://www.globalissues.org/article/74/the-arms-trade-is-big-business

Simpson, L. (2017). Indigenous resurgence and co-resistance. *Critical Ethnic Studies*, 2(2), 19–34.

SIPRI. (2013). *Yearbook*. Retrieved 31 July 2013, from https://www.sipri.org/sites/default/files/2016-03/SIPRIYB13Summary.pdf

Sutton, B. (2010). *Bodies in crisis: Culture, violence and women's resistance in neo liberal Argentina*. New Brunswick, NJ: Rutgers University Press.

Tripp, A.-M., Ferree, M., & Ewig, C. (Eds.). (2013). *Gender, violence and human security: Critical feminist perspectives*. New York, NY: New York University Press.

UN. (2017). International migration report. Retrieved from https://www.un.org/en/development/desa/population/migration/publications/migrationreport/docs/MigrationReport2017_Highlights.pdf

UN. (n.d.). A new era of conflict and violence. Retrieved from https://www.un.org/en/un75/new-era-conflict-and-violence

UN-IOM. (2022). World migration report. Retrieved from https://worldmigrationreport.iom.int/wmr-2022-interactive/

UNHCR. (2021). Refugee statistics. Retrieved from https://www.unhcr.org/refugee-statistics/

von Holdt, K. (2013). The violence of orders, orders of violence: Between Fanon and Bourdieu. *Current Sociology*, 61(2), 112–131.

Walby, S. (2012). Violence and society: Introduction to an emerging field of sociology. *Current Sociology*, 6, 95–111.

Wallis, P. (2014). *Understanding restorative justice*. Bristol: Policy Press.

Yea, S. (Ed.). (2014). *Human trafficking in Asia: Forcing issues*. London: Routledge.

Yuhas, A. (2019, January 1). US agents fire tear gas across Mexican border. *The New York Times*.

Zia, A. (2013). Restorative justice. The chessboard of litigation and American Indian land rights. *Global Journal of Comparative Law*, 2. Retrieved from https://doi-org.ezproxy.lib.uconn.edu/10.1163/2211906X-00201003

7

Sociology's Bipolar Disorder

Michael Burawoy

There is a lot to be gloomy about in this world of ours. Throughout this International Sociological Association (ISA) meeting in Toronto in 2018, I heard from friends and colleagues about the dark clouds of authoritarianism gathering over their countries – Turkey, Argentina, Brazil, Philippines, Hungary, Poland, India and South Africa, not to mention Russia, China, Syria, Iraq, Iran, Egypt and the United States of America. I heard about how democracy can be used to undermine democracy and how democracy can be a tool of oppression. The pessimism has been overwhelming.

How different from the ISA meetings just 4 years earlier when we were celebrating the rising tide of social movements – Indignados, Occupy Movement, Arab Spring, Piqueteros, Gezi Park, newfangled feminism and novel labour movements. Even though these movements had already dissolved or were in remission by the time we met in Yokohama, still those 4 years, 2010–14, were ones to celebrate, full of growth and possibility. Meanwhile, 2014–18 have been years of retreat and subjugation. If in 4 years the tide has turned from one of optimism to pessimism, 4 years hence we could potentially be back to optimism. The present is not fixed, and it is not the end of history. We cannot replace one limited one-sided view with another.

We are sociologists, our point is to show that what exists is not natural and inevitable, we have to examine the social forces that conspire to produce the changes of which we are a part. We are against the current, both against the tide but also the present. In the face of optimism, we must be pessimists, in the face of pessimism, we must be optimists. While I don't want to underestimate the very real suffering that besets our world, still we are sociologists, we cannot succumb to wild swings, we should be burrowing beneath the surface, we have to seek counter-trends, emergent forces, new spaces – what persists despite change, in and through change.

While it gives little comfort to Brazilians, as sociologists we have to recognize both the disintegration of the social fabric in Brazil (together with the imprisonment of the former President Lula, the impeachment of President Rousseff) along with the victory of Lopes Obrador in Mexico. How to see both as expressions of the present conjuncture? Just one deviant case should be enough to set our sociological saliva flowing. How is it that right-wing populism can assert itself in one country and left-wing populism in another country? How is it that there is populism at all? Differences *between* nations call for an examination of forces *within* the nation, and to see that with Trump there is also Sanders. Let us not ignore the resurgence of socialism and the Democratic Socialists of America as we focus on the atrocities of Trump's administration. Let us not forget the atrocities of the Obama administration. The methodological rule is simple: we must look for counter-trends as well as trends, and we must look at both together, how the one produces and reproduces the other, and, moreover, how they both can be the product of a third force.

By themselves these methodological imperatives cannot tell us how to proceed. Theory without sociology is empty, but sociology without theory is blind. To appreciate the specific forces at work requires social theory, an inherited body of knowledge that has shown itself able to illuminate and anticipate tendencies and counter-tendencies. Social theory is a parsimonious organization of the knowledge we have accumulated in our discipline – knowledge that bundles together into intellectual traditions and research programmes, often linked to founding figures – Marx, Weber, Durkheim, Beauvoir, Fanon, Du Bois, Bourdieu and so forth. Theory does not spring from nowhere, nor does it spring from data. There is a danger, in an era of 'big data', where theory is seen as springing tabula rasa from sophisticated modelling. There is, however, no way to extract meaning from data without some prior selection mechanism, some prior lens. Theory is but making that prior lens explicit.

My lens today is Karl Polanyi, author of *The Great Transformation*, first published in 1944 – a book that has become canonical in economic sociology. Why Karl Polanyi? Karl Polanyi fought against the liberal economists – Hayek and von Mises – attacking their market fundamentalism as a dangerous utopia, more dangerous than the socialism they themselves attacked. Polanyi (1944) argued that the attempt to implement market fundamentalism threatens to destroy society, which in turn reacts by sponsoring state regulation, taking the form of the New Deal, Social Democracy, Stalinism but worst of all Fascism. The treatment could be as bad as the disease. The appeal of *The Great Transformation* – which refers to a reaction to the market – lies precisely in the prophetic account Polanyi offers of the present epoch: how market fundamentalism (spurred on by the collapse of state socialism) would, and has, for the last half-century, spread across the globe with devastating consequences. The virtue of *The Great Transformation* is not only that one can use it to trace the devastation wrought by market fundamentalism but also the divergent reactions – and to see the positive with the negative.

Like any influential and lasting theory, *The Great Transformation* contains anomalies and contradictions that drive the research programmes it has inspired. Focussing on power, violence and justice directs us to the limits and possibilities of the research programme, leading not to the dismissal but the reconstruction of Polanyi's original theory.

Polanyi believed that humanity would never again experiment with market fundamentalism. We now know he was wrong. But why? Polanyi believed that market fundamentalism was driven by an ideology of political economy, both in the 19th and 20th centuries. Polanyi missed, therefore, the source of market fundamentalism in the dynamics of capitalism. In criticizing the Marxist idea that exploitation rather than commodification drove human reactions, including the labour movement, Polanyi overlooked capitalist accumulation and its contradictions. He, therefore, failed to see how the resolution of crises of overproduction through state regulation of markets causes crises of profitability, which, in turn, are resolved by liberating markets from social and political protections. Thus, the appearance of so-called neoliberalism springs from capitalism. It is not the first wave of marketization nor the second, but the third wave. Two sources of power are at work here: a structural power built into the capitalist system, tending towards self-destruction, and a class and state power that averts crisis by orchestrating an expansive marketization. The power of ideology is to present market fundamentalism as being in the interests of all – the role of economists is to provide an elaborate justification.

Polanyi saw marketization in terms of the commodification of 'fictitious commodities', entities that lose their use value when subject to unregulated exchange. He had in mind three such entities: labour, land and money. The unregulated commodification of labour creates precarity; the unregulated commodification of land, or more generally nature, accumulates waste; and the unregulated commodification of money, i.e. making money from money (finance capital), creates debt. Each of these three threaten social existence, leading to the self-defence of society – the regulation of commodification or *decommodification*. While Polanyi does pay attention to the commodification of labour and land through the Enclosure Acts that lead to proletarianization and the commodification of labour power, he downplays the violence of expropriation. The problem for Polanyi was the speed of social change rather than the violence of dispossession.

The violence of dispossession lies not only in the genesis of capitalism, Marx's so-called primitive accumulation, but is part and parcel of the expanded reproduction of capitalism – a point made by Luxemburg (1951[1913]) and more recently by David Harvey (2003), Mike Levien (2018) and others. Forcible commodification and *recommodification* are inextricable from the dynamics of capitalism. To sell a human organ it has to be forcibly separated from the human body as well as implanted into another body – that is the metaphor and reality of contemporary capitalism. Violence is not only part and parcel of commodification – the dispossession of land, labour and money from the institutions that support them – but also of *excommodification*, the expulsion of entities from the circuits of exchange, the production of waste and when labour loses employment, or when land, water and air are polluted, as well as when money becomes useless.

In terms of social justice, Polanyi claimed that there was always a double movement, and the expansion of the market led to a reaction against the market. He traced the liberation of the labour market in 19th century England, from all forms of protection, including the Speenhamland system of wage subsidies and outdoor poor relief, followed by the counter-movement organized by voluntary associations, factory movement, cooperatives, trade unions, communalism of Owenism, eventually leading to the Labour Party. While these movements were real and significant, one has to ask whether they were a response to dispossession leading to commodification, or to the commodification itself. Subsequent studies have shown that it was resistance to the expropriation of control over the labour process by craft workers, rather than the unskilled commodified factory labourers, that instigated collective action. Today we have to examine whether it is the process of commodification itself or ex-commodification that prompts the struggles of workers, peasants, students etc. While there have been collective reactions to the expansion of commodification, they are often local, sometimes national, but very rarely reaching a global scale where markets operate. Movements pursue diverse goals without a common anti-market vision; some seek the expansion of democratic freedoms, and others the reduction of such freedoms. Each has its own conception of justice – as sociologists we cannot dismiss and 'irrationalize' the justice we don't like, and embrace or 'rationalize' the justice we support. We have to see how rationality and irrationality combine in each. We have to study their divergences, how they may spring from a common grievance, how they may define themselves through hostility to others and how their interests are organized politically through relation to the state.

At least in the West, relations between different responses to the market have been organized on the terrain of capitalist democracy, but for Polanyi this was never a stable terrain. Just as markets and society are opposed, so are capitalism and democracy. Democracy unfurls struggles that threaten capitalism. Either democracy is pushed aside, and we have fascism or capitalism pushed aside in favour of democratic deepening, i.e. socialism. And, of course, that made sense in 1944. As Adam Przeworski (1985) has shown, as long as capitalism could deliver concessions to the subordinate classes, so liberal democracy was viable, as it has been in the North but not the South. As Frantz Fanon (1963[1961]) has shown for the countries of Africa, and one might say more broadly in the Global South, peripheral and dependent capitalism couldn't deliver the concessions that are the lifeblood of democracy. Here the choice was stark – between an emerging dictatorship on the one side and a democratic socialism on the other. Yet the global conditions of possibility for socialism were inauspicious.

With third-wave marketization, concessions have become thinner, even becoming negative. Democracy thereby loses meaning as it becomes a vehicle, not for the distribution of concessions to the mass of the population, but rather, brazenly benefitting the 1%. Collective responses to the market are no longer channelled through orthodox political parties, but increasingly circumvent democracy. Thus, Cihan

Tugal (2019–2020) has argued that the United States left, critical of Leninism, abandoned parties for direct democracy, autonomism and anarchism, while the right learned from Leninism to build a powerful movement. In mapping the field of politics, we might follow Fidan Elcioglu (2020) who studies the immigration politics of diverse groups at the US–Mexican border. For pro-immigrant groups the border marks a 'strong state' that denies crossers basic human and legal rights, that tears children from their parents and locks up 'illegals' found in the desert. For restrictionist groups, on the other hand, the border marks a 'weak state'. They help Border Patrol root out illegals or provide technological solutions to detect their movement. When the restrictionists charge that immigrants are the arm of drug cartels, the pro-immigrant groups reply that the strong US state stimulates the cartels, which then force immigrants to carry drugs. When the pro-immigrant groups charge the restrictionists with racism, the latter deny this by claiming that they are just interested in upholding the integrity of the border, bolstering the weak state. Here, then, is a sociological account in which each side has its own rationality – one that cannot be understood outside its real and imagined relation to the other side, and to the state.

With the bipolar disorder comes the moral imperative, almost a call to arms, to right the wrongs of the world. As sociologists, we hold a particular place in the world, we are differentially situated in an academic field that is itself undergoing transformation. Can Polanyi help us? A feature of third-wave marketization is the creation of a fourth fictitious commodity: knowledge. Knowledge used to be a public good, something to be shared by all, but increasingly it has become a private commodity, with both production and distribution. Increasingly, universities have to finance themselves, they have to produce their own revenue, they brand and rank themselves, and they are increasingly administered by financiers who expropriate control from the direct producers, the academics who used to control them. Their autonomy has eroded, and they move from being a university in a capitalist society, to being a capitalist university. Sociologists have their work cut out, surviving in their new workplaces. In UK financial assaults on university pensions, generated an effective strike that woke everyone up. In South Africa, an uprising of students that moved from #RhodesMustFall to #FeesMustFall, created havoc with the inherited autonomy. The state moved in with repression as it has in other countries. In Turkey academics lose their jobs for signing a petition. In Russia the European University in St. Petersburg was closed down on a flimsy pretext, but there the community resisted, turning their teaching outwards, creating public debate in community centres. The commodification of knowledge is a violent process that can be thwarted only by organizing beyond the university, where the political terrain has to be reconnoitered as more or less hospitable. At the same time the university becomes part of a global field of higher education that imposes another layer of alien and arbitrary standards on academic output. Here, then, are the social roots of our bipolar disorder – the destabilization of our home terrain.

References

Elcioglu, F. (2020). *Divided by the wall: Progressive and conservative immigration politics at the U.S.-Mexico border*. Oakland, MA: University of California Press.

Fanon, F. (1963 [1961]). *The wretched of the Earth*. New York, NY: Grove Weidenfeld.

Harvey, D. (2003). *The new imperialism*. New York, NY: Oxford University Press.

Levien, M. (2018). *Dispossession without development: Land grabs in neoliberal India*. New York, NY: Oxford University Press.

Luxemburg, R. (1951 [1913]). *Accumulation of capital*. New York, NY: Monthly Review Press.

Polanyi, K. (1944). *The great transformation*. Boston, MA: Beacon Press.

Przeworski, A. (1985). *Capitalism and social democracy*. New York, NY: Cambridge University Press.

Tugal, C. (2019–2020). The Euro-American left's abandonment and the right's surreptitious adaptation of Leninism. *Trajectories (Newsletter for CHS Section of the American Sociological Association)*, 31(1–2), 20–22.

8

The Iron Bars Get Closer

Anormative Social Regulation[1]

Margaret S. Archer

Introduction

At its most general, legal normativity is a concept within law that explores the role that society's moral or value systems, norms and conventions, play in social regulation. Traditionally, both legal and social theorists have used the concept of normativity to account for the 'bindingness' or crucial sense of obligation held to inhere in the law (Pufendorf, 1964/1988). Fundamentally, it was shared normativity that put the 'ought' into social action and accounted for legal conformity. But the central question was which way round it worked? Is it a shared normativity that orchestrates social change, or does social transformation engender changes in norms and values? This chapter will explore this question.

Radical social change, accompanied by changes in the law, has always been problematic in legal philosophy since it challenged the grounding of lasting legal *validity* in lasting *social normativity*. For example, French Revolutionary law, was swiftly displaced by the Napoleonic Code, and proved exercising for other independent States. This was yet more challenging to the philosophy of law as both legal systems broke with previous social norms, were at variance with one another, and yet valid within their time. If legality is granted to either, then legal validity cannot then be seen as reliant upon its grounding in the normativity particular to every nation-state.

The morphogenetic approach does not treat this central problem in either/or terms, siding neither with Durkheim's conviction that changes in the 'collective conscience' *follow* transformations in the division of labour,[2] nor with Hans Kelsen (1945), that legal regulation, derives from its rooting in a foundational 'groundnorm

groundnorm, underwrites its normative validity' (Kelsen, 1945). The reason for not taking sides is principled: the explanation of any social phenomenon must incorporate the interplay between structure, culture and agency, rather than causal primacy automatically being accorded to one of them (as was assumed by Durkheim and Kelsen in opposite ways). Given the complexities of this interdisciplinary debate, I shall spell out the three main propositions to be advanced in this chapter.

(a) To most legal philosophers, the connection between law and normativity is fundamentally *morphostatic*, working in terms of negative feedback between them. To philosophers of social science, the relationship today is *morphogenetic*, with positive feedback amplifying both legal and normative changes, without assuring their compatibility.

(b) For Sociologists, the demise of a shared normative system results in reductions in social integration, an increasing deficit in social solidarity, a growing 'macro-moral disconnect'[3] between religious/ethical systems and members of society, all of which have negative repercussions upon the traditional normative components of the legal order: the law, norms/ rules, conventions, customs and etiquette.

(c) In consequence, all elements above are held to be giving way to the 'Anormative Regulation' of the contemporary social order, or, if preferred, its 'Bureaucratic Regulation' – replete with Weber's 'iron bars' growing closer. In other words, normativity plays a reduced role in furnishing guidelines for social action because the law and social custom diminish proportionately in relation to non-normative forms of regulative social control.

Social change has intensified over the last three decades as a consequence of the synergy between digital science and economic financialization (Archer, 2014, 2015), and novel opportunities for crime have created a novel problem for legislative regulation, namely 'how to keep up?' This inverts the traditional relationship between the legal order and the social order. Increasingly, the law lags behind innovative malfeasance, and, since morphogenetic variety generates more variety in ways that are unpredictable, it outdistances the possibility of jurisprudence ever catching up. There are two legal alternatives. Either the law can try to 'run faster', but this inflates the quantity of legislation and still remains a retrospective tidying up operation.[4]

The alternative to this futile legislative frenzy consists in an increasing cascade of regulations, passing downwards through a plethora of agencies, culminating in increased bureaucratic rather than legal regulation.

The next section is devoted to the growth and role of administrative regulation in late modernity (after 1980), focusing upon its morpho-genetic importance in relation to earlier hegemonic forms of socio-legal regulation.

Why Morphogenesis and Normativity Part Company and Its Main Consequence, Namely Bureaucratic Regulation as Anormative Social Regulation

This is a broad trajectory where 'culture' is gradually displaced from the driving seat and from steering the social order when (Durkheimian) 'mechanical solidarity' prevailed, diminishing further with 'the diversity of morals' (Ginsberg, 1962)[5] and yet further as it confronted *fin de siècle* 'multiculturalism'.

While allowance must be given for the growth in international law, human rights law and the definition of new universal legal prohib-itions(for example, 'Crimes against Humanity'), these developments do not nullify the fragmenting bindingness of normativity in most parts of the life-world (locally, regionally, generationally, sexually, ethnically, linguistically etc.). This is what Doug Porpora (2001) has described as the 'macro-moral disconnect', where the guidelines for behaviour show a growing detachment from systems of social nor-mativity (religious and secular alike), which are then increasingly confined to the private domain (Porpora, 2015; Porpora et al., 2013).

During the 20th century, the phrase 'rules and regulations' was common in ordinary speech; but now the two terms have come apart. Today, 'regulations', which are but one form of rules, are not accompanied by normative justification. The societal sense of obli-gation to these has been displaced among those conforming to them, along with feelings of 'shame' or 'guilt' about potential infringements. Instead, these traditional moral responses have been replaced by considerations for escaping detection, or cost–benefit analysis of the price of a fine versus one's personal convenience (for those who can afford it). For example, using a mobile phone when driving with no 'hands free' device, and frequently disgruntlement about bureaucratic intrusions. This is what is meant by social regulation having become increasingly anormative.

Is it, however, justified to attribute this social tendency to morphogenesis?

The reason given for the proliferation of regulatory bodies in different countries is sometimes the simple speed of change, as accentuated by 'acceleration theory' (Rosa, 2003), which is straightforwardly empiricist. This is illustrated in a UK Cabinet Office Paper (2013), entitled 'When Laws become too complex', showing that since 1979 laws have decreased in number, though increasing in volume, whilst Statutory Instruments have more than doubled; from the late 1980s to 2006. On the other hand, some stress the increased expertise required, especially in complex or highly technical sectors, where '*legitimation* resides in the need for expertness and advanced technical competence' (Casini, 2007, p. 21). Here, the connection with the novel practices and techniques introduced through morphogenesis in the last three decades is more prominent.

However, it is salutary to note that within legal studies, where the growth of regulatory bodies has captured considerable attention, discussion has been restricted to an 'in house' debate about whether or not their increase subtracts from the powers of the state through 'decentring' control and results in its 'polycentricity', often referred to as the 'hollowing out of the state'. This is a debate largely without a social context because, at most, references are made to the changing political philosophies of those in office. Moreover, the concern of 'regulatory studies' is with the workings of regulation, in terms of 'good governance' or the opposite, rather than with the explanation of its growth, social form or relation to normativity. Consequently, there is little meeting point between this corpus of work and my present concerns, which accounts for why the main positions sequentially adopted in 'regulation studies' are of little service to the sociological issues under discussion.

(a) Regulation by 'command and control' (CAC) is the preserve of the state, using legal rules backed by criminal sanctions. 'It is "centred" in that it assumes the state to have the capacity to command and control, to be the only commander and controller, and to be potentially effective in commanding and controlling. It is assumed to be unilateral in its approach (governments telling, others doing), based on simple cause-effect relations, and envisaging a linear progression from policy formation through to implementation' (Black, 2001, p. 106). These substantive assumptions are rejected here and also by those advocating position (b).

(b) Conversely, in the 'decentred understanding of regulation, regulation happens in the absence of formal legal sanction - it is the product of

interactions not the exercise of the formal, constitutionally recognized authority of government' (Rhodes, 1997). Partly based on the
manifest failures of CAC, partly on the simple recognition that regulation has many locales (polycentrism), taking place 'in many rooms'
(Nader & Nader, 1985), and partly on Teubner's (1993) anti-centrist
systems theory (pp. 19–34), this popular approach also eschews any
explanatory generative mechanism producing decentred regulation,
and settles for a list of contributory factors such as 'complexity',
'fragmentation of government', 'loss of steering power', 'new knowledge', 'novel networks' and so forth, whose permutations result in
diverse sources of prescriptions.

(c) Finally, there is the millennial hybrid that combines the above positions,
by accentuating the combination of institutional centralization with
decentred regulation. Hence, in the quest for enhanced steering capacity,
Moran (2004) argues that the state spearheads a 'legibility: installing
systems of comprehensive reporting and surveillance over numerous
social spheres; the consequential pressure to standardize and to codify,
which is to make explicit what had hitherto been tacit; and the creation
of new institutions (notably specialized regulatory agency) to help
enforce all of this'. As the title indicates: *The British Regulatory State:
High Modernism and Hyper Innovation,* Moran's (2004) preoccupations
come closest to my own, but not his conclusions.

The unhelpfulness of these positions can ultimately be attributed to
their empiricism. Such 'tendencies' are merely extrapolations from
current data; there is no mention of generative mechanisms. All the
same, it was hoped that this corpus of literature would have furnished
a brief lexicon of fairly consensual and useable definitions. Yet, to
Black (2001), 'definitional chaos is almost seen as an occupational
hazard by those who write about regulation' (pp. 129–44).[6] Instead, I
have resorted to self-help in the following Ideal Type, with the aim
being of accentuating the most salient features of 'anormative regulation', without pretending to exhaustiveness.

- Regulations do not attempt to meet any form of 'normativity requirement', legal, conventional or personal (such as Korsgaard's 'reflective
  endorsement' 1996, 2009), but are the means of *avoiding* such appeals.
- Regulations exert a *causal force* not a *moral one.* They are unrelated to
  the approbation, approval or assent of those to whom they apply (in
  some of their actions), but whose agreement to any given regulation is
  rarely directly sought. Nevertheless, it is not one associated with a high
  rate of non-compliance.

- Regulations do contain 'normative operators', words such as 'ought' or 'must' is 'required'/'prohibited' or 'permitted'. However, they work – insofar as they do – through the instrumental rationality of the subjects in question, who feel no obligation but, rather, are calculative or prudential in their responses according to their means.
- Regulations have a heteronomous character, depending upon fines, penalizations and prohibitions, which are punitive without incurring either a criminal record or involving social sanction.
- Regulations have to be actual (it would sound odd to talk of the 'dead letter of the regulation'), but they can be displaced and replaced overnight without appealing to the 'democratic defence of validity'.
- Regulations do not necessarily stem from authorities within the legal order. Many do (as in planning regulations), but many others originate from retailers (concerning conditions for return, reimbursement or recompense for products), train and bus services, private utilities, landlords (no pets), hotels, companies, banks, financial services, libraries and taxi drivers. The law may or may not uphold any of the above.
- Regulations do not depend upon existing social conventions. Often their avowed aim is the opposite, as in combatting discriminatory practices or policing acceptable vocabulary and behaviour. (It is not illegal to swear, conventionally many do, but we are sternly warned not to affront railway personnel or cabin crew in this way.) *In fact, convention is now more frequently re-made by regulation than vice versa.*
- Regulations are basically concerned with the social co-ordination of action and practices rather than with issues of social co-operation or re-distribution. As such, they are at most binding (without entailing a sense of obligation) but never socially bonding. Hence the connection with a decline in social integration.
- Regulations differ from laws or other forms of rules in terms of what makes them social. In the latter cases, this depends upon their internal relations within complexes of roles and rules. Conversely, what makes bureaucratic regulations social is simply that people (largely) behave in conformity to them, thus producing a manifest social regularity.
- Regulations are ultimately intrusive of previously unregulated (or more loosely regulated) domains.[7]

Anormative Social Regulation Takes Over

In linking anormative bureaucratic regulation to the intensification of morphogenesis, one socio-political characteristic of regulations is crucial. Since regulations do not rely upon consensus among, or consultation with, the public affected, they are not dependent upon the relatively slow development typical of social conventions and of norms. This feature thus recommends their suitability for a ready response to the novel changes introduced through morphogenesis and its generic tendency for new variety to generate more variety. Nevertheless, more than just ready regulative capability is required to explain why regulations have become the weapon of preference for governance in the 21st century.

The post-war 'golden age', prior to multinationalism and financialization of the economy, was the product of mutual regulation between industrial employers and their workforce, the state of one mattering to that of the other with the two sides enjoying the sponsorship of political parties alternating in government and opposition. Thus, Western democracies could fairly be characterized as 'lib/lab' (Donati, 2000, 2014).[8] The regular alternation of such parties in government (or the equivalent alternation of centre-right and centre-left coalitions) gave half a loaf of bread in turn to those they represented. Hence, such mutual regulation between these distinctive political parties was a form for protracting *morphostasis*.

This did not last, because voter turn-out in general elections plummeted throughout Europe as electorates recognized the diminishing powers of national governments, given international finance capitalism, multi-national corporations and supra-national institutions such as the EU. A decade later, with the onset of the economic crisis, any residue of 'lib/lab' oscillation had disappeared to be replaced by a politics of 'centrism'. Very few (an exception is Bobbio, 1996) still maintained that 'right' and 'left' retained any meaning – unless prefixed by the term 'ultra'. Slogans of the 'We are the 99%' variety indicated that the economic crisis and the response to it of 'austerity' had eroded the residual class basis of political support in Europe, and with it the 'lib' versus 'lab' distinctions between parties. At that point, its successor, 'centrist' politics had no alternative to attempting to cope with the consequences of *morphogenesis* that were no respecters of national boundaries. It was this above all (though not alone) that enhanced the appeal of administrative social regulation.

Politics Without Conviction: From Strategic to Tactical Government

Politics without conviction means a drastic shrinkage (*crispation*) of normativity in political life. Political parties are preoccupied with tactics; with a St Simonian 'administration of things': the day-to-day management of austerity and the reduction of public spending with minimum backlash. The 'government of people' based on a normative conception of the good society, has been replaced with tactical governance, with its 'about turns', absorption in today's latest 'scandal', and the announcement of a 'quick fix'. It behaves like the fire service attending only to emergency calls. It ejects commitment from the political domain, whether in the form of expansive political philosophies or explicitly normative organizations, with a broad conspectus on the good life. Thus, religion in general is banished from the public domain (Trigg, 2008), henceforth supposed to be a depoliticized matter of private belief and practice. If functionalists had once held that values articulated every system of social action, they have become the antithesis of today's political aversion towards social normativity.

Tactical governance works through bureaucratic regulation whose highest aims are measurable efficiency and effective control. Institutionally, the public domain is carved into decreasingly small pieces, each with its own Regulator, meaning that the problems occurring in any fragment can be addressed technocratically. Consequently, the pieces are never put back together and assessed for their coherence, let alone for their contribution to the obstruction of any normative definition of the good society.

Ultimately, politics without conviction generates a huge shrinkage of normativity itself within public life. What matters is that epistemically we, the people, live together in overt 'political correctness'; real ontological differences are not acknowledged, addressed, assisted or ameliorated in this semantic displacement manoeuvre. If those lower down the social hierarchy are not addressed as 'plebs', 'slags' or 'pakis', then a veneer of civility conceals the endurance of real inequalities of class, sex or ethnicity. By implication, any form of society could claim to be 'good' provided it had somehow eliminated improper speech. Thus, the role of political correctness is to mute the expression of normative differences and places a stranglehold on their potential to justify demands for greater justice. Anormative regulation inserts a solid wedge between social policy and normativity.

Social Institutions and Governance by Performance Indicators

From their emergence in Europe, the distinctive feature of the professions was the adherence of each to a specific and demanding code of ethics, departures from which were usually disciplined by a governing body of peers (usually for doctors and lawyers). This ethical regulation, symbolized by the Hippocratic Oath, approximated to a secular vow of service. It both bonded members of a profession together and provided assurance to those they served that the skills in question were being used in their interests and thus that their relationship differed from a market transaction.

Over the last quarter of a century, all of the above groups have become subject to governance by performance indicators. Schools, hospitals, universities and so forth became managed by 'objective' performance indicators with results published in League Tables, which undermined the solidarity amongst 'free professionals' and the relationality between them and those they served. The use of performance indicators represents an extension of the logic of competition from the business world to one previously held to consist of the quality of human relations. The indicators deployed could capture measurable quantitative differences in crude empiricist terms (hospital through-put, waiting times for operations and so on) but were incapable of assessing the quality of care, of teaching or of research.

Internally, within each organization (schools, medical centres, hospitals and universities), and externally between the potential public of users, the logic of competition constitutes an assault upon solidarity. Externally, the effects of governance by performance indicators may not be fatal, but it does damage the social solidarity among users. In seeking school placement for their children in establishments highly ranked on the League Tables for their measurable results, English experience shows parents moving house in order to be eligible for entry and cases of legal prosecution for some who lied about their addresses so as to place themselves in the desired catchment area. Parents are thus placed in competition with other parents and their children, under an obligation of gratitude for these manoeuvres. It is unnecessary to mention the transformation of our students into 'consumers', reluctant to do more than minimal reading unless this 'counts' towards their results. Corporate employers raise the non-academic stakes by the expansion of seductive internships, the appointment of 'student ambassadors' and other forms of colonizing the campuses.

Internal and external effects coalesce. The use of journal 'impact factors' by Heads of Department to control where colleagues publish, the appearance of Google 'hit' rates in academic references (common in Switzerland), the expectation that research grant holders must demonstrate 'impacts' before the research is even completed, embroil all in the situational logic of competition. Collegiality gives way to mutual suspicion, collaboration to strategic considerations and peer review segues into a procedure for enforcing academic correctitude. Who benefits from this competitive turn? The answer is: hardly anyone, except those – usually not the most creative – who have re-invented themselves as academic administrators, but not the state of research and not academia as a solidary body. By working under this form of governance professionals become inoculated against the robust normativity that was once their patrimony.

Governance by Bureaucratic Regulation

It is worth noting that Canada, the United States and the EU have commissions or committees whose aim is to reduce it. In other words, bureaucratic regulation is a strange animal in the sense that some of the agencies most responsible for its proliferation, such as the EU, at least wish to be seen to be unenthusiastic about it. What accounts for this paradox?

Bureaucratic regulation is about control, and no democratic institution wants to be seen as a 'controller'. Yet, there has to be more to it, because so many organizations that increasingly operate through this form of regulation make no claims about their governance being democratic: public utilities, banks, supermarkets, manufacturers, public transport, leisure facilities and hotels amongst others. I maintain that one reason for this profusion and proliferation lies in low social solidarity amongst the relevant populations (of users, consumers, clients etc.) and one consequence of its growth is to drive solidarity even lower.

It is when normative consensus is lowest in a target population that bureaucratic regulation can be applied most easily. Where there is higher solidarity, entailing shared concerns amongst group members, the basis exists for potential (organized) opposition to bureaucratic fiat. Although solidarity does not necessarily imply a state of affairs even approaching normative consensus, the holding of shared concerns cannot be devoid of normativity. Some of the same things matter to those with concerns held in common and the most important of them is that this ought to be fostered rather than damaged. Conversely, low solidarity signals heterogeneous concerns meaning that regulation will have a mixed reception, but one too fragmented for resistance. In that case, control is simply control.

A bureaucratic regulation is usually satisfied if each and every member of the target population behaves as specified (e.g. not parking except in designated bays). What makes a regulation social is simply when a social outcome is its objective, such as avoiding a definition of overcrowding ('No more than 8 standing passengers permitted'). Nevertheless, regulations influence real social relations – specifically social solidarity – in excess of the behavioural conformity sought.

Let us quickly glance at an improbable instance, that of the EU regulation governing the sale of carrots. Commission Regulation (EC) No 730/1999, of 7 April 1999, states that carrots must be 'not forked, free from secondary roots'. One consequence has been that horti- culturalists have to dump or find some industrial outlet for their offending carrots, being paid by supermarkets for only perfectly straight specimens. Another is that the price of the latter rises. Farmers are disgruntled and so are customers. Yet, considering the price, customers may conclude that farmers growing carrots are doing very well. Meanwhile, the grower, returning home with a half a truck load of rejected forked carrots that have now lost freshness and value, curses customer perfectionism. Ironically, neither party may be fully aware of EC Regulation No. 730/1999, and both, if consulted, might well be normatively opposed to it. The attitudes they do share are discounted bureaucratically and the practices imposed by regulation serve to diminish solidarity between them.

Can one generalize from this ludicrous example? Perhaps, to the extent that when social solidarity is low, the weaker are the networks along which information flows and the less the bonds that mitigate or offset a person or group behaving in a way that is the product of regulatory control. Conversely, bureaucratic regulation enables competitive individualism to infiltrate more readily with every new decline in solidarity, thus serving to promote it. Additionally, collec- tivities invent informal regulations of their own. For instance, pas- sengers seated in rows towards the front of the plane have a right to disembark first, whether ready or not. Recognizing this practice, some airlines introduced a priority boarding fee.

Conclusion

This chapter has tracked how sources of normativity within the legal order – laws, rules, norms, conventions and etiquette (Abrutyn & Carter, 2014) – have responded to the intensification of morphogenesis over the last three decades. I have maintained that the task of normative control has passed to processes of *anormative* bureaucratic regulation. These can respond faster to novel social changes but have largely severed their links to traditional legal concerns about legitimacy yet are not imbued with social concerns about legitimation (Turner, 2010). Consequently, the legal and social orders are linked instrumentally, meaning that instead of supplying normative guidelines for actions, which are both constraining and enabling, social regulation is increasingly sought through regulative prohibitions and sanctions that are anormative.

In terms of the three main tasks that legal instruments can perform for the social order – assisting co-ordination, co-operation and redistribution – bureaucratic regulation focusses exclusively upon co-ordination, working causally to promote conformity rather than supplying guidelines fostering how we live together in fairness.

Moral concerns cannot be obliterated but their social diffusion is discouraged as voluntary initiatives prompted by them are colonized. Economic philosophy is curtailed into 'there is no alternative', political philosophy truncated into 'getting by' without vision, and human philosophy reduced to political correctitude unrelated to humanistic ideals of flourishing. In consequence, all the resources most capable of fostering happiness and well-being are repressed by the top-down imposition of anormative social regulation. They are fragmented into the specific remits of each regulative organization, which at most stimulates single-issue pressure groups as a form of opposition. These are hampered from coalescing because they compete for governmental recognition at election time in relation to their numerical strength.

In sum, the major top-down effect is to augment the overall decline in social solidarity, since bureaucratic regulation operates through instrumental rationality and is therefore fundamentally individualistic. Thus, there is no encouragement for the majority to become reflexive relational subjects (Archer, 2007, 2012; Donati & Archer, 2015) but, rather, anormative social regulation constitutes both structural and cultural barriers against effective relationality and creative reflexivity. It follows that we should not be surprised that 'those born here' can be recruited as jihadists, that migrant groups form residential enclaves, and that affluent retirees are retreating into gated communities. These at least have some form of social integration surpassing the absence of solidarity encountered in the developed world and a source of values sustaining normativity, albeit not ones promoting the common good.

Such are the results when the generative mechanism fueling intensive morphogenesis becomes systematically skewed towards market competition, with its intrinsic tendency to produce winners and losers, but one that increases the disproportionality between the two (we are the 99%). From this perspective, the potential for the same generative mechanism to diffuse 'win-win' contexts cumulating in an integrative commons is overshadowed by the proponents of the situational logic of competition, having made common cause with the political promoters of anormative social regulation. With it, the prospects of a eudemonic morphogenic social order appear to be paralyzed.

Notes

1   This paper is abridged from my 'Anormative Social Regulation: The attempt to cope with Social Morphogenesis' (2016), in *Morphogenesis and the Crisis of Normativity*, M. S. Archer (Ed.), Dordrecht, Springer. This paper was presented at Toronto ISA World Congress of Sociology, 2018.

2   Durkheim's position was nuanced by his concern that the Third Republic in France required substantial increases in civic morals and moral education as essential normative reinforcements to produce a stable and just society. See the last chapter of *The Division of Labour* dealing with remedies for its pathologies.

3   Doug Porpora (2001) coined the term the 'macro-moral disconnect', where the guidelines for behaviour show a growing detachment from systems of social normativity (religious and secular alike), which are then increasingly confined to the private domain .Porpora, D. V. (2001). *Landscapes of the Soul: The loss of moral meaning in American Life*. Oxford: Oxford University Press. Porpora, D. V, et al. (2013). Post-ethical society. Chicago, IL: Chicago University Press.

4   This has been attempted and abandoned. For example, between 1983 and 2009 the British Parliament approved over 100 criminal justice bills and over 4,000 new criminal offences were created. In response to that trend, the Ministry of Justice established a procedure to limit the designation of new crimes (Cabinet Office, 2013). In fact, the volume of Government primary legislation diminished between 1979 and 2009, whilst the quantity of Statutory Instruments increased (House of Lords, 2011).

5   An evolutionary exploration that is matched by many in legal philosophy texts on moral development (Joyce, 2007; Krebs, 2011).

6   Compare the following three definitions: 1. To the OECD, regulation is 'the full range of legal instruments by which governing institutions, at all levels of government, impose obligations or constraints on private sector behaviour. Constitutions, parliamentary laws, subordinate legislation, decrees, orders, norms, licenses, plans, codes and

even some forms of administrative guidance can all be considered as "regulation"' (OECD, 1995). 2. To the UK government's Better Regulation Taskforce, regulation is 'any government measure or intervention that seeks to change the behaviour of individuals or groups, so including taxes, subsidies and other financial measures' (BRT undated). DE3. Hall et al. (1999) provide the broadest and vaguest definition when they simply talk of people being regulated by culture.

7   Such as such as EU regulation No. 730/1999 on the retail of carrots, banning the public sale of forked specimens or those with secondary roots.

8   Donati also uses the term to refer more broadly to the *lib-lab* configuration of society, one that is a compromise between the liberal (lib) side of capitalist markets (free economy) and the socialist (lab) side of the welfare entitlements and 'equal' opportunities funded by the state (political system).

References

Abrutyn, S., & Carter, M. J. (2014). The decline in shared collective conscience as found in the shifting norms and values of etiquette manuals. *Journal for the Theory of Social Behaviour, 43*, 2.

Archer, M. S. (2007). *Making our way through the world: Human reflexivity and social mobility*. Cambridge: Cambridge University Press.

Archer, M. S. (2012). *The reflexive imperative in late modernity*. Cambridge: Cambridge University Press.

Archer, M. S. (Ed.). (2014). The generative mechanism re-configuring late modernity. In *Late modernity: Trajectories towards morphogenic society*, Vol. II. Dordrecht: Springer.

Archer, M. S. (2015). How agency is transformed in the course of social transformation. In *The generative mechanisms transforming late modernity*. Dordrecht: Springer.

Better Regulation Taskforce. (no date). Principles of better regulation, 1.

Black, J. (2001). Decentering regulation; understanding the role of regulation and self-regulation in a post-regulatory world. *Current Legal Problems, 54*(1), 103–146.

Bobbio, N. (1996). *Right and left*. Cambridge: Polity Press.

Cabinet Office Paper. (2013). Retrieved 21 November 2014, from www.gov.uk/government/publications/when laws become too complex

Casini, L. (2007). Models of public administration. Comparative analysis of administrative organisation. In *Formez, Innovazione amministrativa e crescita. Rapporto con raccomandazioni, Ricerca Giannini-Formez II Fase*, Vol. VIII. Rome, Formez: International Comparisons.

Donati, P. (2000). *La cittadinanza societaria*. Roma-Bari: Laterza.

Donati, P. (2014). Morphogenic society and the structure of social relations. In M. S. Archer (Ed.). *Late modernity: Trajectories towards morphogenic society*.

Donati, P., & Archer, M. S. (2015). *The relational subject*. Cambridge: Cambridge University Press.

Ginsberg, M. (1962). *The diversity of morals*. London: Mercury Books.

Gov-UK. (2013). *When laws become too complex*. Cabinet Office and Office of the Parliamentary Counsel. Retrieved 21 November 2014, from https://www.gov.uk/government/organisations/publications/when-laws-become-too-complex

Hall, C., Scott, C., & Hood, C. (1999). *Telecommunications regulation: Culture, chaos and interdependency inside the regulatory process*. London: Routledge.

House of Lords. (2011). *House of Lords*, Library note, LLN 2011/028.

Joyce, R. (2007). *The evolution of morality*. Cambridge, MA: MIT Press.

Kelsen, H. (1945). *General theory of law and state*. New York, NY: Russell & Russell.

Korsgaard, C. M. (1996). *The sources of normativity*. Cambridge: Cambridge University Press.

Korsgaard, C. M. (2009). *Self-constitution: Agency, identity, and integrity*. Oxford: Oxford University Press.

Krebs, D. (2011). *The Origins of Morality*. Oxford: Oxford University Press.

Moran, M. (2004). *The British regulatory state: High modernism and hyper-innovation*. Oxford: Oxford University Press.

Nader, L., & Nader, C. A. (1985). Wide angle on regulation: An anthropological perspective. In R. Noll (Ed.), *Regulatory policy and the social sciences, Berkeley CA*.

OECD. (1995). https://www.oecd.org/officialdocuments/publicdisplaydocumentpdf/?doclanguage=en&cote=OCDE/GD(95)95

Porpora, D. V. (2001). *Landscapes of the soul: The loss of moral meaning in American life*. Oxford: Oxford University Press.

Porpora, D. V. (2015). *Reconstructing Sociology: The Critical Realist Approach*. Cambridge: Cambridge University Press.

Porpora, D. V., Nikolaev, A. G., May, J. H., & Jenkins, A. (2013). *Post-ethical society*. Chicago, IL: Chicago University Press.

Pufendorf, S. v. (1964 [1688]). *On the law of nature and nations*. London: Wiley.

Rhodes, R. (1997). *Understanding governance*. Buckingham: Open University Press.

Rosa, H. (2003). Social acceleration: Ethical and political consequences of a desynchronized high-speed society. *Constellations, 10*(1), 1–33.

Teubner, G. (1993). *Law as an autopoietic system*. Oxford: Blackwell.

Trigg, R. (2008). *Religion in public life: Must faith be privatized*. Oxford: Oxford University Press.

Turner, S. P. (2010). *Explaining the normative*. Cambridge: Polity.

9

The Rise of National Populism in Western Democracies

Alberto Martinelli

Introduction

National populism has been on the rise in Western democracies in recent years, on both sides of the Atlantic. A growing literature is highlighting the increasing use of national-populist rhetoric and policies, for example, those of Donald Trump, and European leaders such as Marine Le Pen of Front National, Nigel Farage of UKIP, Matteo Salvini of Lega, Viktor Orban of Fidesz, Jaroslaw Kaczynski of Prawo i Sprawiedliwość, and others. In this chapter, I concentrate on key member states of the European Union, arguing that the diffusion of both nationalism and populism are symptoms of a crisis in European democracies. The convergence of nationalist ideology and populist rhetoric is a major challenge that the European Union faces and it can be effectively countered by developing the political project of a truly democratic and supranational union. I will first outline the distinctive features of nationalism and populism, and then analyse the major factors fostering the rise of national populism in European Union countries. I will conclude by discussing more effective alternatives.

Nationalism

Nationalism is a key concept in the political lexicon of modernity (Breuilly, 1982). Although polysemic, ambiguous and changing in time and space, the concept connotes a defined and well-structured ideology, with a strong emotional appeal, which has been a powerful factor in the political struggles of the last two centuries, by shaping mass political behaviour. Nationalism can be defined as the ideology – or discourse – of the nation. It fosters specific collective movements and policies promoting the sovereignty, unity and autonomy of the people gathered in a single territory, united by a distinctive political culture and sharing a set of collective goals. The concept of nationalism is strictly related to that of the nation-state, since, on the one hand, the nationalist ideology coordinates and mobilizes collective action in nation-building through a sense of belonging to the nation as a primary identity, and, on the other hand, the centralization of power in a sovereign state (i.e. the unification of territory, language, culture and tradition). This allows the national ideology to prevail over the many regional/local and social/cultural autonomies of pre-modern societies. Nationalism is the political principle that affirms the necessary congruence between political unity and national unity, and helps to achieve the political project of the fusion of state and nation.

Nationalism is historically specific. It is a basic aspect of the culture and institutions of modernity, although, both as an ideology and a political movement, it uses and re-elaborates pre-modern symbolic materials, such as ethnicity, with the aim of forming a new collective identity and a new base of solidarity in a modern society of individuals. Performing three key functions: coordination, mobilization and legitimacy, nationalism has played a key role in both major forms of response to the crucial question of how modern societies can establish an effective state–society connection and reconcile the public interests of citizens and the private interests of selfish individuals. One response is 'political' and rests on the idea of citizenship: the nation is simply the body of citizens who participate in liberal–democratic institutions. Another response is 'cultural' and stresses the idea of a collective identity: the nation is made by all those who feel they belong to the same cultural community. This is an idea that is initially upheld by political elites confronting the problem of securing the support of the masses, since the idea can provide a common national identity for members of different social groups.

Nationalism is also a modern phenomenon, closely related to the interconnected set of economic, political and socio-cultural transformations that characterize the various roads towards and through modernity (industrialization, bureaucratization, democratization and mass communication). The role of nationalism varies in the different roads to modernity (Greenfeld, 1992), but there are common processes and recurrent features to it as well (Martinelli, 1995). Modern industrial societies require the free movement of labour, capital and goods throughout the national community, universal schooling and a standardized national language, and intensified social and geographic mobility. Nationalism responds to the need of securing cohesion in the face of fragmentation and disintegration caused by rapid industrialization. It is reinforced by the development of mass politics when the insertion of hitherto excluded social groups into politics creates unprecedented problems for the ruling elites, who find it increasingly difficult to maintain the loyalty, obedience and cooperation of their subjects. It contributes to the development of a national culture by destroying both the exclusiveness of elite high cultures and the parochialism of local cultures (Gellner, 1983). Nationalism grows through the development of primary education, the invention of public ceremonies and the mass production of public monuments, to the point of becoming a new secular religion.

The 19th century and the first half of the 20th century was an age of irresistible nationalism. The nationalistic fever did not decline among the peoples of Europe after the useless slaughter of the Great War; to the contrary, it reached a new apex with the advent of totalitarian regimes and the global conflagration of the Second World War. Only the death of tens of millions, the shame and horror of concentration camps and the enormous destruction perpetrated by the war induced peoples that had fought against each other for centuries to put an end to the 'European civil wars', to establish peaceful relations, and to outline the supra-national regime of the European Union.

After the end of the Second World War, however, nationalism did not disappear from the world, rather, it took other forms. One can find nationalism in the anti-colonial independent movements of Africa and Asia. At the end of the 20th century, it also re-emerged in Europe, where the collapse of the USSR caused an explosion of ethnic, religious and national conflicts and tensions that had been latent, and, to a great extent, absorbed into the Cold War confrontation between the two superpowers. The surfacing of these old conflicts became linked to the new conflicts stemming from the economic and political changes taking place in the post-Soviet world.

The nationalist parties and movements of Eastern Europe are not, however, the only instance of resurgent contemporary nationalism. In many European countries national populism grew as a reaction to the threat of deterritorialization and the uprooting caused by globalization. It has been encouraged as a response to the problems raised by the economic financial crisis and the poor functioning of representative democracy both at the level of the Union and the member states.

Populism

Populism, like nationalism, is both an ideology and a strategy of consensus organization, but with a thin and less elaborated core (Mudde, 2007). Its diffusion has been favoured by mass politics and has been on the rise to the point of becoming a 'catch-all word'. For some scholars (*cf:* Taguieff, 1986), populism does not even have a specific ideological character, but is rather a rhetorical style, an attempt to connect empathically with the masses, that can apply to different ideological models. Populist rhetoric is actually present in the language of almost all political leaders, but, in some cases, populism acquires the distinctive features of a specific ideology, thin but very strong. It is organized around two concepts, people: as the legitimate source of power, and community: as the legitimate criterion for defining the people. It is used to emphasize, if not create, an antagonistic relationship between two homogeneous groups: *We* (the pure, virtuous people) and *Them* (the corrupt, inefficient and negligent elite or establishment). Populism purports to uphold the right of the majority against the minority. Populism is a controversial, slippery polysemic concept: it can refer to the sovereign 'demos' (the legitimate foundation of the political order), or to the people-mass (the common people), or to the people-nation with its ethnic roots (Meny and Surel, 2000).

Populists differ on who should be included or excluded from notion of the people, and on which elites or minorities, besides established party leaders, should be blamed (e.g. Eurocrats, global finance, transnational elites, asylum-seekers, specific immigrant groups). Common ideological elements are: the mistrust of any elite, though all of the political elites, and an emphasis on the people as the true legitimate actor of public decision-making; the antagonism against international finance; the affirmation of social bonds within organic communities, which goes together with the diffidence and refusal of any recognition for Others (immigrants, strangers, ethnic minorities, worshippers of other religions). The vagueness and plasticity of this ideological core, thin and strong at the same time, allows the populist rhetoric to be combined with a variety of 'thick' ideologies, such as nationalism (Martinelli, 2013) or leftist radicalism, that add more specific content to it. Conceiving populism as a thin ideology allows one to account for the variety of political contexts, and the diverse orientation of populist movements (both from the right and left), while simultaneously stressing a set of common features. It also illustrates the dependence of populism on more comprehensive ideologies that provide a more detailed set of answers to key political questions (Stanley and Ucen, 2008). The link with nationalism is the most widespread and dangerous variety of populism, since it can imply violent conflicts and non-democratic drift. Although not present in all forms of contemporary European populism, the link with nationalism reinforces and organizes the populist ideology around key questions of inclusion into/exclusion from the community, and of the re-affirmation of national sovereignty against the EU 'super-state' in opposition to the project of 'an ever-closer union'. There is a widespread belief that some immigrant groups (as a whole, not single members of them) are culturally incompatible with the native community and are threatening to national identities; EU institutions are blamed for fostering the threat by upholding the free movement of people. Nationalism and populism have a lot in common: the demonization of political opponents, a conspiratorial mindset, the search for scapegoats, the fascination with more or less charismatic leaders, but, first and foremost, an anti-European stance. The hostility towards the European project of an ever-greater union, the opposition to the euro, and anti-Europeanism in general, represent the connecting link between populism and nationalism, the point at which nationalism and populism merge. The national-populist ideology makes instrumental use of the popular resentment against institutions and the establishment to spread their nationalistic and anti-European message. An attitude of anti-politics fascinates voters and fuels the consensus for populist leaders who attack both EU institutions and national parties supporting them. EU institutions are the main scapegoats and targets of criticism, together with those national elites who are considered complicit in Europe's supranational technocracy, and should therefore be replaced by the true defenders of national interest (Martinelli, 2013; Martinelli and Cavalli, 2020).

The relationship between the national principle and the democratic principle has evolved in a complex and sometimes contradictory way. Populism is against political pluralism and is the permanent shadow of representative politics (Muller, 2016). In contemporary Europe, national populists are not anti-democratic and actually claim to be the true interpreters of democracy; but they have an illiberal conception of democracy that stresses the democratic component ('government of the people, by the people, and for the people', the absolute power of the majority) at the expense of the liberal component (division of powers, constitutional guarantees, institutional checks and balances, minority rights) (Urbinati, 1998).

National Populism in Contemporary Europe

The main causal factors of the rise of national populism in contemporary Europe are only partially common to this kind of political phenomenon in other regions of the world. The European leaders of national populist parties – France's Front National, Ukip, the Dutch Freedom Party, Italy's League, Alternative fur Deutschland, Hungary's Fidesz, Poland's Prawo i Sprawiedliwość – welcomed Donald Trump's victory as a sign of new times and new opportunities for the majority that has been betrayed by globalization, and they agreed with Trump's protectionism and demagoguery('produce American', 'buy American', 'today power returns to the people'). They, however, exaggerated the similarities between European and American politics, since European populism has also specific features that combine in different ways in the various EU member states.

In contemporary Europe, various interrelated causes contribute to the national-populist upsurge. The impact of the post-Cold War scenario has brought to light old cleavages and old nationalisms and has created difficult problems of regime change, fostering the political career and access to power of populist leaders in Eastern Europe. There is also the double crisis of legitimacy and efficiency in representative democracies: on the one hand, mainstream political parties are less and less able to mobilize voters and to structure political conflict; on the other, global trends erode national sovereignty and limit the capacity of national governments to implement effective policies, whereas the EU governance system does not yet have the legitimacy and scope of action that is necessary to deal with problems that are too big to be coped with at the national level. Finally, there is the impact of a long-standing economic crisis, which interacts with the implications of the political Middle Eastern and African crises (asylum-seekers and terrorist attacks against European cities), with the result of feeding uncertainty, resentment and fear for the future, and of creating a favourable ground for anti-establishment parties.

The first set of causes – and opportunity structures – specifically concern the family of national-populist parties of Central and Eastern Europe that in the 45 years after the Second World War have experienced limited sovereignty, authoritarian regimes and planned economies. The implosion of the Soviet Union has awakened cleavages and conflicts that during the long Cold War had been absorbed into the bipolar confrontation between the United States and the USSR. The end of the struggle between two alternative *Weltanschauungen* helps explain the resurgence of national, ethnic and religious identities and the related geopolitical conflicts that had been anaesthetized and hidden behind the rhetoric of the competing universalistic ideologies of free society and communism.

Old cleavages inherited from the past intersect, and partly overlap, with the new conflicts stemming from the political, economic and cultural transformations of the 21th century and its new global processes. With the collapse of ancient regimes, as the planned economy and the social security system break down, and as traditional social relations are in flux, a sentiment of general insecurity grows, ethnic groups are brought to rely on their cultural and linguistic communities. Where society fails, the nation then seems the only guarantee, and national populism prospers. Moreover, the eurosceptic attitude of many leaders and citizens, from countries like Poland, Hungary, the Czech Republic and Slovakia, can also be traced to a reluctance to give up (though partially) the recently regained national sovereignty to supranational institutions. The four countries forming the Visegrad Group, for example, share a notion of the EU 'à la carte': they gladly accept the financing of the social cohesion policy, but they refuse to accept the agreed quotas of asylum-seekers within their national borders.

The second group of causes that favour the rise of national populism concerns the pathologies of representative democracy and the crisis of its main actors – political parties. A representative democracy works well when a government, legitimized by the free vote of the majority and accountable to all citizens, can effectively handle complex issues. Today, both legitimacy and efficiency are in crisis. This double crisis has been going on for decades. Its root causes can be

traced to the contradiction between growing economic interdependence at the global level on the one hand and persistent political
fragmentation in sovereign nation-states on the other. Until the 2008
global financial crisis, opportunities seemed to outweigh costs, not
only for the large emerging economies of Asia and the United States
but also for the EU. After 2008, however, the balance reversed with
economic stagnation, unemployment and sovereign debt severely
affecting the EU countries.

Traditional mass parties have been losing consensus and influence
as a result of different interrelated processes of change: first of all, the
declining appeal of the great ideological narratives due to the failure
of communism and the Soviet Union's collapse; but also the help-
lessness of social democracy in the face of growing inequalities, and
the boiling down of liberalism to a self-regulating market doctrine.
The great cleavages – both of a political-cultural nature (state vs.
church, center vs. periphery) and of a socio-economic nature (land vs.
industry, capital owner vs. worker) – that marked the formation of the
modern European society and gave birth to traditional parties, have
been weakened by the combined impact of secularization, the growth
of the service economy, feminization of the workforce and the
extension of welfare. Together these processes lessened class and
religious conflicts and undermined the traditional bases of the mass
party system. The economic and cultural processes of globalization
then deepened this transformation.

Global interdependence and interconnectedness creates new technological and economic opportunities, but also growing social and
environmental inequalities; by distributing costs and benefits unequally,
it fosters new cleavages in society between those social groups that are
favoured by the global economy and a multi-ethnic society, and those
that are harmed. These new cleavages exacerbate a misalignment
between traditional parties and their voters. Traditional parties seem
less and less capable of channeling, filtering and processing the
increasingly fluid and heterogeneous demands coming from civil society, with the result that their integration into coherent government
programmes becomes more and more difficult.

Globalization has created problems not only for representative
democracy but also for performing democracy, i.e. effective government, as well. Four decades of globalized economy have eroded
the sovereignty of the nation-state. It has reduced the range of

government policy options and their effectiveness, thus enlarging the gap between what is promised by leaders and what is delivered. This has then exacerbated a shrinking and redefinition of the welfare state, and has jeopardized the traditional intermediary role of parties, unions, business organizations and professional associations. All of this has fostered citizens' disaffection with and distrust of leaders' skills and democratic governments. In the European Union, the erosion of the national sovereignty of member states could be compensated for by supranational governance, but this has happened only to a limited extent because the Union is still unaccomplished and suffers from a democratic deficit.

The third main root cause of this democratic drift is the global financial crisis and economic stagnation. These have amplified globalization's negative impact on some social groups, particularly among low-skill workers in traditional industries with diminishing wages, unemployed and underemployed youth finding only precarious jobs, and other globalization losers, which has then furthered the antagonism against migrants who compete for jobs with the natives and against transnational corporations who cut jobs at home through offshoring (a major propaganda item in Trump's electoral campaign). This prolonged economic-financial crisis and growing unemployment and underemployment fosters a climate of psychological uncertainty, fragmentation and precariousness, with consequences for the political system of EU countries, specifically resulting in the rise of national-populist movements.

Mainstream government parties, already under stress, have become the target of national-populist propaganda that portrays them as the docile instruments of supranational technocratic and financial elites. For Marine Le Pen's Front National, for instance, 'le mondialisme' is the new contemporary slavery, and the vagrant, anonymous bosses of international finance are the new slave-traders, who in the name of profit want to destroy everything that tries to oppose their tyranny – primarily, the identity and sovereignty of the nation. The euro is involved in this condemnation: those supporting it are seen as traitors not only of France's national interest but of the European interest as well, since it is argued that the euro means the forced integration of the European economies into a US-dominated world market. Together with global elites, the EU superstate, and the euro, immigrants are easy scapegoats: the long-standing crisis revives the denunciation of migrants stealing jobs and welfare subsidies from the native population. National-populist parties in many European countries – like Ukip, Italy's Lega, Party of True Finns, Dutch People Party, Flemish Vlaams Belang and Austria's Freedom Party – uphold policies of welfare state chauvinism that restrict social protection only to citizens (Kitschelt and McGann, 2000). The anxiety related to the economic crisis intersects with the fear caused by the consequences of Middle Eastern wars and African failed states; the terrorist attacks of Islamic fundamentalism against European cities and the pressure of asylum-seekers who escape from war, political instability and the social disintegration of many territories foster a diffuse sense of insecurity, resentment and fear, and create favourable ground for the growth of populist parties and movements.

The rise of national populism can also be traced to the cultural dimension of globalization – namely, to the explosion of digital communication, which has amplified the role of mass media in the political space. Traditional media, and commercial television in particular, have exerted a significant influence in politics for many years, insofar as they contribute to the increase in the costs of electoral campaigns and the connected influence of political lobbies, to the personalization of leadership, to the weakening of internal party dialectic and to the depoliticization of mass protest. Communication specialists have replaced party cadres, traditional propaganda methods like the 'militant distribution' of the party newspaper have been replaced by spin doctors, opinion pollsters, image consultants, social media experts, a radical change that has been fostered and foster in its turn the personalization of leadership. The marketization of mass media dictates its own logic, to which political actors have to adapt. Televised talk shows treat politics as any other message or entertainment, fulfilling the need of drawing viewer attention by turning everything into something spectacular, oversimplifying and overdramatizing every issue, stereotyping and demonizing rivals, and focusing on scandals and personal accusations. Commercial TV is coherent with the populist rhetoric of glorifying the common sense of the man on the street, even when it equals prejudice, disinformation and false messages.

The new digital and social media has turned out to be even more influential than television (Kriesi and Pappas, 2015) and has further weakened political parties' capacity to mediate or control its message.

This has ultimately undermined the authority of scientists and intellectuals. Authority based on knowledge and experience is challenged daily by millions of web users who pretend to be experts on everything and are perpetually indignant. The refusal to listen to the opinion of an expert or to verify the reliability of a presumed scandal/information is part and parcel of the populist distrust and hostility towards any type of elite, especially intellectual elites, with the consequence that many people then fall victims of false news, manipulations, conspiracy theories and 'post-truths' (a 2016 neologism). This paints an alarming picture: while the digital revolution offers many opportunities, it also raises concerns about the fate of the public democratic discourse. Blogs and social networks are primarily used for personal gain and notoriety, seldom used in order to better the knowledge, of reality, or to develop the critical mind, to experiment with forms of deliberative democracy, or educate citizens with respect to different opinions and be open to dialogue, debate and compromise, as much as it purports to be so. The Internet is, on the contrary, more often used for naming and shaming, creating scapegoats, expressing frustrations and prejudices, complaining while putting the blame always on others for misdoings and failures in a game of collective lack of responsibility. The field is thus open for the diffusion of messages with a strong and immediate emotional impact, such as those of nationalism, populism and anti-Europeanism.

An Alternative to National Populism

The main symptom of the crisis of democratic representation in contemporary Europe is the rise of national-populist leaders, movements and parties (Martinelli, 2017). The risk exists that the rationalizing power of parties and institutions might be severely reduced by the ebbs and flows of volatile and ephemeral political moods, triggering a vicious circle between weak and short-sighted governments and protest populist movements without perspectives. This is particularly dangerous at a time when the need for legitimate and efficient governments, able to face a series of intertwined crises (low economic growth, high unemployment, massive migration, terrorism and climate change) is stronger than ever. The supporters of populist anti-EU parties criticize real pathologies of democratic life and sincerely wish to 'cure' them, but their conception of democracy is often rudimentary and incomplete, fostering the rise of intolerant, plebiscitarian leaders who, once in power, prove incapable to govern complexity, or govern in a competent or responsible manner.

National populism can provide an answer, although limited, to the legitimacy crisis of contemporary democracies insofar as it offers an identity to the many losers in the globalization game. The rhetoric that creates this identity focuses on transnational elites and the EU bureaucracy and technocracy as the roots of all evil, and as those responsible for all problems of unemployment, precariousness, declining income and general insecurity. The underlying strategy, however, of restoring full national sovereignty and of renationalizing policy-making cannot respond effectively to the interrelated crises of unequal development, poverty, terrorism and war because the constraints on sovereignty imposed by globalization do not disappear through this rhetoric, but are, rather, on the contrary, made even stronger and more pervasive by it, as it encourages political entities that are smaller and weaker than a supranational union.

The rhetoric of national populist parties and movements is contradictory. On the one hand, it denounces the dysfunctions, aporia and pathologies of representative democracies in EU countries; however, the nationalist ideology advocates the re-nationalization of policies in those same malfunctioning democracies. Populist leaders argue, of course, that when in power they will fix problems and cure pathologies, making government more efficient, honest and transparent; however, in reality, when these types of parties win elections, their governments revert to technocratic, corrupt and opaque decision-making, exposing themselves to the same type of criticism that populists direct at European institutions in Brussels and Frankfurt.

National populism is Eurosceptic and often Europhobic: EU institutions are easy scapegoats for both the crisis of efficiency/ effectiveness and the crisis of legitimacy of European democracies. A deficit of democratic representation does exist in European governance, and communitarian treaties do put constraints on the autonomous policy choices of member states; however, one cannot attribute democratic pathologies to only these causes. Likewise, it is an illusion to think that in a globalized world separate nation-states could have the resources of power necessary to govern the complexity of the present crises and to mitigate their effects. Most importantly, one should avoid the serious risk of entering upon a path already tragically traveled in European history, since national rivalries has been a major cause of the 20th century's devastating wars.

The challenge of national populism must be faced quickly and forcefully. The critiques directed at economic and cultural globalization (deepening inequalities, the fomenting of intercultural conflicts) and at representative democracy (legitimacy deficit, scarce effectiveness, mismanagement and corruption) must be taken seriously and encourage reforms aimed both at bettering the quality of democracy and avoiding the illiberal and anti-EU drift that populism implies. The growing consensus for this type of Euroscepticism should not induce the political actors upholding the project of an ever-closer union to pursue populist slogans and proposals, but, rather, to uphold an entirely alternative project. The key aspect of this project is a thorough reform of EU institutions, granting more power to the European parliament, developing a truly European public space, and striking a reasonable compromise between intergovernmentalism and supranationalism, between economic competitiveness and social cohesion.

A supranational governance could be achieved by transferring further quotas of national sovereignty to the EU level in order to implement pan-European decisions in macroeconomic, social, fiscal, foreign and security, environmental and migration policies, adopting the method of reinforced cooperation among those members that already share the common currency. However, the decisive argument for preferring the communitarian over the nationalistic option is the motivation that has been at the root of the European project: the need to put a definite end to the centennial history of the European 'civil wars'. As François Mitterand (1995) warned in his last speech in the European parliament: 'le nationalisme, c'est la guerre'.

Note: An abridged version of this chapter was first presented at the ISA World Congress of Sociology, 2018.

References

Breuilly, J. (1982). *Nationalism and the state*. Manchester: Manchester University Press.

Gellner, E. (1983). *Nations and nationalism*. Oxford: Blackwell.

Greenfeld, L. (1992). *Nationalism: Five roads to modernity*. Cambridge: Harvard University Press.

Kitschelt, H., & McGann, A. J. (2000). *The radical right in western Europe. A comparative analysis*. Ann Arbor: University of Michigan Press.

Kriesi, H., & Pappas, T. S. (Eds.). (2015). *European populism in the shadow of the great recession*. Colchester: ECPR Press.

Martinelli, A. (1995). *Global modernization. Rethinking the project of modernity*, London: SAGE.

Martinelli, A. (2013). *Mal di nazione. Contro la deriva populista*. Milan: Università Bocconi Editore.

Martinelli, A. (2017). *Beyond Trump. Populism on the rise*. Milan: ISPI.

Martinelli, A., & Cavalli, A. (2020). *European society*. Leiden/Boston: Brill.

Meny, Y., & Surel, Y. (2000). *Par le peuple, pour le peuple*. Paris: Fayard.

Mitterand, F. (1995). *Speech at the European parliament*, January 17, 1995.

Mudde, C. (2007). *Populist radical right parties in Europe*. Cambridge: Cambridge University Press.

Muller, J. W. (2016). *What is populism*. Philadelphia: University of Pennsylvania Press.

Stanley, B., & Ucen, P. (2008). *The thin ideology of populism in central and astern Europe: Theory and preliminary mapping*. (unpublished).

Taguieff, P. A. (Janvier 1986). La doctrine du national-populisme en France, *Etudes*, *364*(1), 27–46.

Urbinati, N. (March 1998). Democracy and populism, *Constellations*, *5*(1), 110–124.

10

Mapping Violence

A Comprehensive Perspective

T. K. Oommen

Introduction

Violence is a contested concept in social science although used widely. In the Durkheimian perspective it is a normal phenomenon, in that a society from which violence is completely eliminated is not an empirical possibility. For Karl Marx, violence can be a positive force, as implied in the dictum 'the end justifies the means', and for Max Weber, violence can be positive or negative, in that he considered state violence to be legitimate. Without falling into the trap of a 'retreat into the present' (Elias, 1989, pp. 223–248), and re-calling the fact that we were all unborn in the hoary past (to reverse the phrase of economist Lord Keynes who observed, 'in the long run we are all dead'), I attempt a conceptual history of violence, taking into account a reasonable chunk of time beginning with colonialism, passing through the Cold War period and ending with the ongoing Global Age.

Usually analyses of violence are confined to physical violence, but some have enlarged the scope of this analysis by including structural violence (Galtung, 1969) and symbolic violence (Pierre Bourdie, 1977) into their analytic frame. These types of violence, in turn, can manifest in genocide, culturocide and ecocide (Oommen, 2006). As Galtung (1969) sees it, structural violence impairs access to fundamental human needs, arising out of inequalities in the distribution of wealth, power and privilege. Symbolic violence manifests in non-recognition of identity and stigmatization around various cultural dimensions of people, i.e. their religion, language, legal system, art, music etc.

I

We need to understand the three 'cides', genocide, culturocide and ecocide, and their meanings to undertake a comprehensive analysis of violence. Genocide is defined as the 'deliberate extermination of a people or nation' (Stoett, 1999, pp. 29–50). A multi-national or multi-cultural State, however, can also be a party to genocide by inaction and/or by 'facilitating' the extermination of a people or nation by another party within the State. Resolution 260 III of the United Nations, passed on 9 December 1948, entitled *The Convention on the Prevention and Punishment of the crime of Genocide*, as any of the following acts committed with the:

> intent to destroy, in whole or in part, a national, ethnic, racial or religious groups as such: (a) killing members of the group; (b) causing bodily harm or mental harm to the members of the groups; (c) deliberately inflicting on the group conditions of life calculated to bring about its destruction in whole or in part; (d) imposing measures intended to prevent birth within group; (e) forcibly transferring children of the group to another group. (cited in Stoett, 1999, p. 35)

This is a minimalist definition, however, and presents serious limitations to understanding physical violence within a territory or State. That is why when the Khmer Rouge campaign in Cambodia killed a million people it had to be termed 'auto genocide'. This has also been true of the extermination of political dissenters within other one-party states. Consequently, a large proportion of human killings have not been able to be labelled as genocide. It is, however, necessary to designate all deliberate extermination of human groups as genocide, characterizing them as violence.

Part of the problem arises from the assumption that (a) the State population is socio-culturally homogeneous and (b) that the State is a protector to all its citizens. Empirical evidence suggests that a large number of States have multi-cultural populations and that the State is perceived and experienced as a predator, as much as it is as a protector. Until the 1980s, information about the State-sponsored genocide of civilians was a well-guarded secret. During the 1980s, organizations such as Amnesty International, Human Rights Watch and the International Crisis Group started documenting and publishing about State violence against its own citizens. Rummel (1994) provided information regarding 141 State governments, as well as 73 quasi-State regimes and rebel groups from 1900 to 1987. He referred to 'democide' as the killing of civilians by an organized group, be it a State, quasi-State or rebel group. Valentino et al. (2004) provided information from 1945 to 2000 regarding mass killings, including genocide and politicide, wherein the victims are primarily political opponents to the regime and/or dominant groups within the State territory. A third set of data on genocide and politicide came from the State Failure Task Force (SFTF), collected by Barbara Harff (2004), for the years 1950–2000. These sources delegitimize the idea that violence inflicted by the State is 'legitimate'.

Although the principle of self-determination by the people is widely believed to be the founding principle of the nation-state, how is 'the people' determined? Jennings (1956) astutely wrote: 'The people cannot decide until somebody decides who are the people' (p. 56). Furthermore, in the case of 'democratic' nation-states, smaller and weaker national identities have been deliberately liquidated through state violence (Oommen, 1997, pp. 135–159). In the case of socialist states, political dissenters, even those from cultural mainstreams, have been murdered, disappeared or marginalized (Oommen, 1997, pp. 115–134). This illuminates the need to re-conceptualize violence, particularly State violence. One of the avowed objectives of the nation-state was to develop cultural homogenization because: 'no citizen can imagine his state or make it the object of his political affection unless he believes in the co-existence of a national type to which the individual inhabitants of the state are assimilated' (Wallas, 1921, p. 287), a sentiment in tune with the pre-globalization era.

The Doctrine of Assimilation guided the formation of nation-states in western Europe and was ruthlessly pursued. For example, the Republic of France encapsulated several nations – Alsations, Basques, Bretons, Catlans, Corsicans, Flemings and Occitanians. In 1789 half the population in France spoke no French at all, and even by 1863 about 20% of the population did not speak what was considered to be French in official circles (Hobsbawm, 1990, p. 60). Gradually all citizens were forced to learn French and their mother tongues were forgotten. In independent India, an utterly multi-cultural country, the dominant language (Hindi) and the majority religion (Hinduism) gained prominence marginalizing other languages and religions, and I have designated this process as culturocide (Oommen, 1986, pp. 53–74).

The term ecocide entered social science vocabulary in the context of the US war operations in Vietnam and the deliberate destruction of the ecological systems of the enemy territories (Weisberg, 1970). Ecological degradation can also occur because of the production and deployment of nuclear weapons and the disposal of nuclear waste. Failure to take long-term policy measures, so as to avoid famines, floods and droughts, can also result in ecological devastation. Natural disasters can lead to disastrous ecological destruction if early warning systems are not instituted. Above all, rash deployment of high technology for rapid economic development leads to the displacement of people in large numbers causing ecocide if appropriate rehabilitation programmes are not in place (See, for example, Oommen, 1992, pp. 131–139). Therefore, in a comprehensive analysis of violence ecocide should constitute an integral dimension.

Nature of Colonialism and Types of Violence

Colonialism has been characterized by the racial and cultural sense of superiority of the colonizers (e.g. the white man's burden, and the civilizing mission). There are two types of colonialisms, however, the replicative and retreatist. The distinction between replicative and retreatist colonialisms is made by me for the first time in 1991 while explaining the development and distinction between sociology in the First and the Third Worlds (See Oommen, 1991). These are vastly different in terms of the nature and intensity of the violence they require (Oommen, 1991, pp. 67–84). Replicative colonialism produced the New World, consisting of the Americas, Australia and New Zealand. These areas were inhabited by indigenous people who were subsequently framed as 'savages', they were described as being both wild and barbarous, as well as simple, peaceful and innocent. In the 17th century English men believed that without their religion and notion of the Deity, men would live like 'Savage Beasts' (Ascheroft, 1972, p. 150). This was the rationale behind the civilizing mission of colonialism in these areas, of which Christianization formed a part; however, in the process of this, both genocide and culturocide was perpetrated.

In Australia the aboriginal population was 100% in 1787, but after 200 years of colonization, by 1988, it had been reduced to a mere 1%, according to the statistics of the Government of Australia

(Department of Prime Minister and Cabinet Office of Multicultural Affairs National agenda for a multicultural Australia, Canberra, ACT Australian Government Publishing Service, 1989, p. 6). Estimates of Native Americans at the time of European contact vary between two and five million, but after 500 years of European occupation it diminished to a mere 250,000 (Snipp, 1987). Half of this population lives in 260 reservations, and half are integrated into mixed localities. As Jarvenpa (1985) observed: 'Reservations and reserves (have) perpetuated social segregation, administrative paternalism and a lower-class status to the Indian people' (p. 29). One looks in vain to the New World for a nation-state governed by the 'Noble Savage', who has instead been subjected to both genocide and culturocide. The civilizing mission has left hardly any trace of the 'Savage Other'.

The trajectory of retreatist colonialism has been quite different; it revolves around the existence of the 'Black Other' and the 'Oriental Other'. The Dark Continent, Africa, was the traditional abode of the Black Other which included the Egyptian civilization region. Here, the religion of the colonizers, Christianity, had to face stiff competition from Islam. Because of this, two identities had to be stigmatized, both racial (Black) and religious (Islamic). There were also two areas of Africa, the pagan or indigenous, and the Arab; the former being 'primitive', and the latter 'civilized'.

Francois Bernier, the French philosopher, was the first to attempt a biological classification of the human race in 1648. He argued that the brachycephalic African was inferior to the dolicocephalic European. Voltaire likewise held that whites were superior to Negroes. David Hume was categorical in his view that Negroes, and in general all other species of humans, were inferior to the whites.

The 'Black Other' was invented in the 16th century and by the 19th century its select physical features, intelligence and culture had become linked to a specific narrative and an inferior biological model of humanity had been constructed. A new discipline called Anthropometry emerged, which measured the various parts of the body, be it the length and shape of the nose, or the texture of one's hair, an obscured Cephalic Index had been created to understand intelligence and the capacity to build institutions or create cultures. The argument was that those who were Black (and, of course, derivatively Browns and Yellows) lacked mental capacity and, therefore, needed to be civilized. This is the reason why 'the Civilizing Mission' became the motto of colonialism in Africa. Convinced that the Blacks who inhabited the Dark Continent were incapable of self-rule, the Europeans apportioned Africa at the Berlin Conference, held in 1885, in a haphazard way, completely ignoring, and subsequently shattering the integrity of, the existing 'nations' of Africa. As people without a history, Africa had no right to 'nations' in Colonial Europe's perception, and were incapable of national self-determination. Therefore, European colonizers appropriated the right to govern African people, ignoring the fact that the colonial state was a totally illegitimate institution.

The strategy was different in the case of the Indian subcontinent, as it had a long and enduring civilization. The Aryan myth also complicated matters as it claimed a shared ancestry for Indians and Europeans (Poliakov, 1974). The Oriental peoples of India and Egypt were subsequently marginalized based upon a narrative around their inability to self-govern. In 1810, Chateaubriand justified the conquest of the Orient thus:

> Of liberty they knew nothing, of propriety they have none, force is their god, when they go for long periods without seeing conquerors who do heavenly justice, they have the air of soldiers without leaders, citizens without legislators, and family without a father. Hence they should be conquered and colonized. (quoted in Said, 1991, p. 172)

Exactly 100 years later, in 1910, Balfour wrote:

> Western nations as soon as they emerge into history, show the beginnings of those capacities for self-government. You may look through the whole history of Orientals, and you will never find traces of self-government. (quoted in Said, 1991, p. 32)

What one witnesses here is an attempt to marginalize the Black and Oriental Other through biased conceptualization. European thinkers irrespective of their ideological polarities endorsed this conceptualization, begetting enormous violence.

Emergence of the Three-World Schema

By the end of World War II colonialism disappeared and the Cold War period began, continuing for nearly 45 years, from 1945 to 1989, a trichotomy of three worlds – the First, the Second and Third – came into focus, replacing the realities of the colonial era. If the mission of the colonial period was 'civilizing', the motif of the Cold War was modernization. But as the orientations of the First and Second worlds drastically differed from one another, there was enormous competition to attract and annex the Third World into one of the modern identities being espoused. This was a significant theme of the Cold War.

The First World, signified by capitalism, was totally modern, the Second World of socialism was partially modern; this was thanks to its technological feat, but the absence of multiparty democracy and civil society made it only partly modern. The Third World was considered negative in all respects. It was 'a world of tradition, culture (culture in the bad sense of the term, that is religion), irrationality, underdevelopment, over-population, political chaos and so on' (Pletsch, 1981, p. 574). In this perception the society of the First World is the least violent, and the Second and Third Worlds are violent due to the absence of civil society and liberal democracy.

There was a serious anomaly in this conceptualization of the Third World, consisting of Africa and Asia largely, the sites of retreatist colonialism and Latin America the product of replicative colonialism, it being an extension of European society and culture. What was most common among the Third World countries was their economic underdevelopment. Academics in the Third World started interrogating the notions of modernity and development, those postulated by the intellectuals of both the First and Second worlds. The Second World, led by the Soviet Union, floated the idea of 'neo-orientalism' mirrored in the speech of A.I. Mikoyan delivered to the 25th International Congress of Orientalists in 1950. He observed: 'The peoples of the Orient create for themselves their own science, elaborate their own history, their own culture, their economy; in this way, the peoples of the Orient have been promoted from being objects (matter) of history to the rank of creators' (Quoted in Abdel-Malek, 1963, p. 122).

The delinking of the institutions of State and nation, and the identities attached to them, has been the most important work done in the transition from the Cold War era to the Global Age (Albrow, 1996). The Global Age has also witnessed the emergence of a trio of institutional complexes – State, market and civil society (Oommen, 1996, pp. 191–202). Notwithstanding the presumed democratization of the world, however, violence has not decreased.

Structural violence as manifested through both poverty and hunger has persisted, if not grown. In 1950, almost 790 million people were found to be food insecure, and half a century later, in 2000, that number stood at 800 million according to the Food and Agriculture Organization (FAO). In 1997, the G7 countries, with 11.8% of the world's population, had 64% of the world's GDP. In contrast, the G77 countries, with 76% of the world population, had only 16.9% of the world's GDP. Evidence suggests that economic disparity is constantly increasing in all countries of the world, particularly after the Structural Adjustment Programme (SAP) was introduced. This suggests that, insofar as the hegemony of the market persists and the State retreats from welfare programmes, structural violence will not only continue but also is likely to increase. What I have designated as culturocide, the systematic denial of identities and the blocking of possibilities, of living their preferred way of life continues. This is mainly conditioned by the institution of the nation-state. As Tilly observed, even after 500 years of nation-building:

> only a tiny proportion of world's distinctive religious, linguistic and cultural groupings have formed their own states, while precious few of the world's existing states have approximated the homogeneity and commitment conjured up by the label 'nation-state'. (Tilly, 1994, p. 137)

Violence continues to exist in most nation-states, which are racially and culturally heterogeneous. In a study undertaken by Ted Gurr (1993), data from 127 countries, that is, all the countries in the world with a population of more than one million, found that 93 had 233 minorities who faced violence. The largest concentration of these minority groups were in Africa; with 55 countries and 41 minorities at risk. In Asia, out of the 21 countries 15 had minorities at risk, and there were 43 such groups. These two regions were subjected to 'retreatist colonialism' (Oommen, 1991, pp. 67–84). Thus, the majority of minorities at risk in the world are arguably the result of the ruthless policies of State formation pursued by colonial administrations. In Latin America, with 21 countries, 17 have minorities at risk and there are 29 such groups. But because of colonialism these States are ruled mainly by immigrants. In western Europe, which followed the policy of ruthless cultural homogenization, it too had 15 countries out of 21 with minorities at risk, and with 24 such groups. In contrast, eastern Europe and the USSR, with nine countries, have five countries with minorities at risk, and 32 such groups. The point of theoretical interest here is the emergence and persistence of violence – both physical and symbolic – as a function of state policy, vis-à-vis minorities.

Technology and Violence

I have referred above to the role of high technology in causing ecocide and its role in bringing about violence. But technology has no agency; it is in the hands of decision-makers, leaders of powerful nation-states who are instrumental in creating violence through rash development and prescribed policies. Huntington (1992) proposes: 'To preserve western civilization in the face of declining western power, it is in the interests of the US and European countries ... to maintain western technology and military superiority over other civilizations' (p. 47).

What is pertinent to the present analysis is to note that technology is perceived as an instrument to uphold military superiority – not so much for economic development and human welfare, but to achieve the purpose at hand one needs a conjunction between high technology and a value orientation, viz. homocentrism. Although this value orientation was in existence for at least 20 centuries in the west, high technology based on inanimate energy emerged only in 17th-century England. Before that the human capacity to intervene in nature was limited. The root of ecological crisis that humanity is facing today was at the conjunction of four factors: the institution of the nation-state, modern technology, western Christian values and capitalism.

Notwithstanding the tremendous contribution of science and technology towards human progress and development, science and technology also pose the greatest threat to human existence. More than 50% of the world's scientists and engineers are engaged in military research. In the last quarter of the 20th century, 95% of the funds for military research were expended by six countries: the United States, Soviet Union/Russia, China, the United Kingdom, France and Germany. The destruction of the enemy's environment is a frequently employed war strategy, thereby causing ecocide. Many of the 'minorities at risk', in the Third World countries were controlled by weapons imported from World Wars I and II (Krause, 1992; Neuman, 1988). One need not labour the point that reckless production and deployment of war technology results in ecological imbalances and degradations.

Some eastern religions consider nature to be divine, through pantheistic beliefs and polytheistic practices. According to these religions divinity is transfused throughout nature. Such beliefs should have restricted human intervention in nature; however, in practice this does not happen. In contrast, Semitic religions facilitate the exploitation of nature by withdrawing divinity from nature. Both these value orientations do not provide the mix appropriate for economic development and the nurturing of nature. For material development, selective and careful intervention in nature is required. To preserve nature we need to retain a reverential attitude towards it. That is, we need to blend the homocentric and cosmocentric perspectives to avoid ecocide.

In the dominant world views of the 21st century, the relationship between humanity and nature is viewed either as dependent and dominant, or as independent and autonomous. However, we need to conceptualize the relationship between humanity and nature as being interdependent, reciprocal and complementary, if we want to sustain the integrity of nature without arresting material progress. This would be a step towards reducing the violence manifesting through ecocide.

Violence at the Micro Level

So far I have discussed violence at the macro (civilization and State) and meso (primordial identity groups) levels. Presently I will focus on micro level, that is, everyday violence. The two sets of victims targeted in this context are drawn from organic collectivities (gender) and aggregate collectivities (class). Organic collectivities are targeted as they belong to specific identity groups. Aggregate collectivities, such as class, are drawn from a variety of organic collectivities (Oommen, 2014, p. 9). Some individuals from organic collectivities (such as Blacks in the United States or lower castes in India) may experience upward mobility and the intensity or frequency of violence against them may decrease.

Violence against women is universal and has existed for millennia. However, its documentation has grown since the 1980s, thanks to the scholarship propelled by the feminist movement. Traditionally, women have been perceived as a symbol of the 'honour of the nation' or community, and therefore attacking and mutilating women's physical integrity was a means of terrorizing and humiliating the enemy. Similarly, women's bodies have been treated as cattle, and made available to victorious forces. At another level, mass rape has been used to drive out entire communities from their homeland. In Rwanda, rape and social violence have become tools of genocide. In Afghanistan, abductions, forced marriages and violence against women are perpetrated daily (Khan, 2004). While gender violence is nothing new, the proclivity and normalization of attacking civilians within the context of warfare has increased. While the civilian casualty rate in World War I was only 5%, by 1990 it had gone up to 90%, according to one estimate (Sivard, 1991). Thus, the tendency to target civilian populations, and within that, to focus on women and children, has been multiplied. By the end of the 20th century there were more than 30 million refugees and internally displaced persons worldwide, the majority of whom were women and children (USCR, 1999).

Domestic violence (against women) increases during and after war. Ristanovic (1994) has documented this. Those who indulged in such violence were primarily soldiers who had returned from war, and victims included mothers, wives and daughters. Men who have married from other nationalities also have been shown to express their anger against family members when the media reports crimes against their own nationalities. The conjunction of deteriorating economic conditions and national identity often accelerate these forms of violence. In situations of conflict between the State and militants, women also experience intense violence as in the cases of Kashmir Valley (Bhatia, 2001, pp. 37–41) and Sri Lanka (Maunaguru, 1995, pp. 158–175).

Violence against women can begin even before birth through amniocentesis, resulting in the abortion of female foetuses. Although the natural birth ratio produces same female ratios, in the most populous countries of the world, such as China and India, because of the abortion of female foetuses, the sex ratio is adverse to females (Heise, 1989, pp. 1–18; Patel, 1987). In many societies girls are fed less, given less nutritious food, breastfed for a shorter span of time, provided less medical and health care leading to higher rates of physical and mental retardation as compared to boys (Ravindran, 1986). Even after the attainment of adulthood, women are often denied the right to control their bodies in a variety of different ways. This is particularly gruesome in the case of women who are below the poverty line (Taylor, 1985). Thus, intersectionality between gender and class produces violence through a variety of causes. The common manifestation of physical violence against women is wife battery, rape, incest, genital mutilation and female sexual slavery (Heise, 1989; Slack, 1988, pp. 435–448).

Violence against women in families is reported from countries all over the world, irrespective of their level of economic development and cultural background (Connors, 1989). The Human Development Report (1990) concluded: 'In most societies women fare less well than men. As children they have less access to education and sometimes to food and health care. As adults they receive less education and training, work longer hours for lower incomes and have few property rights or none' (p. 31).

The 'MeToo' phenomenon that arose in the early 21st century, in media all over the world, with regard to the rampant and normalized sexual harassment of women, is an ample testimony to the sex discrimination even in sophisticated work contexts, such as academia, theatre and film. Human society is on the brink of collapse due to gender violence.

If 50% of humans experiences violence because of their gender, at least 25% of human beings experience violence because of class background. For the overwhelming majority of people on planet earth absence of violence means: a proper shelter and food to eat, to be able to care for their children and to live with dignity, to have good education for their charges, their health needs cared for and to have access to paid employment (Nelson Mandela, cited in Camdessus, 2000).

Camdesus himself observed:

> Poverty is the ultimate systemic threat facing humanity. The widening gaps between the rich and poor nations ... are ... potentially socially explosive ... if the poor are left hopeless, poverty will undermine societies through confrontation; violence and civil disorder. (cited in Thomas, 2000, p. 3)

The meaning and significance of these statements unfolds when one notes that the total number of persons killed during the two World Wars was estimated to be about 30 million. The two wars together had a span of 11 years. Thus the average number of persons killed during the span of two wars was 2.7 million persons per year. World War II concluded in 1945. Between 1945 and 1990, in war, and war-related conflicts, 22 million people died (Sivard, 1991). That is, during the

45 years following World War II, half-a-million persons died per year due to inter-state and intra-state physical violence. In contrast, the number of persons who currently die of hunger and hunger-related causes each year is 15 million (Thomas and Reader, 1997, p. 109). Thus during the 45 years which followed World War II some 675 million persons died due to hunger-related causes. Admittedly, deaths occurring due to structural violence (death due to hunger being just one such factor) are several times higher than deaths due to physical violence, due to wars and related conflicts A recent media report (*The Hindu*, 22 June 2018) said that the under-nourished people in the world had risen from 777 million in 2015 to 815 million in 2016, according to the UN's Sustainable Development Goals 2018 report, which points to the persistence of structural violence in the world today.

Mapping the Violence Scenario

In light of the analysis so far, one can map violence scenarios as shown in Figure 10.1.

Figure 10.1 Mapping the violence scenario

S.No.	Manifestation	Responsible Agencies	Motives/reasons
1.	Inter-state wars and conflicts	Existing sovereign states	Maintaining sovereignty of states; hegemony over client/weak states.
2.	Civil wars/ insurgencies	Aspiring primordial groups/communities within sovereign states to establish their sovereign states.	Erosion of state sovereignty/ legitimacy; collective alienation of primordial groups within states
3.	Inter-group conflicts: Racial, religious, caste, tribal, regional, linguistic groups	Hegemonic state, rapacious market, intolerant groups in civil society.	Fear and mistrust between primordial communities.

(Continued)

Figure 10.1 Mapping the violence scenario (Continued)

S.No.	Manifestation	Responsible Agencies	Motives/reasons
4.	Extreme disparity in income/wealth and/ or concentration of power.	Iniquitous state policies and rapacity of market.	Excessive and illegal profit and concentration of power.
5.	Domestic violence, persisting patriarchy	Authoritarian undemocratic society and civil society.	Domination of adult males over women and children.
6.	Institutionalized inequality sanctioned by traditional value.	Tradition, lack of democratic ethos.	Hegemonic orientation of the traditionally 'superior' groups over the traditionally 'inferior' ones.
7.	Disaster through famines, floods, droughts, pollution	Wrong state policies, exploitation by market and civil society.	Non-action or delayed actions by responsible agencies.
8.	Non-availability or non-affordability of education and health.	Defective state policies, intense competition in civil society groups and excessive profit-orientation by the market.	Abdication by the state its responsibility to citizens, the tendency on the part of market and civil society to make profit through welfare measures.

References

Abdel-Malek, A. (1963). Orientalism in crisis. *Diogenes, 44*, 103–140.

Albrow, M. (1996). *The global age*. Cambridge: Polity Press.

Ascheroft, R. (1972). Leviathan triumphant: Thomas Hobbes and the politics of wild men. In D. Edward, & M. E. Novak (Eds.), *The wild man within: Western thought from renaissance to romanticism*. Pittsburgh, PA: University of Pittsburgh. pp. 141–182.

Bhatia, A. K. (2001). *Transcending faultlines: The quest for a culture of peace*. (A Report). New Delhi: Women in Security Conflict Management and Peace.

Bourdie, P. (1977). Foundation of a theory of symbolic violence. In P. Bourdie, & J. C. Passeron (Eds.), *Reproduction in education, society and culture*. SAGE: London. pp. 1–68.

Camdessus, M. (2000). Poverty reduction and growth: An agenda for Africa at the dawn of third millennium, (Opening Remarks at the Summit meeting of African Heads of State, Libreville, Gabon), January, 18, 2000.

Connors, J. E. (1989). *Violence against women in the family*. New York, NY: United Nations.

Department of Prime Minister and Cabinet Office of Multicultural Affairs. (1989). *National agenda for a multicultural Australia*, Canberra, ACT: Australian Government Publishing Service, p. 6.

Elias, N. (1989). The retreat of sociologists into the present, *Theory, Culture & Society, 4*(2–3), 223–248.

Galtung, J. (1969). Violence, peace and peace research, *Journal of Peace Research, 6*(3), 179–191.

Gurr, T. R. (1993). *Minorities at risk*. Washington, DC: US Institute of Peace Process.

Heise, L. (1989). International violence against women, *Response, 12*(1), 1–18.

Hobsbawm, E. (1990). *Nations and nationalism since 1780 – programme, myth and reality*. Cambridge: Cambridge University Press.

Human Development Report. (1990). Delhi: Oxford University Press.

Huntington, S. (1992). The clash of civilizations, *Foreign Affairs, 72*, 22–49.

Jaruenpa, R. (1985). The political economy and political ethnicity of American Indian adaptations and identities. In R. D. Alba (Ed.), *Ethnicity and race in the USA: Toward the twenty-first century*. London: Routledge & Kegan Paul. pp. 29–48.

Jennings, I. (1956). *The approach to self-government*. Cambridge: Cambridge University Press.

Khan, I. (2004, December 18). Violence against women: The unacknowledged casualties of war, *The International Herald Tribune*.

Krause, K. (1992). *Arms and the state: Patterns of military production and trade*. Cambridge: Cambridge University Press.

Maunaguru, S. (1995). Gendering Tamil Nationalism: The construction of women in projects of protest and control. In P. Jagannathan, & Q. Ismail (Eds.), *Unmaking the nation: The politics of identity and history in modern Sri Lanka*. Colombo: Social Sciences Association. pp. 158–175.

Neuman, S. G. (1988). Arms aids and super powers, *Foreign Affairs, 66*(5), 201–214.

Oommen, T. K. (1986). Insiders and outsiders in India: Primordial collectivism and nation building, *International Sociology, 1*(1), 53–74.

Oommen, T. K. (1991). Internationalization of sociology: A view from developing countries, *Current Sociology, 39*(1), 67–84.

Oommen, T. K. (1992). Restructuring development through technological pluralism, *International Sociology, 7*(2), 131–139.

Oommen, T. K. (1996). State, civil society and market in India: The context of mobilization, *Mobilization: An International Journal, 1*(2), 191–202.

Oommen, T. K. (1997). *Citizenship, nationality and ethnicity*. Cambridge: Polity Press.

Oommen, T. K. (2006). *Understanding security: A new perspective*. New Delhi: Macmillan India Ltd.

Oommen, T. K. (2014). *Social inclusion in independent India*. New Delhi: Orient Blackswan.

Patel, V. (1987). *In search of our bodies: A feminist look at women, health and reproduction in India*. Mumbai: Shakti Publishers.

Pletsch, C. E. (1981). The three worlds or the division of the social scientific labour, circa 1950-75, *Comparative Studies in Society and History, 23*, 565–590.

Poliakov, L. (1974). *The Aryan myth: A history of racist and nationalist ideas in Europe*, London; Chatto: Heineman for Sussex University Press.

Ravindran, S. (1986). *Health implications of sex determination in childhood*. Geneva: World Health Organization.

Ristanovic, V. N. (1994). Domestic violence against women in the conditions of war and economic crisis. Paper read at the International Symposium on Victimology, August, 21–26, 1994.

Rummel, R. J. (1994). *Death by government*. New Brunswick, NJ: Transactions.

Said, E. A. (1991). *Orientalism: Western conceptions of the orient*. London: Penguin Books.

Sivard, R. L. (1991). *World military and social expenditures*. Washington, DC: World Priorities.

Slack, Al T. (1988). Female circumcision: A critical appraisal, *Human Rights Quarterly, 10*, 436–448.

Snipp, C. M. (1987). *The first of this land*. New York, NY: Basic Books.

Stoett, P. (1999). *Human and global security: An exploration of terms*. Toronto, ON: University of Toronto Press.

Taylor, D. (Ed.). (1985). *Women: A World report, a new internationalist book*. Oxford: Oxford University Press.

Thomas, C. (2000). *Global governance, development and human security: The challenge of poverty and inequality*. London: Pluto Press.

Thomas, C., & Reader, M. (1997). Development and equality. In B. White, R. Little, & M. Smith (Eds.), *Issues in global politics*. Basingstoke: Macmillion, pp. 90–110.

Tilly, C. (1994). States and nationalism in Europe, 1492-1992, *Theory and Society, 23*(1), 131–146.

US Committee for Refugees (USCR). (1999). *The world refugee survey 1999*. US Committee for Refugees: Washington, DC.

Valentino, B., Huth, P., & Black-Lindsey, D. (2001). *'Draining the Sea': Mass Killing and Guerrilla Warfare*. International Organization 58: 375–407

Wallas, G. (1921). *Human nature in politics*. New York, NY: Alfred Knopf.

Weisberg, B. (Ed.). (1970). *Ecocide in Indo-China: The ecology of war*. Boulder, CO: Lynne Reinner Publishers.

11

Moral Capital

A Much Needed Resource

Piotr Sztompka

No free society shall survive long without solid moral traditions and social conventions.

The alternative to such standards is not individualism and autonomy, but coercion and social pathologies. (John Gray, 1994, p. 77)

In the Simmelian tradition of social theory which I adopt in my work society is but the network of relations among individuals, and social process is the endless permutations and transformations of this network. Society is neither a supra-individual whole, nor a random collection of individuals. It is a space 'in-between'. From this perspective, an individual is not an isolated, autonomous, entity, but is, rather, a unique knot in the tapestry of all social relationships. Each of us is simply the occupant of a specific location in the inter-human space. All that, which is truly human (the self, language, culture, knowledge), is derived from and manifested in our relationships with others. The only meaning through which people can be understood as separate, fully individual entities, is biological. As Herbert (2007) 'the poet puts it in a rather brutal way, they are 'the bags of skin in which the old meats are fermenting' (p. 181).

According to this view, which I call 'the third sociology' (as distinct from the sociology of systems, and the sociology of action) two concepts grasp the static and dynamic aspects of society: 'inter-human space' and 'social becoming' (Sztompka, 1991, 1993). Society is thus the inter-human space in the process of social becoming. In other words: society is what happens between and among individuals, the constantly changing network of relations. What people do vis-à-vis other people is neither fully haphazard and spontaneous, nor predictable and controlled. Rather, it is to a great extent regulated, it follows some pre-existing scenarios, social rules. People act on the basis of meanings, which they ascribe to be based upon various types of social relations, and their personal interpretations of these scenarios they encounter. Such meanings are embedded in social values, among which are moral values, and it is this category that I will be discuss in this chapter.

The path of development for a society is not pre-determined. There is no necessity in the direction of progress. We have to purge the theory of social change from the Hegelian and Marxian overtones and admit that all which happens in society, including social change, is directly dependent on the actions of the people. 'The greatest generalizations in history are not propositions about the processes of history but about the actors in history, that is, men' (Homans, 1967, p. 47). Development, or progress, is a contingent achievement produced by human choices among a spectrum of possibilities. History is thus made by humans, and may take various courses. Societies may be successful, developing and moving forward, or they also may stagnate, disintegrate and collapse. Therefore, I propose a concept of social becoming as being the constant self-transformation of society by society, driven by actions taken by societal members, through their praxis (Sztompka, 1991). Societies differ in their potential capacity for transforming praxis. Here then comes the notion of agency, and the potentiality of society for successful praxis and creative self-transformation. Agency and praxis are the two sides of the incessant social functioning; agency actualizes in praxis, and praxis reshapes agency, which actualizes itself again in changed praxis. In this way social change proceeds.

The agency of society is the combined product of two dimensions: structures and agents. The shape of society thus depends, on the one hand, on the traits of the whole society, and, on the other, on the endowment of specific individuals. In the studies on social development, modernization and more general transformations in societies, the most common emphasis is on hard, tangible factors: at the macro level, the emphasis is on economic resources and viable organizational forms (e.g. efficient legal order or administrative frameworks), and at the micro level, the emphasis is on the level of education and skills (often labelled as 'human capital'). Another crucial resource is often neglected: the moral values, and the culturally embedded and individually internalized rules indicating the proper quality of interpersonal relations. These constitute moral capital. At the level of the social wholes, from the family to the nation-state, moral capital determines the quality of overall arrangement, and the organization of inter-human space. At the level of individual members, from family members to citizens, it determines the ways in which we establish relations with other people. Thus, moral values appear in both capacities as a network of normatively prescribed moral relations, and as the internalized moral attitudes of individuals expressed in their actions vis-à-vis other people. Ultimately, this comes down to people acting, involved in a moral praxis. If a sufficient, critical mass of people behaves morally, there then appears a general recognition that 'this is done', and finally that it 'should be done'. In this way the moral culture emerges. In the optimal situation, these values at a structural level coexist with the same values at a personal level. This mechanism operates at all levels of social complexity, from the family to the state.

Now let us disentangle the notion of moral capital: why 'moral', and why 'capital'? Moral values are those which regulate the most important forms through which people relate to each other, safeguarding our collective and individual well-being. Together they provide a model, an ideal, for a good, happy society. They define the duties of societal members. Duty, i.e. normative meaning, applies to three aspects of inter-human relations: acting, thinking and feeling. In general, social rules associate duty with the behavioural level, with actions (relegating what we should do). Two examples: in the relationship of friendship we should be loyal to our partner, and in the relationship of employment we should provide fair wages to our employees, proportional to their effort and merits. Values, then associate duty at the mental level, with aspirations, desires and ambitions (they regulate what we should want). Again, two examples: in the relationship of friendship we should wish our partner well, and in a therapeutic relationship the doctor should strive to make the patient healthy. Additionally, values relate duty to the level of emotional expression (they regulate the nature and intensity of our emotions). An example can be found in the relationship of friendship: we should sympathize with our partner in his troubles and enjoy his/ her success; and in the relations in the family the death of a loved person should fill us with sadness and grief.

What are the most important moral values? Perhaps the following list is not exhaustive, but there are at least six core moral values governing crucial inter-human relationships: trust, loyalty, reciprocity, solidarity, respect and justice. These constitute specific positive and negative vectors of moral space; they prescribe what should be done, and also prohibit what should not be done. Within the spectrum of these values there is a hierarchy, some are more important than others. Trust, for example, is integral to the core of the moral space, in terms of moral relations; trust is a prerequisite for all other five values. They cannot exist without some measure of underlying trust. In this sense, trust is a necessary moral imperative.

The importance of trust in social life is due to the fact that human beings are essentially social. We cannot survive without others. The trouble is that we can almost never be sure how others will act towards us, nor react to our own actions. Part of this uncertainty is epistemological: we simply lack full knowledge and information about our partners, about their intentions and motivations, as well as the contexts or situations in which they act. But even more importantly, there are ontological limits as well. Human actions are always under-determined, or as philosophers put it, people are endowed with free will. The determinants of action are extremely complex, and can be influenced, even simultaneously, by the past, present and/or future. The unique combinations of influence are impossible to detect. There is also the phenomenon of reflexiveness: people act upon beliefs, but not only adequate beliefs, upon gossips, rumors, prejudices, stereotypes and false information. The hints and cues that inspire action, selected from a sea of ideas and random pieces of knowledge floating about, is impossible to fully understand or predict. Additionally, people are rule-directed creatures, they consider the values and norms of their community and wider society, yet, which rules they will accept and use among the multiple, often vague, mutually conflicting and even contradictory precepts indicating prescriptions, prohibitions, permissions and preferences is a subjective choice and never easy to know (Merton, 1982, p. 180).

In the realm of human action and choice there is thus pervasive uncertainty. Yet, it is crucially important for us to determine whether others will act in ways that are beneficial for us or harmful. We must act despite our ignorance, and engage in society with others. Hence, we turn to trust, a substitute for prediction and certainty. We formulate a belief about our partners that they are trustworthy, and that they will act in ways beneficial to us. But this is largely conjectural and may be labeled as confidence. A second step is needed. Trust in a full sense occurs only if we decide to act on our belief, to test it when we commit ourselves in action: marrying another, lending money to a friend, signing a contract, making an investment, voting for a politician. Trust is then belief expressed through action. We trust that others are trustworthy and will meet our expectations and behave properly towards ourselves. Because we cannot be certain, the action in such conditions of uncertainty involves risk. Turning our confidence into action we take the risk, we gamble, we make ourselves vulnerable. Hence, I propose: Trust is a bet about the future, contingent actions of others (Sztompka, 1999, p. 25).

There are five other moral values. Second to trust is loyalty. Loyalty is the reverse side of trust, a duty to someone who trusts us. Loyalty allows us to believe that someone whom we trust and whom we treat considerately will not take advantage of this against us, will not gossip about us behind our backs, will keep silent about our secrets, will defend us against third parties and will properly protect and return in due time whatever we have entrusted to them (a cash loan, a car, an apartment, a child for baby-sitting, etc.). We can also count on them to support our views and help us in what we do. The opposite of loyalty is opportunistic obedience imposed by the force or threat of repercussion. The concept of loyalty does not apply to fawners. Obsequious yes-men obey their boss without reservations because they do not wish to be thrown out of the party or sect. This offers them numerous benefits, and if one belongs to the mafia, one does not want to end up in a lake with bricks attached to legs. Such opportunism, however, becomes uncomfortable, so yes-men then rationalize their conduct, and begin to really believe in the infallibility and genius of their leader. The American psychologist Irving Janis called this phenomenon 'groupthink' (Janis, 1972). It consists in people losing, or rather dissolving, their personalities in a closed group, the members of which then mutually strengthen their beliefs and gradually move further and further away from reality.

Next in the hierarchy of moral values is reciprocity. Reciprocity, in the view of some authors, is an innate, universal human impulse. Bronislaw Malinowski discovered it among the primitive tribes of Trobriand islanders (Malinowski, 1932/1967). Marcel Mauss (1971) considered it a spontaneous reaction to any received gift. In contemporary sociology, Alvin Gouldner (1960) has argued for its central role among all moral precepts. Reciprocity allows us to expect that the person to whom we have given something will feel obliged to return the favour, even if delayed in time or of a different nature from the original gift. Reciprocity requires us to repay for the good we have received from others. As Marcel Mauss (1971) wrote, a 'gift' initiates a network of relationships between the donors and the beneficiaries, and forms the basis of a community. The essence of a gift is spontaneity and selflessness. The opposite of a gift is a bribe, a benefit conveyed with an instrumental intention to obtain something specific. It contributes to the emergence of a 'corrupt community', only outwardly based on mutual trust, but in fact united by a common fear of sanctions. Such a community is only apparently based on loyalty, but in reality, on mutual blackmail, on the fact that both parties can blackmail each other.

The fourth moral value in our catalogue is solidarity. Solidarity means the readiness to sacrifice one's own interests for the good of a community (family, neighbours, professional, ethnic, religious, national, continental, all-human) in the hope that said community will show concern for our problems and will reciprocate with compassion, help and care when we are in need. We show solidarity with those whom we refer to in our conversations and thoughts as 'we' or 'us'. The personal effect of solidarity is social identity, linking our individual aspirations, goals and hopes with the aspirations, goals and hopes of a defined social group. When authentic solidarity is lacking, a pathological, xenophobic and intolerant form of solidarity emerges, which was described by the American social anthropologist Edward Banfield (1967) as, 'amoral familism'. This denotes solidarity within a limited group – formerly a tribe, today a professional circle, trade union, political party, religious sect or mafia organization. The strength of such amoral familiasm relies on blind loyalty and absolute obedience to a leader, while being separated from society at large by a tight wall of reluctance and aggression. Such a solidarity does not unite, but divides, it does not integrate, but excludes, creating an insuperable dichotomy of 'us vs. them', reserving all the virtues to us, and attributing all the sins to them, even denying them human dignity. This is not a solidarity of cooperation, but a solidarity of the besieged fortress. A common ethical space exists only inside a closed group, while outside, tolerance towards others is replaced by xenophobia, trust is thus replace by paranoid suspicion, kindness by hostility, debate by insults, and the common good by particularistic group interest.

The fifth value in my list is respect. Respect regulates relations between people who are unequal – for better or worse – in various ways. It copes with the fundamental fact that people have unequal talents, skills, knowledge, achievements, exceptional biographical records and consistent moral standards. We direct respect at elderly people emphasizing their experience and wisdom, some people, myself included, are still sticking to the traditional rule of giving an extra measure of respect towards women. There are also some occupations and professions endowed with particular respect, so-called 'helping professions' (Merton et al., 1983). Medical doctors, firemen, attorneys, soldiers, policemen and priests, all receive a measure of respect based upon their occupation. The value of respect allows us to believe that our services, achievements and successes will be noticed and appreciated in proportion to our efforts, talents and contribution. By the same token, we are compelled to treat the achievements of others in the same way. The opposite of respect is contempt and flattery. This includes false compliments, sham applause, the purpose of which is to make others dependent on our praise, or to force the flattered person to give us something in return. As with all rules, respect may be abused or misdirected. The notorious case of misdirected respect in its highest form is fame, which one can see in the category of so-called celebrities. Their elevated status in popular awareness is usually the product of media marketing, rather than authentic achievements.

Finally, the sixth moral value is justice. Justice is supposed to ensure a fair balance and proper proportion between what we give to others and what others return to us. It requires that such proportion be equally respected with reference to all people, regardless of their social status, with the help of universalistic criteria. Depending on the kind of proportion that is at stake we may distinguish five forms of justice: distributive, communitarian, retributive, transactional and attributive.

Distributive (or meritocratic) justice concerns the proportion of achievements (merits) and gratifications. Higher achievements should be more rewarded. For example: one's effort at work should be compensated by proper wages. Second, communitarian justice concerns proportion between contributions, service to a community, a group, society and what the community provides for its members. Beneficial membership should be matched by more contributions, and vice versa more contributions should be matched by more benefits from the group. For example: the level of dues in the association should be proportional to the benefits or services that the association provides for its members. Third, retributive justice demands proportional repayment for the losses, harms or pains inflicted by other people. For example: repair or replacement of damaged property. Particularly important to this is the proportional inflicting of penalties for the violation of laws and other social rules. This is the role of the courts of law, but also of parents vis-à-vis their children, or teachers vis-à-vis their pupils, etc. Fourth, transactional justice has to do with the proportion of prices between goods, commodities or services and exchanged between people. For example: sellers and buyers in the common trade, employers and employees in the labour agreement, suppliers and receivers in the industrial contract. Finally, attributive justice relates to the opinions and evaluations of other people. The rule demands proper proportion between achievements and the received amount of praise, respect or fame. It may be therefore considered as a particular variety of meritocratic justice. For example: it is expected of professors to give grades to their students, or, employers to give recommendations to their employees.

The important meta-rule in all these forms of justice is that they should be applied without regards to any particularistic criteria, in equal, universalistic way to all, irrespective of their social status, gender, race or role. As in fact in all cases the application of the procedures of justice eventually produces or enhances some inequality – e.g. of unequal wages, unequal rewards, unequal penalties, unequal measures of verbal or symbolic respect – the general definition of justice may be formulated in a paradoxical way: it is the equal application of the equal principles of inequality. The opposites of justice include partiality, nepotism, undeserved privilege, unjustified pay gaps, undeserved penalties, excessive prices and unfair opinions.

To summarize: moral values demand that partners be reliable, fulfil their mutual obligations, act loyally, reciprocate the good deeds of others, acknowledge their achievements, reward others commensurately with their effort and be ready to make sacrifices for the benefit of their community. Moral space decays if others fail our trust, act disloyally, take advantage of us to promote their selfish interests, refuse to respect us, ignore the achievements of others, unfairly distribute the available goods, honours, and privileges or egoistically turn their backs on their community.

In my work on trust I have singled out six factors determining the emergence of a culture of trust (or metaphorically 'the climate of trust'), understood as the widespread conviction that people are generally trustful and trustworthy, accompanied by the normative expectation that one should trust others, at least as long as they do not violate that trust (Sztompka, 1999). The same factors operate in the case of the other moral values as they are conducive towards the emergence of moral culture. Thus, the reasoning presented earlier can be applied to the wider concept of moral culture, or in more metaphorical terms the 'moral climate'.

There are six factors which determine the emergence of the moral culture, or its opposite the culture of immoral egoism and cynicism. They operate at all levels of social complexity, from small groups to entire societies, from families to nations. The first is axio-normative coherence versus 'anomie', i.e. axio-normative chaos. If rules of conduct are precise, non-contradictory and consistently enforced, then such a situation allows for the predictability of the behaviour of others. This provides security in the approach to others and therefore breeds a good 'moral climate'. On the other hand, when the rules are eroded, unclear and contradictory, the resulting anarchy does not allow for any certain predictions; it produces insecurity and defensive reactions by means of purely egoistic, cynical individualism.

The second factor conducive for moral culture is the stability of the social order versus traumatogenic change (Sztompka, 2004). If there are established institutions, frames of social action and routines of everyday life continuing over long periods of time, people know what they can expect of others, they feel secure and thus a 'moral climate' appears. The opposite conditions reign when social change occurs in a rapid, comprehensive, deep and unexpected way, derailing people from their accustomed routines of life, engendering cultural trauma and producing the defensive reaction of a widespread violation of moral rules (Sztompka, 2004).

The third factor is the transparency of social organization versus its opposite: secrecy and anonymity. Transparency is a condition for predictability, and the latter breeds predictability, security and readiness to follow mutually beneficial moral rules. Secrecy and anonymity easily evoke conspiracy theories and suspiciousness, blocking good, moral relations with others.

The fourth factor is the familiarity of the social environment as opposed to estrangement or alienation. If people feel 'at home', or interact with others similar to themselves, they are more apt to follow moral rules, whereas encountering a foreign environment or others who look different, dress different, or behave in different ways, eat different food and pray to different gods easily leads people to embrace xenophobia, intolerance, stereotypes and prejudices, opening up opportunities for immoral conduct.

The fifth factor is the accountability shown by the people and institutions with which we are dealing, as opposed to arbitrariness and lack of responsibility. If the agencies enforcing obligations are operating effectively and are easily accessible, we have a sort of insurance policy around this, in case our trust in others turns to be misplaced, in such cases our losses will be compensated, and hence we are more ready to engage in moral conduct. On the other hand, if arbitrariness rules, if our partners or institutions are not responsible, we have to take things into our own hands and develop all manner of precautions. Widespread suspiciousness, defensiveness and egoistic, cynical behaviour are a natural consequence.

The sixth factor is a rich space of personal contacts, as opposed to isolation and loneliness. If people have extended networks of good, rewarding social relationships, ties and bonds, strong families, intimate friends, dependable coworkers, and resourceful acquaintances, they feel rooted and secure, able to count on others in times of crisis. Good experiences of reciprocated moral behaviour within the network also encourage moral attitudes towards others, including strangers. On the other hand, the condition of loners raised in pathological families, unhappy in marriages, lacking friends and poorly adjusted at work tends to lead to social isolation, insecurity, suspiciousness and readiness to use others for their personal gain.

The other component of the concept of moral capital has to do with the notion of 'capital', by which is meant a valuable resource. Capital is a resource which is self-multiplying if put into use, and fungible, i.e. convertible into other resources. Referring to the social meaning of capital, James Coleman (1988) described it as, 'the aspects of social structure which facilitate some actions of social actors – individual or corporate – within this structure. It allows to reach goals which in the absence of such features of structures would not be possible' (p. 96). Why is it so important to possess positive moral capital? The answer is again the social nature of humanity, as we function within a network of relations with other people. This fact, codified since antiquity as our 'social nature' (Aristotle), recognizes that people live and act surrounded by other people. We enter into certain kinds of relationships with others, and are never alone. As Józef Tischner (2006) observed, 'we always live with someone, next to someone, close to someone, towards someone and for someone' (p. 68). This is an existential necessity: 'All social animals cooperate because solitary bee, wolf, or man will not secure survival' (Sennett, 2013, p. 96).

We need other people for a variety of reasons. The function of moral capital for individuals is tied to our social nature, insofar as a rich moral capital makes life happier and easier. It provides existential security, and feelings of rootedness. But it also satisfies some of our basic needs as a human species. One of these is the need to talk, and in order to talk one has to have partners, others with whom you can communicate. Erving Goffman (1959) argues that we are constantly occupied by the presentation of self, attempting to impress others and particularly those who are important audiences for us, 'significant others' to use George H. Mead's phrase (Mead, 1962/1934). With such audiences we need to develop extensive and rich relations. These relationships then offer in return, a reflection of ourselves. The mirror of others is how we appraise our appearance, and physiognomy. Our social status, prestige, esteem and support are likewise generated through relationship, acquired by perceiving the reactions of others, and shaping our self-evaluation accordingly. This is what is meant by the idea of the 'looking-glass self' (Cooley, 1902/1964).

Apart from such intrinsic, autotelic functions, moral capital is useful instrumentally, as a means for our extrinsic ends. We use others who appear in our inter-human space to obtain help, support and encouragement. We use others as sources of information, advice and expert knowledge. In the conditions of a complex division of labour, others are necessary to provide goods which we cannot obtain or produce ourselves. Similarly, there are some ends which we may want to achieve, that can only be achieved in cooperation with others. We are influenced by others, particularly by those around us through personal power or informal contacts. This is grasped by a saying in business, that it is more important whom you know than what you have.

In a similar way we may classify the function of moral capital for whole groups, as a societal function. On the autotelic side here as well, there is an obvious and well-confirmed importance of team spirit and morale, of the need for a good social climate for the effectiveness of groups. Rich social networks and a dense social life infuse dynamism, innovation and help with the mobilization of energy in the group. It was Georg Simmel who noticed, in the 19th century, how life in the cities, with innumerable interpersonal contacts, the rich inter-human space, differed in developmental potential from life in the country, in the dispersed and isolated village-type communities (Simmel, 2008). His insights were then confirmed by research in urban sociology.

Apart from these autotelic functions, there are also instrumental functions for groups. Rich social capital facilitates cooperation and raises efficiency, because it allows one to utilize a pool of knowledge, competence and the skills of various members of society, made freely and openly available. It also lowers transaction costs, as it replaces miniscule contracts with services of mutual trust. The famous research of James Coleman in the Jewish Orthodox community, involved in diamond trading in New York City, shows how close bonds of ethnicity and religion allow for huge informal transactions based on trust, which brings unmatched competitiveness and great profits drawn from monopolized trade (Coleman, 1988).

Moral values permit individuals to be open, innovative and creative, thanks to a sense of existential security, often due to a strong social identity. This then allows for the predictability of others' actions and the ability to plan one's own actions. Without a place in the inter-human space and without recognized values, the fate of a person, as Thomas Hobbes (1651/1946) wrote, is 'solitary, poor, nasty, brutish, and short,' entangled in 'the war of all against all' (pp. 82–83).

The benefits of moral capital, for the community, are vitality, efficiency and developmental dynamics (social order and social emergence). This is due to several circumstances. First, thanks to community integration, moral values constitute 'the cement of society,', or 'the glue that keeps society together' (Elster, 1989, p. 251). Second, moral values encourage cooperation with others. They mesh together 'the gears of the social machine' (Sennett, 1998, 2013). Third, they support coordination of various activities, enabling harmonious relations. They serve as the 'social lubricant' (Ossowska, 1968). Moral capital is an important resource in shaping the robust agency that is then able to push society forward, to produce creative self-transformation and progressive social development.

Alas the realities of many societies are witnessing the opposite of this in the first few decades of the 21st century. The levels of distrust, both horizontal and vertical, are alarmingly high. The citizens' loyalty towards the state and public institutions is very low. In place of reciprocity there is widespread exploitation. The idea of a common good is treated as an abstraction replaced by rampant egoism. Abuse, hostility and violence replace respect. Injustice of all sorts prevails. It is a mistake to treat these as intangibles and imponderables, as 'soft' irrelevant factors. Distrust, suspiciousness, egoism, interestedness, contempt, hostility and injustice are catalysts for social disaster. History shows persuasively that the decay of the moral space precedes the collapse of even the strongest empires. Without moral capital social development cannot be achieved.

References

Banfield, E. (1967). *The moral basis of a backward society*. Glencoe: Free Press.

Coleman, J. (1988). Social capital in the creation of human capital, *American Journal of Sociology*, *94*, 95–120.

Cooley, C. H. (1964 [1902]). *Human nature and the social order*. New York, NY: Shocken Books.

Elster, J. (1989). *The cement of society: A study of social order*. Cambridge, Cambridge University Press.

Goffman, E. (1959). *The presentation of self in everyday life*. New York, NY: Anchor Books.

Gouldner, A. (1960). The norm of reciprocity; a preliminary statement, *American Sociological Review*, *25*(2), 161.

Gray, J. (1994). *Liberalism* (Liberalism). Kraków: Znak.

Herbert, Z. (2007). *Wiersze wybrane* (Selected poems). Kraków: Wyd. a5.

Hobbes, T. (1946 [1651]). Leviathan. Oxford: Basic Blackwell.

Homans, G. (1967). *The nature of social science*, New York, NY: Harcourt Brace.

Janis, I. (1972). *Victims of groupthink*. Boston: Houghton Mifflin.

Malinowski, B. (1967). *Argonauci Zachodniego Pacyfiku (Argonauts of the Western Pacific)*. Warszawa: PWN.

Mauss M. (1971 [1923]). *Essais de sociologie*, Editions de Minuit, Paris.

Mead, G. H. (1962 [1934]). *Mind, self and society*. Chicago: University of Chicago Press.

Merton, R. K. (1982). *Social research and the practicing professions*. In A. Rosenblatt, & T. F. Gieryn (Eds.) Cambridge: ABT Books.

Merton, R. K., Merton, V., & Barber, E. (1983). Client ambivalence in professional relationships. The problem of seeking help from strangers. In J. D. Fisher, A.

Nadler, & B. M. Depaulo (Eds.), *New directions of helping (Vol. II)*. New York, NY: Academic Press.

Ossowska, M. (1968). *Socjologia moralności (Sociology of morals)*. Warszawa: PWN.

Sennett, R. (1998). *The corrosion of character*. New York, NY: Norton.

Sennett, R. (2013). *Razem; rytuały, zalety i zasady współpracy* (Together; the rituals, pleasures and politics of cooperation). Warszawa: Muza.

Simmel, G. (2008). *Pisma socjologiczne* (Sociological writings). Warszawa: Oficyna Naukowa.

Sztompka, P. (1991). *Society in action: The theory of social becoming*. Cambridge: Polity Press.

Sztompka, P. (1993). *The sociology of social change*. Oxford: Blackwell.

Sztompka, P. (1999). *Trust: A sociological theory*. Cambridge: Cambridge University Press.

Sztompka, P. (2004). The trauma of social change. In J. Alexander, R. Eyerman, B. Giessen, N. Smelsor, & P. Sztompka (Eds.), *Cultural trauma and collective identity* (pp. 155–195). Berkeley, CA: University of California Press.

Tischner, J. (2006). *Filozofia dramatu* (Philosophy of the drama). Kraków: Znak.

12

Preventing and Exiting Violence

A Domain for Sociology?

Michel Wieviorka

Introduction

Violence is an issue of significance for the humanities and social sciences. Most researchers and schools of thought have at some point explored it or dealt with it. It has been the central theme of countless theories and empirical studies in sociology and more broadly speaking for the humanities and social sciences.

Defining violence is not easy. A universalist, objective approach will, for example, propose a quantification – the number of crimes in a country, of persons killed in a war, of suicides, etc. But violence is also subjective. Its definition depends on what a person, a group, or a society considers as such at any given point in time. Various people, groups, societies, and even different groups within the same society, will have different perceptions of this, which makes it difficult to generalize. It also encourages a tendency towards relativism. This difficulty around the definition of violence is particularly obvious with terrorism. As we already know the terrorist for some is the freedom fighter for others.

Suffice it to say that the humanities and social sciences have by no means exhausted the attempts to conceptualize violence, and go further than the non-scientific definitions of daily life or found in the media. But such an endeavour demands discussion.

At the beginning of the 1980s, during a time when the Red Brigades and other armed organizations were operational, I had the opportunity of attending a meeting in Florence. The historian Charles Tilly, a leading exponent for the mobilization of resources school of thought, discussed his approach to terrorism as being opposed to that of Ted Robert Gurr. Gurr was a leading proponent of the trend in American political sociology that considered the participation of actors in organized violence to being explained by their relative frustration (Tilly, 1970). On another occasion, during the Congress of the International Sociological Association in Goteborg, in 2010, I had a fascinating discussion about the analysis of violence with Randall Collins; we continued this discussion in an Italian sociological review (Collins, 2008). He defended an interactionist approach, in a book which has become a classic, whereas I advocated research based on the subjectivity of the actors, which exists well before the point of the intersubjective encounter in which the violence may break out. Finally: there emerged, in 2016, in France, an interesting discussion concerning Jihadis, which rapidly had an impact at the global level. The discussion focussed on the motivation in the decision to take action. Was it primarily Islam, or was it the radicalization resulting from situations and social processes associated in particular with a history shaped by poorly assimilated decolonization, precarity or exclusion, discrimination, etc.? Gilles Kepel focused on the radicalization of Islam, while Olivier Roy discussed the Islamization of social radicality; finally Farhad Khosrokhavar demonstrated that there is no one reply, but a wide variety of possible situations (Khosrokhavar, 2018). Other important discussions have posed the question of the relations between religion and political violence, for example in relation to Salafism –cf. Mohamed-Ali Adraoui, *Salafism Goes Global,* Oxford University Press, 2020.

On occasions, the academic conflict has become heated, even extremely so in some cases. This happened, for example, around the genocide in Rwanda. There was a confrontation, shown in the media, in which two schools of research disagreed with one another. One school of thought went so far as to accuse the other of negationism (an example of negationism would be holocaust deniers) (Rwanda, 2017).

Typically, researchers listen to one another, and consider where they agree as well as what separates them, even if at times some do disagree vociferously in public.

Two Domains, Separate and Different

In a joint article, John Gledhill and Jonathan Bright (Oxford Internet Institute) (Bright and Gledhill, 2018) demonstrate that, generally speaking, more space is devoted to the study of violence than to the study of peace. They point out that there is little academic exchange between those who study war, and those who study peace; they report the existence of methodological divisions but also divisions in the regions studied or whether or not gender is an issue.

This finding is in keeping with my own observations and emphasises the difference between research on violence, which is well developed and varied, and the research focused on exiting and preventing violence, which is much less studied. Closer consideration reveals a fragmented space in which technical, militant and institutional technical skills are mobilized. These may include medical doctors dealing with traumatisms associated with the experience of terrorism, transitional justice lawyers, international consultants in 'peacekeeping', 'conflict resolution', 'nation building', etc. However, this cannot be said to be sociological research as such; it is much more testimony, reporting or professional expertize.

If we have to start, as Gledhill and Bright do, with the image of a separation between two registers, we observe that the second, unlike the first, is in no way reminiscent of a structured domain of research in the humanities and social sciences. It must also be admitted that exiting, or preventing, violence is not simply the reverse of violence – the two are not symmetrical – as if for example, once the causes of an episode of violence are known, one could deal with it simply and erase it, by dealing with these causes. There are specificities inherent to the prevention of, and exit from, violence, which also demand consideration. To articulate the two sets of issues, we first have to consider the exit from violence as being a domain for sociological research in its own right, with its own specificity. Once its autonomy has been ensured, we then must consider how this domain can define its relation to the pre-existing domain constituted by research on violence.

Throughout the world, countless actors intervene in the reduction, prevention or ending of violence, including its ongoing effects, or its impact after it has ceased. Each element of these issues is part of an extensive arena (Wieviorka, 2015). In some cases, the question is precize and more or less limited; it is of avoiding, minimizing or ending what, in violence, affects or has affected individual persons as such, people whose physical and moral integrity has been affected. What can be done for the American Vietnam war 'vets', who witnessed, and/or participated in killings and atrocities, and cannot recover? What about child-soldiers enlisted at a very young age in guerrilla movements, in Africa or Latin America, which has now surrendered? In other cases, the question is one of confronting global issues: global terrorism, organized criminality and international drug trafficking, whole regions of the planet devastated by war, as is the case today in the Middle East.

Between the two extremes, there is no shortage of problems at town, village, local area or nation-state level, but also at community level in a locality beset by problems.

Consequently, countless skills are mobilized and, over and above the material results, the outcome is the knowledge produced by the actors. Doctors, psychiatrists, lawyers, diplomats, consultants of all sorts, militants and officials from humanitarian NGOs, soldiers, national or international politicians, etc. may draw lessons from their experience and think about their actions, thus contributing to a fund of knowledge, which has the advantage of being based on experience. Occasionally there are documents prepared by authors who are capable of adopting a sociological or anthropological viewpoint, if only as a result of their training. But this in no way affects the overall image which we retain from all this production and, for example, from the reports of humanitarian organizations, international institutions or consultants. As far as they are concerned, the prevention of and exit from violence in no way constitutes in their opinion a specific domain in the humanities and social sciences. At best, they constitute a domain which is loosely structured, dominated by empirical knowledge with no recourse to theorizing.

If this is the case, it is not because these questions are of little interest to citizens, political actors, public-policy-makers or diplomats, humanitarian organizations, or social scientists, etc.; quite the contrary. It is perhaps because our traditional conceptions of violence have long rendered the project of constituting a domain in sociology, or a field in sociological research devoted to violence, unnecessary.

The Emergence of Victims

It is important to understand the evolution of the political and social status of violence within academia. Before extending their sphere of activity to the whole world and becoming globalized, the humanities and social sciences were originally a Western invention; confined in the first instance to countries in Europe, then rapidly and powerfully extending to North America and later to Latin America. In these societies, violence was considered the main threat to social order. This justified the perspective opened up by Hobbes of the State's right to resort to force in order to avoid violence, which he defined as being the natural state of war 'of every man against every man'. The sociological tradition, amongst others, is located in this perspective; we have, for example, Max Weber decreeing that the state has the monopoly of legitimate force, or Norbert Elias considering the role of the State and, in the first instance, the Royal courts, in the decline of human aggression (Weber, 1975). These activities fall within the jurisdiction of the State and its action, which is primarily, but not uniquely, repressive. The State can hardly be questioned from this point of view, except to challenge its abuse of power or shortcomings or when the population resorts to violence to challenge a regime and justify a revolutionary action. This has been an ongoing issue, giving rise to important schools of thought and action, often stressing the need for revolutionary violence. Friedrich Engels, for example, highlighted the 'role of violence in history'. Some explained that a degree of violence may be necessary to ensure progress and social emancipation, or asserted, with Georges Sorel, in his famous *Réflexions sur la violence* that the necessary violence of the working class would encourage the bourgeoisie to become radicalized also, and would, ultimately, raise the level of civilization. Following World War II, many writers, scholars and activists considered violence essential to end colonization. Jean Paul Sartre wrote a celebrated and quite radical preface to Franz Fanon's *Les damnés de la terre* about this.

Whether it be a question of asserting that the State has the legitimate monopoly of the use of violence, or of appealing to the positive and emancipatory role of violence, in both cases, there was no space to make of the exit from violence an issue for research in the humanities and social sciences. These approaches had little vocation for the analysis of the action of the State assuming its monopoly on violence; nor did they have any great interest in questioning sociologically the prevention of violence in the face of revolutionary, Marxist-Leninist, anti-imperialist or decolonizing ideas.

But in the 1960s in the 20th century, the viewpoint of the victims began to be perceptible in the public sphere in Western societies. The ways in which whole groups within these societies had been decimated or brutalized began to emerge as a subject for discussion. These included Indigenous and Black people in the United States, Jews in Europe, Armenians in Turkey, regional minorities everywhere and many others. The voices of those who denounced the violence also suffered by women, children and the disabled began to be heard. In short, the voice of the victims was being considered.

This (r)evolution developed along two distinct paths, which were already perceptible in the context of the processes leading up to the Nuremberg trials (Sands, 2016). On the one hand, there is the personal nature of the suffering endured, and in the most serious cases, offences involving human rights, when the concept of crime against humanity forged by the legal expert Hersch Lauterpacht. On the other, we have the collective nature where the object of the mass violence is the group to which the victims belong, which in extreme cases were subjected to systematic destruction, or 'genocide' to use the term forged by the legal expert, Raphael Lemkin.

Whether it be a question of individual or collective subjectivity, or whether the violence affects individual human beings, or targets a group as a whole, this evolution around our understanding of violence has led to extraordinary changes. These issues have been impelled by organizations devoted to the defence of human rights, movements demanding the recognition of historic suffering affecting certain groups and possibly demanding compensation, intellectuals initiating public discussion and the elaboration of policies, for example in the form of multicultural measures or affirmative action.

Violence has become an issue for analysis. Studying it is often an endeavour to reduce or prevent it, or to adequately manage its impact. It became a matter for scholars and practitioners, NGOs, and was no longer a matter for the State alone. Increasingly it has involved considering demands from civil society. For example, when *Médecins sans Frontières* demanded a 'right to intervene' for humanitarian reasons despite the refusal of the State, it was a matter that went beyond the morals of classical politics. It could also be, as was already the case in Nuremberg, a supranational or international concern.

The legitimate monopoly of the State, sole guarantor of the control of violence, was challenged from both above and from below during the 20th century. The interest taken in the victims and not only in the maintenance of order had had an effect. Numerous actors, whether at State level or not, were working to prevent or exit violence, thus reflecting the view that there should be more systematisation of the knowledge enabling a better understanding of the facts and appropriate action. From this arose the creation of think tanks and specialized institutes, and a platform in the Fondation Maison des sciences de l'Homme, the FMSH, which, with the aid of several institutions, mobilized some 300 researchers to moderate the International Panel on Exiting Violence, IPEV, panel and launched a journal devoted to these questions (Violence and Exiting Violence, 2019).

Loss of Legitimacy and the Destructuration of Political Violence

In Western societies, at least, the past 50 years have been marked by an increasing rejection of violence, which has become almost taboo.

Half a century ago, major intellectuals and researchers within the humanities and social sciences considered State violence to be legitimate. This is not often the case today, which makes it politically easier and more desirable to constitute the exit and prevention of violence as an object of analysis. The debate is no longer a case of opposition between advocates and opponents of certain types of violence, the adhesion or rejection for example of guerrilla or revolutionary movements, as it sometimes tended to be.

Finally, violence itself has considerably evolved. The most spectacular example is political violence, in many ways weakened, its decomposition giving way on one hand to metapolitical violence, in particular religious, as in Islamic, Hindu or messianic Jewish nationalism, and on the other, to infra-political procedures, organised delinquency and criminality. For example: today a guerrilla movement may become a key player in drug trafficking. Let us add that far-right nationalism and white supremacy are today part of this landscape of violence.

From the Analysis of Violence to Its Prevention and Exit: Classical Approaches

The humanities and social sciences offer a wide range of approaches to studying violence, each with the potential to lead to a coherent proposal for the exit from or prevention of violence.

The classical arguments made for ending violence are structured around two main types of approach. The first prioritizes the idea of reaction or response: violence is here seen as individual or collective behaviour enabling an actor to confront difficulties, disruptions or crisis. This type of approach may include the concept of 'relative frustration', which I referenced above in relation to Ted Robert Gurr: the origin of violence lies in changes affecting the position of a person or a group who, as a result, feels frustrated. Researchers, in particular those in North America, who developed this approach in the 1960s and 1970s often quote the Tocqueville of *L'Ancien regime et la Révolution*. In this case, exiting violence, or preventing it, involves preventing or minimizing, or rapidly ending, the crisis. The focus is not on the actors of the violence so much as it is on the social, economic and cultural conditions which cause the crisis and their reaction.

A second type of approach focuses on the calculations of the actors, once again either individual or collective. Violence here is not reactive but instrumental; it is a resource mobilized towards a specific end – in particular a political one. Thus the 'theory of mobilization of resources', illustrated by Charles Tilly, and referred to above, is influential in political science, focussing on the way in which a social movement, at the outset excluded by the political system, endeavours, by using violence, amongst other resources, to enter the political system, establish its presence there, and to either maintain its position or to exclude others. In this case, exiting violence means ensuring that the cost for those who might consider using it would be too high.

Other approaches to understanding violence tend to focus on the culture and personality of the actors and perpetrators. For some, a 'primary socialization' in the family or at school may encourage tendencies towards violence, forging personalities which would be receptive thereto or even shaping a whole culture. A renowned study by Theodor Adorno et al., published in 1950 in the United States, *The Authoritarian Personality*, is often quoted in support of this type of approach. Adorno suggested that an antidemocratic 'authoritarian personality', forms in childhood, and enables the worst collective crimes to be committed (Adorno, 2017). In understanding the violence of the Jihadis today, in particular the dimension of hatred of Jews, some consideration has to be given to their family background. For example, it is important to be aware, as was said to be the case for Mohammed Merah, that anti-Semitism may have been rife within their environment since birth, when he was milked by his mother.

Based upon this perspective, the so-called 'deradicalization' public policies should thus address primary forms of socialization, through education and the family, and these should be implemented as early as primary school.

These relatively classical approaches to violence each have their specificity. While each sheds light, which could be useful, building on one another to exit violence demands considerable caution. It is preferable not to get the explanation wrong. Furthermore, these approaches, while they may be useful in some ways, do also have their limits. The most obvious are related to the gratuitous, even meaningless, nature of some acts of violence, or of certain dimensions to the phenomenon of violence. Why did the jailers in the death camps, described by Primo Levi (1989) in his last book, choose to humiliate the prisoners and treat them like animals? Was this really necessary? What explanation is there for the cruelty of the soldiers in the American army, for example, in the Abu Ghraib prison in Iraq in 2006, or during the My Lai massacre in Vietnam in March 1968? What should we make of the incomprehensible floods of words of the extreme-left terrorists in Italy at the time of the decline of their movement in the 1980s? One explanation is that dehumanizing the other makes possible to by-pass the barriers towards enacting atrocity towards other human beings that are no longer considered as human.

This brings us to the consideration of the rationales of de-subjectivation and re-subjectivation, which deserve our consideration.

The Perspective of the Subject and of Meaning

I have suggested (Wieviorka, 2012) constructing our considerations on violence on the basis of the subjectivity of the actors. My idea is that subjectivity emerges in the course of the process of de-subjectivation and re-subjectivation. To do this, I identify various figures of the subject of violence which I list briefly here to show how they fit together, with possible proposals for an exit from and prevention of said violence.

What I call: the 'floating' subject: here at the outset, the violence is restricted because the subject cannot become an actor in non-violent democratic interactions. For instance, young people in deprived urban areas who take part in a riot in reaction to the announcement that a death in the area has been caused by police 'blunder' express a rage which cannot be conveyed in any other way. In this case, exiting violence involves the accession to a material space transforming the crisis, ending it and enabling these young people to express their subjectivity in action. This is a space which may be conducive to non-violent conflictuality, a point to which I shall return.

The non-subject claims to act in obedience to a legitimate authority, a head of State, for example, like Adolf Eichmann explaining before his judges that if Hitler had ordered him to kill his own father, he would have done so. His defence was that there would be no personal responsibility in his act, since he had to obey, nor would there be any emotion – for example, anti-Semitism – which is difficult to believe. In this case, theorized by Hannah Arendt as being due to 'the banality of evil', exiting violence involves holding the person who resorts to violence responsible for their acts, and restricting the situations in which obedience to a legitimate authority gives rise to violence. It should be noted that today, in some democracies at least, a soldier who receives a barbaric order, that of torturing for example, has the right to refuse to obey.

The hyper-subject moves from the loss of meaning, which could make of the actor a 'floating subject' to the overload or recharging of meaning; this was formerly provided by the grand ideologies, in particular revolutionary and is to be found today primarily in religion. This overload enables the hyper-subject to act, to break with being passive or feeling impotent. The most important thing to ensure here is that this overload does not entirely permeate the conscience of the hyper-subject, so much so that there is a risk of passage to action. Preventing or exiting violence means confronting the use of religion, and specifically quasi religious rhetoric, as a force impelling violent action. This raises a question: is it acceptable to combat religion in general, or one religion in particular, to avoid violence? Or to mobilize one religion to combat another mobilized in the cause of violence? Or, as is the case in some 'deradicalization' programmes, for example in Denmark, rely on the moderate, secularized sectors of the religion which the terrorists take advantage of?

What I call the **anti-subject**, in contrast, attributes no meaning to violence; violence is, for them, an end in itself. Cruelty, when it is not instrumental, aimed, for example, at terrorizing an enemy, is a powerful method of denying any subjectivity to other people; the anti-subject needs this to feel to be aware of being the actor of their own existence. When confronting violence for the sake of violence, it is essential not to allow the actor any space: the presence of witnesses, journalists and photographers, and the prohibition of alcohol or drugs which facilitate disinhibition, all play an important role. If not, only repressive action is efficient.

This typology, even if only an outline and incomplete, is already a contribution to the bases for considering the prevention of and exit from violence. Each subject portrayed has its own specificities. The exit from violence (or preventing entry) depends on the type of subject; for example, the 'floating' subject only wishes to be able to become an actor of non-violent, negotiable conflicts, whereas hyper-subjects are totally involved in a religious approach which is non-negotiable. Each figure has its own variations and its own specific sensitivity to attempts at exiting violence or to a public policy for prevention.

The Applied Humanities, Social Sciences and the Sociological Analysis of Action

Would it be possible to envisage an applied approach for the humanities and social sciences that would throw light on action and decision-making in matters of violence? The listing of a set of considerations and proposals is not sufficient in itself to constitute a genuine domain for violence within the humanities and social sciences. If we are to make progress towards achieving such an aim, it should be ensured that practical action, ultimately informed by the concrete analysis of researchers, becomes an object for research and discussion in its own right.

The preceding observations and remarks reveal a characteristic specific to the issues posed by the exit from and prevention of violence. Contrary to the analysis of violence, which does not require to be accompanied by action, it is difficult to separate the analysis of the exit from and prevention of violence from operational concerns, for example, from the idea of leading to recommendations. Basically, one of two things must be true here. The research on the prevention of and exit from violence must in fact be an extension of the research on violence. This extension may call for co-production or cooperation with actors in the field. However, it does not fall within the scope of an autonomous field of research. The main questions, which the researcher must then consider, concern the nature of the links which they may, or which they must, maintain with the actors. Which relationships should be chosen and how can researchers ensure that these do not jeopardize their independence, their liberty and their difference vis à vis other players? This is what is being considered here up till now in this text.

The other alternative is that the issue at stake in the research is the action and its actors. In this case, a very different approach is involved. Here we must examine the meaning of a specific action, the relationships in which actors operate and through which they contribute to change. We must look at the processes in which they appear collectively, in the form, for example, of an NGO or associations, and the sources of their involvement including both personal and professional reasons. Research opportunities are numerous, whether it be private actors, individual or collective, or actors connected with public authorities at local, national or supranational level. Who are the negotiators, the intermediaries in the meetings leading up to the Oslo Accords or the exit of the FARC from the armed struggle? How do humanitarian organizations recruit and continue to recruit their staff? What type of militants do they target, and what support, what obstacles or opponents do they encounter? Is international justice not, in fact, the justice of the victorious? Is the geopolitical order, which is being prepared by those who purport to be contributing to peace and the return of the rule of law in Syria or in Iraq not in fact consistent with certain interests, which go beyond what is stated?

This second set of approaches is the reverse of what we referred to as the applied humanities and social sciences. Applied approaches consist in finally contributing directly, perhaps with the help of some actors, to improving the knowledge available about the mechanisms and procedures of exiting from or preventing violence. However, from the point at which their focus is on the exit from and prevention of violence, as research objects, their approach is quite distinct. The claim is no longer one of doing more and better than applied sociology by systematising knowledge and organizing it in a global structured space. This second perspective in no way implies that analysts and actors no longer have any contact with one another. It authorizes, even demands, considerable collaboration; for example, researchers may invite the actors to jointly reflect upon the meaning of their action, or discuss with them on the basis of findings of a study carried out on the actors. But this set of approaches makes a clear distinction between roles. The researcher is not an actor, and the actor is not a researcher.

If we accept this duality of approaches, we have a firm foundation on which to base our conviction that the analysis of the exit from violence and its prevention maintains strong links with the analysis of violence itself, but at the same time, also has its own dimensions and scientific autonomy.

The Return of Conflict

What can then be the specific issue at stake in a genuine social science of the exit from violence, integrating the two dimensions, which have just been highlighted? Violence is frequently, but not always, the reverse of conflict, the reverse of a conflictual relation when this relation is institutionalized and negotiable. When no conflictuality of this order is conceivable, the space for violence is much larger. When it is possible to transform the violence which is merely a threat or which is already very present into discussions, by recognizing the other as a person in their own right, the result is that the other will now become an adversary and is no longer an enemy as was the case till then. One can more easily discuss, negotiate, reach a compromise with an adversary than with an enemy.

Thus, when this possibility exists, actors who may be humanitarian, political, religious, diplomatic or other may endeavour to transform a situation of chaos, civil war or guerrilla, into a negotiation in which the protagonists will succeed in finding the conditions for a form of cohabitation, which may be tense but is not murderous. For example: in 2017, the FARC guerrillas in Colombia accepted to sign a peace agreement with the government by which the FARC did not purely and simply disappear but was transformed into a recognized and legitimate political force.

Similarly, the Oslo Agreement between Israelis and Palestinians in 1993 aimed at transforming violent confrontation into the possibility of co-existence. But this possibility was ruined rather quickly.

Sometimes the expression 'post-conflict' is used to refer to the horizon targeted in this type of situation. In fact, this wording is inappropriate. It would be preferable to speak of 'post-violence' or the transition from armed or violent conflict to non-violent conflict.

What applies in political matters or civil war also applies in social affairs. In a firm, which is preferable: a total absence of meetings and discussions between employers and the employed, may unexpectedly lead to a situation of non-negotiable crisis, or even of violence, the kidnapping of managers, or arson? Or a relation with the trade unions which indeed may not always be easy? For a mayor in a deprived urban area, is it preferable to have a network of young people's associations voicing, perhaps vociferously, the demands of the young who feel excluded and subject to discrimination, or nights of rioting?

We see clearly here how research can on one hand formulate this type of question directly, and, on the other, study those on the ground who are endeavouring to provide answers, including negotiators, consultants, diplomats, social workers, trade unionists, etc.

But Is It Really Possible to Exit Violence?

The exit from violence is not necessarily definitive, stable or total. According to Gallup International the five most dangerous countries in the world are Venezuela, South Africa, Salvador, southern Sudan and Liberia. In South Africa, Salvador, and Liberia, political violence has disappeared; but it has been replaced by criminal violence. This is not uncommon.

A society permanently exposed to one sort of violence develops a culture favourable to other forms. It has, for example, been observed that after years of political violence, the incidence of rape and domestic violence or homicides may be particularly high.

In the first instance, therefore, one form of violence may disappear, only to be replaced by another, possibly because this violence was embedded in the previous one. Thus, to turn to the example of Columbia again, if the peace agreements ended the armed struggle waged by the guerrillas, here and there these forces have been replaced by forms of behaviour (rape, murder, extortion, all sorts of mafia-type practices, etc.) which bear witness to the total absence of any State or guarantor of order which the guerrilla had ensured in their own way. We should add that in some cases, the exit from one violence is instantly replaced by another violence, in others the processes overlap and yet others are more distant in time.

Violence leaves traces that may be profound and last long after it has ended. Trauma, difficulties to project oneself into the future, a profound conviction of having experienced something irreparable, an intractable tension between the desire for peace and the desire for justice, etc. The period of adjustment after violence for both the individual and the community, for the victims as well as for the guilty, may assume one of at least three key modes:

The first is in keeping with what Ernest Renan set out in his lecture 'Qu'est-ce qu'une nation?' in 1882 – when he explained that to function a nation must know how to forget *'les violences au cours desquelles elle s'est formée':* How can we live together if we are obsessed by the past? The second mode consists in living in the past, what Sigmund Freud referred to as melancholy, refusing to leave the past behind and constantly brooding over this 'never-ending past' in the words of the historian Henry Rousso.

The third option is 'mourning' – a term to be used with caution because it might lead us to imagining that we are forgetting, whereas the issue is one of projecting ourselves into the future while not forgetting, but not being a prisoner of the suffering linked to the past. This option is never easy because the past, even if it is in some way transcended, can always resurface painfully in the memory and eclipse the present. Genuine 'mourning' implies that the sensitive questions of forgiveness, justice and peace or even reconciliation be settled. How can we accept an unjust peace, or a form of justice which does not bring with it peace? Who is in a position to propose to forgive – the guilty, their descendants or a community? Who has the right to give forgiveness: the victims, or their descendants? What can we expect from the State in this respect? How can the victims live alongside neighbours who have participated in extreme violence, as is the case in some situations in the former Yugoslavia or in the Great Lakes region in Africa?

Conclusion

These are sensitive issues, all the more so as in the approach we adopt we cannot ignore considerations of the timescale. In the short term, exiting violence means above all preventing it from happening again, if it has just been intercepted; this entails an immediate, possibly pragmatic response. In the long term, however, it may be possible to envisage much more far-ranging economic, political, social or educational issues and to distance oneself from the actual violence in its material aspects.

The actual way in which an experience of violence was halted may play a determining role in the long run. Thus a statistical study carried out by the Swedish researcher, Peter Wallensteen, (who presented it in my seminar at the EHESS on 31 May 2017) compared two modes of resolution of armed conflicts: one was based on the victory of one side over the other, the other involved the conclusion of a peace agreement through negotiation. The findings are informative: after a negotiated agreement, the percentage of a return to violence within 10 years was much lower than after a victory.

The exit from, or prevention of violence, are complex questions which remain as practical issues with a substratum of concrete aims. But they cannot be settled uniquely by the expertise of specialists – consultants in 'Peace building' or in 'Conflict resolution' for example – respectable as they frequently are. These issues demand a capacity to think in terms of different time scales, to analyse different sub-jectivities and to consider the reconstruction of subjects through processes of subjectivation, which are always complex. In the last resort, these issues demand the acceptance of the idea that democracy, and the associated non-violent processing of differences, is the best tool for the management of divisions and tensions, which, whatever one may think, are the lot of all human societies. In other words, these issues call for the social sciences to extend their approach to violence, on the one hand, and on the other, to focus on action to counter it. The analysis of action should be conducted by researchers who do not live in isolation in their ivory towers but engage in discussions with the actors who construct their own analyses. In return, these analyses can shed light on action, even while being distinct from it.

References

Adorno, T. W. (2017). *Etudes sur la personnalité autoritaire*, éd. Allia, Paris.

Bright, J., & Gledhill, J. (2018). Divided discipline? Mapping peace and conflict studies. *International Studies Perspectives*. DOI:10.1093/isp/ekx009

The polemic between a collection of historians, in the article Rwanda : the 'Que sais-je ?' – the book that re-writes history. http://www.lemonde.fr/idees/article/2017/09/25/rwanda-le-que-sais-je-qui-fait-basculer-l-histoire_5190733_3232.html#hZesgGtp02 c7qXOX.99, and Filip Reyntjens 'Le difficiledébatsur le Rwanda en France', Mediapart, 11 October 2017.

In Sociologica, n°2/2012. Cf. Collins, R. (2008). *Violence: A micro-sociological theory*. Princeton: Princeton University Press; I clarify my approach further in Retour au sens, éd. Robert Laffont, Paris, 2015.

International Panel on Exiting Violence (IPEV).

Khosrokhavar, F. (2018). *Le nouveau Jihad en Occident*, Paris, éd. Robert Laffont.

Levi, P. (1989). *Les naufragés et les rescapés : Quarante ans après Auschwitz*, éd. Gallimard, Paris.

Sands, P. (2016). *East west street: On the origins of genocide and crimes against humanity*. London: Alfred Knopf/Weidenfeld; Nicholson.

Tilly, C. (1978). *From mobilization to revolution*. Reading (Mass.): Addison-Wesley Publishing Company; Ted Robert Gurr, Why Men Rebel, Princeton University Press, 1970.

Violence and exiting violence, n°1, Janvier 2019.

Weber, M., *Politiks als Beruf, 1917, in Le Savant et le politique, Plon 1959, Norbert Elias, sur le processus de civilisation, deux vol., La Civilisation des mœurs, Calmann-Lévy, 1973, et La Dynamique de l'Occident, Calmann-Lévy*, 1975.

Wieviorka, M. (2012). *La violence*, Paris, éd. Pluriel-Hachette.

Wieviorka, M. (May 2015). Sortir de la violence. Un chantier pour les sciences humaines et sociales. *Socio*, 221–240.

13

White Women in the War on Immigrants

Framing Anti-Immigrant Discourse Against Migrant Mothers

Mary Romero

Introduction

Traditionally, many of anti-immigrant images tended to be masculine, from the president, attorney general, border patrol agents, to the detention guards. However, white women posing as mothers are more bolden about their anti-immigration politics and now their white bodies opposing migration from the Global South are alongside angry white men. In 2018, as the news showed images of US Immigration and Customs Enforcement (ICE) pulling children and babies from their mothers' arms, crying and traumatized children in cages, and distraught parents, Ivanka Trump posted a picture of herself embracing her 2-year-old son. She was immediately criticized for her insensitivity in sharing a photo of a 'sweet family moment', while ICE enforced her father's 'zero tolerance' policy of separating children from their asylum-seeking parents at the border (Heil, 2018). Reponses to her post included:

> Too bad all mothers in America can't enjoy the same.

> What would you do if you were separated from your children? Would be rather painful, don't you think ... and nobody would care??? Especially your father ... SAD!

> Imagine being the mother of a child born in a country your father would describe as a 'shithole'. Would you also try to leave to try to give your child a better future?

> Glad you know where your kids are. Now what about the 1,500 moms whose kids were taken at the border ... and now are lost? What about those children, Ivanka?

Juxtaposing Ivanka's photo with the shocking images of children in cages, ICE buses fitted with booster seats for children and reports of the painful cries from migrant mothers and their children as they are separated, is as troubling as the message, 'I really don't care. DU?' on the jacket that Melania wore to tour an immigrant children's shelter. Migrant women's stories of motherhood and Ivanka and Melania's could not be further from each other. Contrasting the privileged white feminine photos of Ivanka and Melania to the brown mothers depicted as risking their children's safety in seeking asylum from violence in their home countries or as economic and climate refugees sends a message of white women as representing motherhood and ideal mothering.

In the Trump administration, both Ivanka and Melania play central roles highlighting themselves as ideal mothers. Yet, never opposing Trump's cruel and barbaric policy that separated children from their migrant mothers. *Guardian* columnist Arwa Mahdawi's (2018) expresses the reaction of many who were appalled by Ivanka's lack of sensibilities, both as a mother and as a member of the Trump administration. She writes:

> When Ivanka tweeted that photo on Sunday, I don't think it was a gaffe—I think she knew exactly what she was doing. Which was playing to Trump's specific base; reminding them that its white families like hers – like theirs – who are important, not the brown families who Trump is breaking up; using the image of herself as a loving mother to provide a human face to Trump's inhumane administration. Ivanka is an important complement to Trump's messaging. He does all the crass dehumanisation of immigrations, lumping them together with the gang MS-13 and calling them dangerous "animals" the US needs to protect itself from; she provides the aspirational imagery of the US that needs protecting. (Mahdawi, 2018)

Against the horrific backdrop of images of children separated from their parents, Ivanka's pose serves to remind US citizens what real motherhood looks like – white mothers and white children, not brown or Black mothers and their children. The simultaneous appearances of these opposing images include coded messaging that appeals to a white mother's concern for her own children's welfare rather than interest in migrant babies and children. Instead, the images reinforce the anti-immigrant narrative of migrant children as threats against their white children.

In addition to Ivanka's role in symbolizing white motherhood, other women in the Trump administration took major steps towards justifying the policies of zero tolerance. In defence of General Attorney Jeff Sessions claim that separating immigrant children and parents is rooted in the Bible, Sarah Sanders argued that 'It is very biblical to enforce the law'. In response to a CNN reporter's question: 'Where does it say in the Bible that it's moral to take children away from their mothers?' she replied: 'It's a moral policy to follow and enforce the law' (Jones, 2018). However, Homeland Security Secretary Kirstjen Michele Nielsen became the point person responsible for defending and carrying out the policy. Nielsen reported to the Senate committee: 'Our policy is, if you break the law, we will prosecute you', suggesting that the only two options are either separating families or not enforcing the law. Nielsen has argued that news coverage of children abused and warehoused in cages are 'hearsay stories'. On June 17, she tweeted, 'This misrepresenting by Members, press, and advocacy groups must stop. It is irresponsible and unproductive. As I have said many times before, if you are seeking asylum for your family, there is no reason to break the law and illegally cross between ports of entry'. She then followed up with the tweet, 'We do have a policy of separating families at the border. Period' (Daniels, 2018).

Homeland Security Secretary Nielsen has been instrumental in supporting immigration policy as a national security issue. In her speech to the National Sheriff's Association, she has referred to the children as 'criminal aliens'. This is consistent with the administration's insistence that the children are MS5 gang members, or that they are future recruits being allowed into the United States The Central American migrant caravans, in early 2017 and 2018, were similarly framed as criminals, even though they included women and children fleeing gang violence, poverty and political repression. Nielsen justified the use of tear gas against families with small children by arguing they were being used as human shields by the organizers. The Department of Homeland Security posted her statement on Facebook, 'I refuse to believe that anyone honestly maintains that attacking law enforcement with rocks and projectiles is acceptable' (Self, 2018). Maintaining the administration's claim that asylum-seeking parents are illegal and criminal, Nielsen later drew the comparison between family separation on the border and parents removed from their families when convicted of a crime and sent to prison (Kopan, 2018). Later, Nielson suggested that asylum-seeking parents were responsible for the death of 7-year-old Jakelin Caal and 8-year-old Gomez Alonso, who both died after they were separated from their parents and under the custody of US Customs and Border Protection. Nielson shifted accountability for their deaths onto their parents because they were 'sending their children across the border alone' and therefore the parents are responsible for 'consequences for their actions' (Jordan, 2018).

In a *Huffington Post* essay, Jessie Daniels (2018) calls attention to the significance in having White House press Secretary Sanders and Homeland Security Secretary Nielsen positioned to defend the policy of family separation. In her opinion piece, *Why the Face of Family Separation is a White Woman*, Daniels argues that 'assumptions about white women's innocence and outsized empathy that have made them some of white supremacy's most effective agents'. By women serving as the administration's voice for this policy, the expectation that women are the caretakers of children and families enhances why migrant mothers and their children are security threats at the US–Mexico border. Like Ivanka and Melania, Sanders and Nielson soften the inhumane policy of family separation in constructing mothers and fathers seeking the safety of asylum with their children as bad parenting and as threats to their own families. Thus, Daniels argues, Sanders and Nielson are positioning the protection of American families as a 'women's issue'.

While migrant and refugee mothers have been the focus of past anti-immigrant sentiment and a target in welfare changes, construct-ing them as a threat to national security is a new discourse that frames white mothers and children as being vulnerable and in need of pro-tection. In his research on news coverage of immigration, Leo Chavez (2011) found that in times of low anti-immigration sentiment, images of the migrant mother–child dyad appeared rather than images denoting danger (p. 73). Images of migrant mothers and children appeared during periods of empathy and a 'recognition of shared humanity'. Anti-immigrant sentiment uses images and metaphors to fuel nativist fear of an invasion, conquest or a crisis (Chavez, 2001; Santa Ana, 2002). In the recent attacks against migrant and refugee mothers in the United States, there are two opposing motherhood discourses side by side. On the one hand, mothering discourse is used to demonize migrant and refugee women as unfit mothers, and on the other hand, white women in the Trump administration use traditional motherhood norms and values to embrace their status as mothers, in opposition to non-citizen mothers. How have these images and met-aphors been used in the recent anti-immigrant discourse? How are they similar and different? Do they have the same goals as past anti-immigrant discourse, or is there an emerging political agenda? How have we reached a point where migrant women and children are viewed as not just unworthy of asylum but also as an economic and security threat? What has been the participation of white women in anti-immigration rhetoric in constructing brown mothers as a danger to their families and the nation?

Juxtaposing the images of Ivanka's white motherhood with brown and Black migrant mothers being separated from their children highlighted the importance of having respectable white ladies normalizing the hatred and violence of white men. The most powerful way of using their white womanhood is to represent ideal motherhood and their role in raising future white generations and white citizens.

White Women in Nativist Movements

Along with identifying the policies, images and arguments used to construct migrant mothers and their children as dangerous and criminals, more research is being conducted on the role of white women in nativist movements in the United States, including the ways of weaponizing white motherhood to support and maintain white supremacy. Previously, feminist historians had focused on white women's fight for equal rights, such as the right to vote. However, more recently, historian Stephanie Jones-Rogers (2019) documents white women's active participation in maintaining slavery by owning slaves, which directly links their wealth and power to white suprem-acy, and their investment in white supremacy. In the early Jim Crow era, journalist and civil rights advocate, Ida Bell Wells-Barnett documented the lynching of Black men in *The Red* Record (1895), which frequently resulted from white women's false claims of assault. The National Association of the Daughters of the Confederacy were instrumental in preserving white supremacy in controlling the narra-tive of public history of the South, along with raising funds for hun-dreds of monuments and statues honouring men who fought to uphold slavery (Daniels, 2021).

White women's participation in white supremacist movements is well documented in Kathleen Blee's (1991, 2002) research beginning with the Ku Klux Klan in the 1920s to their present involvement in organized racist hate movements. Similar narratives of white womanhood virtue and the 'other' posing sexual and moral menace were significant in legitimating Klan activity. White native-born Protestant women represented womanhood, family and female purity. A primarily activity was normalizing the Klan through rituals of birth, death, and other political and community events such as picnics and parades. Unlike popular images of members of hate groups as single-minded, working-class and secretive, Blee found many were unmarried, employed, middle-class and professional women engaged in church groups, women's rights groups, political parties, as well as prohibition and anti-vice groups. While male Klan members adopted traditional gender symbols and ideology, Blee (1996) underlines the 'new gender bargain' made, in which 'women would maintain the home as a sanctuary for men, raise men's children, and assist them in business but in return expected political rights and respect' (p. 53).

White women's participation in right-wing movements, including contemporary hate groups, continues. Like their less visible involvement in the Klan, the increasing number of white women in hate movements has largely gone unnoticed, instead media and researchers focus on men's activities. Again, these women participating in hate groups are from middle-class neighbourhoods, well-educated and are largely responsible for establishing a strong sense of community, family and social bonds inside the organization. In her research on white women in hate movements, Blee (2002) characterized their perception of racial victimization, which views Jews, Blacks and other minorities as threatening to their families. Their presence in the organization preserves ideal womanhood, promotes their sexually virtuous and celebrates them as the mothers of future white generations.

One of the most bolden type of hate organizations in recent decades have been anti-immigration organizations, particularly those engaged in militia patrolling along the US–Mexico border. The most familiar organization is the Minuteman Civil Defence Corps (MCDC). Other hate groups targeting immigrants include American Border Patrol, Sierra Vista, American Freedom Riders, Federal Immigration Reform and Enforcement Coalition, Maricopa Patriots, Patriots' Border Alliance, Riders Against Illegal Aliens, and United for a Sovereign American (Doty, 2009). Most of the research conducted on these militia organizations highlight the leadership and patrolling activities that white men participate in (e.g. Chavez, 2008; Doty, 2009; Shapira, 2017). An exception is Jennifer Johnson's research on Minutewomen's online activism (2011) and older women joining the Minutemen as the Granny Brigade (2014). Minutewomen's primary contribution to the organization is online activism consisting of coordinating boycott campaigns, identifying and promoting multicultural programmes in schools as immigrant advocate propaganda, and working for or against elected officials based on their position on immigration policies. Minutemen recruited older women as grandmothers under Operation Granny Brigade in 2007, primarily to create a spectacle of the Border Granny willing to secure the border and demonstrate their patriotism and contrasting them to President Bush and politicians in general who were portrayed as ignoring the immigration problem. Although described as ready to protect their families by stopping undocumented immigrants at the border, Johnson reported that Border Granny's activities were actually the gendered work of cooking, maintaining membership lists and writing newsletter, and serving and hostess and friends to the men.

Considering Daniels' analysis of the significance of positioning Ivanka Trump, Sarah Huckabee Sanders and Kirstjen Nielson into the zero tolerance policy and shifting the focus to a woman's issue reminded me of the images and metaphors used by Mothers Against Illegal Aliens (MAIA), an Arizona-based women's anti-immigration group active during 2006–2008. Occasionally sharing the same stage at anti-immigration events, MAIA openly supported the Minutemen but did not participate in their patrols along the border. However, they actively protested immigrant advocates' resistance to Sheriff Arpaio's use of racial profiling in arresting low-wage Mexican workers and the use of his posse in stopping and detaining persons who appeared to be Mexican. Mostly, MAIA engaged in online activities promoting anti-immigration policies, multicultural education and opposition to civil rights organizations. Unlike other white middle-class women in anti-immigrant movements, MAIA members did not engage in supporting the Minutemen in traditional roles assigned to women in movements. Dallacroce took an independent and equal stand alongside Minutemen speakers at rallies.

MAIA emerged as one of the first and only women's anti-immigrant organizations vilifying migrant women and children, predominately Mexican mothers and their children. Like past white women's nativism groups, MAIA positions their members as mothers rather than employers, workers or citizens. This stance on the meaning of gender and motherhood in the right-wing white-separatist group is addressed in Joann Roders and Jacquelyn S. Litt's (2004) research on the World Church of the Creator. They argue that '[i[t is not surprising that women in the movement use motherhood or 'maternalism' as a point of departure for activism, as this has been a strategy employed by women, progressive and reactionary, for centuries in the United States and across the globe' (p. 101).

MAIA popularized white motherhood with a Madonna logo, very much like Ivanka's pose. The MAIA Madonna logo is framed as patriotic blending of the US flag into the mother–child image and is surrounded on all four sides with the slogan, 'Protect Our Children. Secure Our Borders'. Like the MAIA logo, Ivanka's photo represents ideal motherhood, which not only draws a stark contrast to migrant and refugee mothers and their children of colour but normalizes her father's immigration policies as necessary to protect US borders and white families. Trump's nativist base supported his remarks about migrants as vermin infesting the country and seeing them as criminals engaged in murder, child abuse and neglect, prostitution, racketeering and rape. Even though crossing the border is an administrative offence and not a criminal offence, Trump followers agreed with Attorney General Jeff Sessions argument when he said, 'If you are smuggling a child, we will prosecute you, and that child will be separated from you, as required by law ... If you don't like that, then don't smuggle children over our border' (Horwitz and Sacchetti, 2018).

Revisiting my research on MAIA, two reoccurring themes appear to have become part of the mainstream discourse, including images and metaphors used to deny migrant women of colour their motherhood (Romero, 2008, 2011). Their motherhood is constructed as a direct threat to US citizen mothers and their children. Like other race-based nativist groups active in the United States, MAIA targeted migrant mothers as responsible for overcrowded schools, low-achieving schools, poor access to affordable health care and draining public benefits. Examining their use of images and metaphors offers insight into the Trump administration's current immigrant rhetoric and policy, justifying the separation and detention of migrant mothers and children. A decade ago, MAIA laid out their campaign against migrant women and their children by framing their message as pro-family and conservative using traditional images of motherhood. Although, first MAIA's internet and media presence was short-lived before posting a new website, their founder, Michelle Dallacroce continued to participate in anti-immigrant campaigns. She has been successful in getting nativist and racist immigration discourse against Mexican migrant mothers in the mainstream through interviews with local, national and international news media, including Fox News, CNN and BBC. MAIA's mission to education citizens on undocumented immigration was used to introduce and promote the term 'anchor baby' to deny them birthright citizenship and to weave nativism with mothering and feminist discourse. MAIA was instrumental in normalizing racist nativism using Homeland Security discourse from the lens of white motherhood.

Having traced MAIA's emergence among other anti-immigrant groups in Arizona, I analyzed data from their website, Mothers Against Illegal Aliens, which included three updated versions over a 12-month period between November 2006 and 2010. Before MAIA completely took down their site, a more polished version went live. This last version eliminated many of the most racist depictions of Mexicans, blogs and links to other anti-immigration movements, but maintained blogs on 'anchor babies', misinterpretation of the 14th amendment, as well as personal attacks to immigration and civil rights advocates. This analysis draws from both the original website and the final site, which is no longer available. Interviews conducted by local, national and international news organizations, and newspaper coverage of the group's activities were also coded for metaphors, images and arguments that migrant women and their children are economic and security threats to white motherhood and their children. I present the analysis in two major themes: undocumented Mexican mothers as breeders for personal gain, highlighting their children as 'anchor babies', and educational propaganda on the evils of Mexican immigration to white families and the nation, claiming the 14th amendment has been misinterpreted and claiming that Mexicans plan to reconquer the Southwest.

Breeders Not Mothers

MAIA claimed that the greatest threat migrant women pose is their ability to have children: 'The biological fact that a woman can birth a child is the instrument by which the illegal alien women utilizes to demand citizenship and residence in the United States' (Dallacroce, 2007a). Mexican migrant mothers are constructed as opposites of the patriotic mothers in the United States, which MAIA claims must protect their families and country. Instead of framing these migrant women as mothers, MAIA depicts their procreation as breeding. In her speech at a Minutemen rally, Stephanie C. Harris, MAIA's media coordinator, expressed outrage that Mexican women were 'outbreeding *our* mothers' (Pela, 2006).

> When the government told Americans, we had to go to zero population, we obeyed ... But these illegals come here with their *Catholic culture*, and they have a bunch of babies and they can't afford them. *They're breeding like rabbits!* Then they go on food stamps and welfare, and Americans have to pay for that. [emphasis in original] (Pela, 2006)

While there is no government policy for zero population growth, white middle-class births have declined for a variety of reasons, none of which are related to immigration from Mexico. Nevertheless, racist nativists frequently identify the birth of non-whites as a threat to their well-being.

Emphasis on migrant women breeding rather than mothering also achieves efforts to dehumanize and deny migrants and refugees any shared humanity with white US citizens. Blogs and other web postings show carefully selected words to reinforce migrants as non-human. The slogan 'isupportpeople' is frequently sprinkled throughout their website to identify US citizens. In reference to non-citizens, the adjectives 'illegal', 'alien', 'foreign' and 'inferior' appear, such as 'illegal alien females' or 'illegal alien infants' (MAIA, 2006, 2007).

The predominant characteristic used to depict migrant women is opportunistic, which is exemplified in the following post that appeared in the original website describing the strategy these mothers use for coming to the United States:

> You sneak over the border.

> You get pregnant *as fast as* possible, *as many times as* possible.

Use your child as your *weapon of choice* to *'blackmail'* the USA to let you stay.

Call every USA citizen a racist and home wrecker who wants you and your child to leave and return to your country. (Dallacroce, 2007a)

This strategy includes attacks against these mothers as: 'stealing the American Dream', having children they cannot afford to raise and demanding assistance from the US government. Using similar tropes as 'welfare queen' and 'affirmative action baby', MAIA relies on their white audience to understand their racially coded language: 'If a legal woman in the USA tried to pull off this scam to get ahead of the line it's called a "GOLD DIGGER". Wanting something for nothing! These women make the choice to have a baby' (Dallacroce, 2007a).

The claim that migrant women have a child in the United States to obtain access to legal residence status and to have the government foot the bill is clearly the argument in the post on Elvira Arellano (Dallacroce, 2007c). Arrested after a raid at the Chicago airport, Arellano took sanctuary at the Adalberto United Methodist Church for a year while she fought deportation proceedings. Arellano protested she had paid a third of her salary on taxes and claimed she was protecting her son, Saul's, rights as a citizen to attend school in the United States (McElmurry, 2009). MAIA posted a blog on 'MAIA exposes the myths surrounding Elvira Arellano':

No one is breaking up families other than Arellano. In fact, she in no way shape or form has produced a biological father for this so called American citizen - and instead, places this child on the footsteps of the USA to become the surrogate father to himself and surrogate husband to his mother - when indeed, he is nothing more than another Illegal Alien welfare child being used by his mother to further her claim that she is somehow entitled to remain in the USA in opposition to laws which she claims are inhumane. ... MAIA refuses to allow women like Elvira Arellano to transport their children over the borders, or by deliberate and wanton impregnations - to steal public services and lay claim to U.S. Citizenship - by birthing them in the USA in order to further their demand that they should be allowed to remain in the USA regardless of their illegal immigration status or the lawful deportation and removal actions levied against them. (Dallacroce, 2007c)

MAIA's description of Arellano using her child to obtain public benefits and to gain access to US citizenship is the basis for their use of the term 'anchor baby'. Drawing from Dallacroce's claim about the misinterpretation of the 14th amendment, she argues that as a non-citizen entering the country illegal, any child Arellano has in the United States cannot be a citizenship. In the most recent version of MAIA's website, the blog, 'Alien born infants are illegal TOO!!!!', Dallacroce cites Senator Howard of Michigan to their slogan in earlier versions of the website, 'it takes a citizen to make a citizen' (Dallacroce, 2007b).

MAIA's postings argue that migrant mothers having children in the United States or bringing children into the United States is a form of child abuse to their own children and to the children of US citizens. As portrayed in the case of Arellano, the migrant mother has a child to use as leverage to gain residency in the United States. Furthermore, MAIA claims the migrant mother is engaged in child abuse towards the children of US citizens.

> A child is the responsiblity (sic) of the parents not a country to raise. A child being used by a mother to "steal" from the mouths of "legal children" in the USA should be charged with child abuse for attempting to benefit from their crime and profiting from additional actions while within the interior of the USA. (MAIA, 2006)

Rather than having traits more commonly attributed to 'motherhood', migrant mothers are depicted as immoral, sneaky, contriving and do not deserve to be mothers.

MAIA's 'Educational' Mission in the Anti-Immigrant Campaign

Since her arrival in Arizona's anti-immigrant discourse in the early 2000s, Michelle Dallacroce has identified as a US Air Force veteran and mother of two children devoted to protecting US families against illegal immigration. In one of the first newspaper interviews with Michelle Dallacroce, a *Los Angeles Times* reporter wrote, 'She formed Mothers Against Illegal Aliens, she said, because she feared for the future of her two young children, who could be ignored in the United States dominated by Mexican-born people. She described the possibility of Mexicans taking over the country as "genocide" and said migrants were "raping" the country by demanding social services' (Riccardi, 2006, p. A1). Working with the conservative Centre for

Security Policy to organize a Million Mother March in 2007, Dallacroce posted the following rallying cry.

> The winds of a new American patriotism, resolve, energy and national purpose are blowing and they are blowing strong! By the millions, American mothers are persuading friends, compatriots and family members to join in demonstrations to restore our country to sanity and respect for our sovereignty while launching veritable renaissance of American exceptionalism. (Dallacroce, 2007d)

Similar themes are evident in MAIA's (2006) mission statements: 'The Mission of Mothers Against Illegal Aliens—(MAIA) is to bring awareness to and educate the LEGAL American families whose children are the silent victims of this Invasion of Illegal Aliens'. Their revised version emphasizes urgency: 'The members and volunteers of MAIA have made a commitment to continue to education and inform all legal citizens of America, since our government and the media are side-stepping the real issues: that our children and our country are at risk of being eliminated!' (ADL, 2008, p. 12)

MAIA's educational mission is not limited to promoting the argument that migrant mothers and their children are the source of society's social problems, particularly cuts in public services and crime. The following appeared in the original MAIA website and cited in the Anti-Defamation League's (ADL, 2008) report, Immigrants Targeted: Extremist Rhetoric Moves into the Mainstream:

> Our beautiful Nation has been turned into a jungle by the mass invasion of illegal aliens– the streets of America; the neighborhoods and communities where we live; the malls and stores where we shop. The schools where our LEGAL [emphasis in original] children attend – and yes, even the churches where we worship– are now the Citadels of fear, bigotry, racism, physical danger and hate! The LEGAL children of America's 21st century have become the scapegoats and victims of this invasion of illegal aliens.. . . As evidenced by Spanish homework being sent with our American children. [Emphasis in original] (ADL, 2007, p. 3)

Rather than recognizing that local and state services reflect decades of tax cuts, MAIA claims that migrants place a burden on healthcare services and have eroded the quality of public education.

The influx of illegal immigrants is having an impact on many parts of the nation's society, much of which is harming children of legal citizens.... The children of illegal immigrants are overcrowding schools to the detriment of providing an education to legal students... For Arizonans, the requirement to find a way to teach English to students is an example of federal interference made even more onerous because of daily fines that are piling up ... (Hess, 2006)

MAIA also considers the children of migrants posing a physical threat to their children as stated by MAIA's media coordinator, Stephanie Harris:

The blond-haired, blue-eyed American kid has to wear baggy clothes and dye his hair brown because otherwise the Mexicans will beat him up.... And these kids are all getting free lunches when the American kids don't. Our kids have no future ... (Pela, 2006)

In her statement to a local reporter, she described migrants as an economic threat when they do work:

They come in and take our jobs away from us. And so *American can't feed their kids* because people are hiring illegals to do all the work.... [Emphasis in original] (Pela, 2006)

Along with claiming immigrant children are engaged in criminal activity and threaten the safety of the children of US citizens, they have also attempted to link sex crimes and drunk driving to the presence of immigrants. During the 12 months that the website was maintained, the homepage carried a link to the 'Family Watchdog' search engine, 'What to see if there are any child predators in your area??' Below the bulldog logo of Family Watchdog was a link to 'Who to call to report illegals'. The website also included reports from across the country of any non-citizen arrested as a suspect of a sex crime (Romero, 2008).

Concern about drunken drivers emerged when Mothers Against Drunk Driving's (MADD) requested that MAIA refrain from using the name 'Mothers Against'. They responded by attacking MADD's policy of including non-English speakers in their education campaign and providing bilingual materials. In addition, MAIA chastised the organizations for not maintaining national statistics on the number of non-citizens arrested for drink-driving (also see ADL, 2008, p. 13).

MADD, a *not-for-profit*, continues to collect millions of dollars each and every year in FEDERAL GRANTS and private donations ....and yet, MADD was, is and remains *conspicuously SILENT* regarding the dangers and the heartbreak foisted upon our Nation and communities when it comes to providing statistics, relative to illegal alien drivers. Drivers who *drink, drive, injure, maim and kill our fellow citizens and our innocent children and whose illegal actions and Illegal presence in the United States instantaneously made and continues to make .... thousands of innocent American families ....grieving victims for life!!* [Emphasis in original] (Dallacroce, 2007d)

Despite only citing one incident of a non-citizen as a drunken driver in an accident, MAIA's website incorporated these drivers as a threat:

ILLEGAL ALIEN DRUNK DRIVERS – TAKE INNOCENT AMERICAN LIFE!!

ILLEGAL ALIEN DRUNK DRIVERS – INJURE INNOCENT AMERICANS FOR LIFE!!

ILLEGAL ALIEN DRUNK DRIVERS – MAIM INNOCENT AMERICANS FOR LIFE!!

ILLEGAL ALIEN DRUNK DRIVERS – DESTROY INNOCENT AMERICAN FAMILIES FOR LIFE!! (Dallacroce, 2007d)

As in all their postings, the crime was secondary to the person's immigration status at the time of the incident. Highlighting their citizenship status reinforced the 'alien' classification as a measure of their criminal status. This is most evident in the press release MAIA made criticizing city government's lack of response against Latino immigrants after an undocumented man shot and killed a police officer:

The times that these meetings are scheduled by the Phoenix police demonstrate a lack of consideration for the families and homeowners in the City of Phoenix. However, when the Baseline Rapist and Shooter was an issue, the Phoenix police department had meetings during evening hours and in locations which were accommodating to the general public. They even held them in Spanish. Notice of these meetings were on the local news channels, the radio and by flyers. Mayor Gordon had no problem attending these meetings. These actions definitely give our neighborhoods and its citizens the strong impression that our mayor, city council and police department do not care about our family's safety and our security. Does this reflect our local government's attempt to appease the illegals for their money and votes? (MAIA, 2007)

The anti-Mexican sentiment is emphasized by condemning the police department's efforts to protect all members of the community against a serial rapist who killed nine of his victims during the summer of 2006. Since non-citizens cannot vote, MAIA includes citizens of Mexican descent as outside the category of 'our' family and security.

While much of MAIA's anti-immigrant discourse was aimed at teaching the families of US citizens about the threats that immigration poses, their major educational platform was a campaign against birthright citizenship. Similar to other white nativist, Dallacroce argues that the 14th Amendment has been misunderstood and misinterpreted.

It is CLEAR, the 14th Amendment and the language used explicitly excluded "aliens" and their offspring, not legally within the United States - from citizenship. Our founding fathers did not have crystal ball to predict that 30 million illegal aliens from Mexico, China, Ireland and every other country would be using the birth of a child to violate the laws of the United States for sympathy and as a means to remain in the USA - and by intent and design - change the face of our nation by strong arming the American people in the name of family and child.

*There can be no argument that Illegal Aliens fall in the "alien" category which is specified in the documents pertaining to the 14th amendment - held in trust for the American people in the Library of Congress in our Nation's Capital. The fact that our forefathers **did not** explicitly state that the Infants of Illegal Alien Female's (sic) were included in this sentence, **DOES NOT MEAN THAT THEY ARE NOT EXCLUDED**.* [Emphasis in original] (MAIA, 2007)

The 'evidence' she cites is only relevant to a few cases, such as the children born to diplomatic representatives of a foreign state. Lacking a strong legal argument, MAIA resorted to posting racist nativist positions against birthright citizenship:

Children born of Illegal Alien parents are about the worse form of Illegal Immigration we will face. Why did Rome fall and whatever became of those great Republics that ignored the same undermining problems that we seem to ignore as well? These children, and there are many now eligible .... are voting and are seeking public office. Their votes and their elected positions will serve to dilute and undermine the importance of our own legal child's vote and political intentions, and will further serve to pollute the social, cultural and political environment that once embraced Americans of all faiths, traditions, races, ethnicities, languages and values. **Anchor baby citizenship is a "coup" in the making** and lending to this conspiracy is the fact that millions upon millions of parents, brothers, sisters, uncles, aunts et al., have been, are and will continue to be sponsored (chain migration) by anchor babies .... that is ....forcign national children born of Illegal Alien parents on United States soil. [Emphasis in the original] (Dallacroce, 2007e)

Among the posts that appear on the current website related to the topic of immigrant mothers' babies born in the United States are the following blogs: 'Anchor Babies, Away', 'Alien born Infants are Illegal TOO!!!', '14th Amendment' and 'Fugitive Elvira'.

Like previous posts, MAIA's thinly veiled racism against people of colour, particularly Mexicans, appears in their stated fears of whites losing political power. A more direct post was found in a blog, 'This is President Fox's Attack on America' that identified Latino organizations. Although not all the names are accurate, they include civil rights and advocacy organizations alongside one relatively unknown racist nationalist one: 'Discover the real threat to America by reading about radical and well-organized "Hispanic" organizations whose goal is the reconquering of the Southwest. These groups are known as Aztlan, La Raza, LULAC, LaMecha (sic), MALDEF, and others not as well-known'. This statement reappears even in MAIA's most updated version of their Mission Statement. Dallacroce claimed the largest Latino non-profit advocacy group, the National Council of La Raza (NCLR), now known as UnidosUS, received government funding:

A politically active organization which sole purpose is for the advancement of one nationality should not be funded by tax dollars from departments of the U.S. government and given ear marks of $4 million dollars by our government to better the way of life, i.e. politically monopolize the U.S.A. by the number of illegal occupants of the U.S.A. and their offspring in order to shift the balance of legal immigrants and citizens of the U.S.A. This is fraud and it is a misuse of funds and justice against the people of the United States of America. The abuse of funds and power from all levels of government and businesses throughout the U.S.A. is being flexed and out reached in order to ignore current laws and protections granted by the Constitution of the United States of America. (Dallacroce, 2006)

Readers are encouraged to explore racist nativist websites that attempt to show the presence of a race war between Mexican Americans and whites. Footage from speeches and marches from the 1970s are used with voice-overs describing the threat.

In other postings, the theory of a 'coup' is elevated to a Mexican invasion and an actual war. Their mission statement goes beyond claiming a cultural invasion (note: this appears in their revision as well as older versions of their website):

> We are not only at war with Iraq, but we ARE at WAR with MEXICO; a silent war with Aztlanders and a war with President Fox who said he will take over the United States with sheer numbers without ever firing a shot. We now have 20–25 million illegal's (sic) in the United States, and the count rises by a minimum of 10,000 every day. [Emphasis in original] (Dallacroce, 2007a)

Mexican immigrants are equated to an alien enemy engaged in a hostile occupation of the United States:

> We find that the United States of America is being willfully and deliberately populated to facilitate the hostile occupation – and the Colonization of our Country by a large number of ILLEGAL ALIENS – males, females and infants and anchor babies who have – unlawfully INVADED OUR NATION. [Emphasis in original] (Dallacroce, 2007a)

Although, the United States colonized the southwest after the war with Mexico, racist nativist groups claim that Mexico is now colonizing the land they once lost. In this argument, migrants and refugees are perceived as being a type of sleeper cell that will rise and reconquer the land for Mexico. Just as in the Oklahoma bombing and the attack on September 11th, there is no evidence that undocumented migrants have ever been engaged in terrorism in the United States.

Conclusion

On 3 August 2019, a Trump supporter and white supremacist drove 9 hours across Texas to El Paso to kill Mexicans in 'response to the Hispanic invasion of Texas' and shot and killed 23 at a Walmart near the border. The manifesto the shooter left cites the white supremacist theory, 'The Great Replacement'. Like MAIA's claims of Mexicans taking over, the theory claims the white race is being replaced by immigrants and refugees. The manifesto also claims his actions will eliminate the threat of the Hispanic voting bloc. During Trump and Melania's visit to El Paso following the mass shooting, Melania posted a picture on Twitter of holding a 2-month-old orphan who survived the shooting when his mother died protecting him and his father was killed when he tried to shield them from the bullets. The child was brought to the hospital at the request of the White House for the photo session. Donald Trump is giving a thumbs up and both smiling. Melania's tweeted photo generated the same outrage that Ivanka's photo had 1 year earlier (Helmore, 2019).

> This is a photo of Trump grinning while Melania holds a baby orphaned by the shooting. A baby who was taken from home and forced to serve as a prop at a photo-op for the very monster whose hate killed her/his parents.
>
> I am genuinely confused and horrified by this image. Am I taking this the wrong way? Why is Trump and Melania posing, GRINNING, and giving a thumbs up with the infant who's parents were murdered by the shooter in El Paso.
>
> This is not how a normal human being would interact with a baby that just lost his parents due to your own inaction. You would hold him and cry. Or at least keep the cameras away while you contemplate.
>
> I am not sure I've even been as angry as I am right now. This photo op is disgusting.
>
> His photo shoot was really disturbing, no empathy and humanity in him or his wife (and definitely none in people who arrange thes stuff). Compare it to what our PM did after the shooting in Christchurch.

This baby's parents were just murdered by a psychopath who was incited by Trump's xenophobia. While at first glance of the photo, the viewer may think of a family photo. However, as Rhonda Garelick (2019) points out 'Melania is the least publicly maternal First Lady we've ever had. She doesn't even pretend to care. ... Baby Paul now stands in for all the children – indeed, all human begins – who, like him, have been harmed and are being held against their will by a white supremacist president'. Even in this moment, Melania attempts to use her white motherhood by cradling the baby but shows no compassion or empathy.

While many of us considered MAIA as an extremist group in 2007, the current migrant crisis created by the Trump administration demonstrates the degree to which MAIA's racist-nativist platform and rhetoric has been incorporated into Trump's zero tolerance policy and his fight for a border wall. State violence in the form of detention, deportation and the use of tear gas against migrant mothers and their children continues to be justified by the Trump administration on the basis that they are criminals because they crossed the border without documentation, fleeing violence in their homeland. Ivanka's manipulation of the classic Madonna symbol of mothers represents white mothers as ideal motherhood. Ivanka constructed an image that is juxtaposed with photos of arrested mothers seeking asylum. Criminalizing the mothering of immigrant women is also evident in the recent trend towards charging parents with smuggling when they migrate with their children. Here again, these mothers are framed as placing their children in harm's way, as well as 'smuggling' them into the country. Nielsen, along with her male colleagues, continues to argue that the separated migrant children are safe and well cared for. The Trump's administration's use of popular anti-immigration metaphors perpetuates images of immigrants as less-than-human in attempts to justify state-sanctioned separation of mothers and children. Cast as illegal females, rather than migrant mothers, the pain and suffering encountered by family separation is attributed to these parents. Both motherhood and reproductive rights are under attack in current refugee and migrant crisis at the US–Mexico border as well as other national borders around the world.

References

Anti-Defamation League (ADL). (2007). *Immigrants targeted: Extremist anti-immigration rhetoric moves into the mainstream.* Retrieved from https://www.fosterglobal.com/policy_papers/ExtremistAntiImmigrationRhetoricMovesIntoTheMainstream.pdf

Anti-Defamation League (ADL). (2008). Immigrants targeted: Extremist rhetoric moves into the mainstream. Retrieved from https://www.fosterglobal.com/policy_papers/ExtremistAntiImmigrationRhetoricMovesIntoTheMainstream.pdf

Blee, K. M. (1991). *Women of the Klan: Racism and gender in the 1920s.* Berkeley, CA: University of California Press.

Blee, K. M. (1996). Becoming a racist: Women in contemporary Ku Klux Klan and Neo-Nazi groups. *Gender and Society, 10*(6), 680–703.

Blee, K. M. (2002). *Inside organized racism: Women in the hate movement.* Berkeley, CA: University of California Press.

Chavez, L. R. (2001). *Covering immigration, popular images and the politics of the nation.* Berkeley, CA: University of California Press.

Chavez, L. R. (2008). Spectacle in the desert: The Minutemen project on the U.S.-Mexico border. In D. Pratten, & A. Sen (Eds.), *Global vigilantes* (pp. 25–46). New York, NY: Columbia University Press.

Chavez, L. R. (2011). Narratives of the nation and anti-nation: The media and construction of Latinos as a threat to the United States. In M. Boss (Ed.), *Narrating peoplehood amidst diversity: Historical and theoretical perspectives* (pp. 183–206). Aarhus: Aarhus University Press.

Dallacroce, M. (2006, June 17). This is president Fox's attack on America. *MAIA Blog.* Retrieved 17 May 2007, from http://www.mothersagainstillegalaliens.org. blog/?page-id=62/

Dallacroce, M. (2007a, March 15). IAI-illegal alien infants! *MAIA.* Retrieved 30 March 2007, from http://mothersagainstillegalaiens.org/site/index.php? option=com_content&task=view&id=19&Itemid=30

Dallacroce, M. (2007b, April 27). Alien born infants are illegal TOO!!!! *MAIA Blog.* Retrieved 9 June 2007, from http://mothersagainstillegalaliens.org/site/index.php? option=com-content&task=view&id=16&Itemid=29. In November 2021 listed under ADMIN-MOTHERSAGAINSTILLEGALALIENS

Dallacroce, M. (2007c, August 19). Elvira Arellano a/k/a criminal fugitive arrested in L.A. *MAIA Blog.* Retrieved 10 October 2007, from https://mothersagainst illegalaliens.org/elvira-arellano-a-k-a-criminal-fugitive-arrested-in-l-a/. In November 2021 listed under ADMIN-MOTHERSAGAINSTILLEGALALIENS.

Dallacroce, M. (2007d, October 25). It's time to get mad at MADD. *Blog.* Retrieved 15 December 2007, from http://www/mothersagainstillegalaliencs.org/site/index. php?option?opettion=com=content&task=view&id=38&Itemid=57

Dallacroce, M. (2007e, November 21). Is Lou Dobbs the Thanksgiving Turkey or the Christmas Goose? *Blog.* Retrieved 15 December 2007, from http://www. mothersagainstillegalaliens.org/site/index.php?option=com-wrapper&Itemid=68

Daniels, J. (2018, June 20). Why the face of family separation is a white woman. *Huffington Post.* Retrieved from https://www.huffingtonpost.com/entry/opinion-daniels-kirstjen-neilsen-family-separation_us_5b2a5774e4b05d6c16c983a4

Daniels, J. (2021). *Nice white ladies, the truth about white supremacy, our role in it, and how we can help dismantle it.* New York, NY: Seal Press.

Doty, R. L. (2009). *The law into their hands: Immigration and the politics of exceptionalism.* Tucson, AZ: University of Arizona Press.

Garelick, R. (2019, August 10). Surrogate angels of death. What to make of the first lady holding the motherless child and youngest survivor of the El Paso massacre. *The Cut.* Retrieved from https://www.thecut.com/2019/08/trump-baby-photo-el-paso-shooting.html

Heil, E. (2018, May 28). Ivanka Trump posted a photo with her son. Some on social media weren't too happy. *The Washington Post.* Retrieved from https://www. washingtonpost.com/news/reliable-source/wp/2018/05/28/critics-pan-ivanka-trump-for-posting-photo-with-her-son-as-migrant-families-are-separated/?utm_term=.2c998973866d

Helmore, E. (2019, August 9). Anger as grinning Trump gives thumbs-up while Melania holds El Paso orphan. *The Guardian.* Retrieved from https://www.theguardian.com/us-news/2019/aug/09/trump-el-paso-melania-orphan-baby-thumbs-up

Hess, B. (2006, February 18). Angry mothers protest to target effects of illegal immigration. *Sierra Vista Herald.* Retrieved from http://www.svherald.com/articles/2006/02/18/local-news3/txt

Horwitz, S., & Sacchetti, M. (2018, May 7). Sessions vows to prosecute all illegal border crossers and separate children from their parents. *The Washington Post.* Retrieved from https://www.washingtonpost.com/world/national-security/sessions-says-justice-dept-will-prosecute-every-person-who-crosses-border-unlawfully/2018/05/07/e1312b7e-5216-11e8-9c91-7dab596e8252_story.html?utm_term=.a9112093202d

Johnson, J. L. (2011). Mobilizing minutewomen: Gender, cyberpower, and the new nativist movement. *Research in social movements, conflicts and change, 32,* 137–161. Bingley: Emerald Publishing Limited.

Johnson, J. L. (2014). Border granny wants you! Grandmother policing nation at the U.S-Mexico border. In N. A. Naples, & J. B. Mendez (Eds.), *Border politics: Social movements, collective identities, and globalization* (pp. 35–59). New York, NY: Mew York University Press.

Jones, E. (2018, June 14). 'It is very biblical to enforce the law': Sarah Sanders, Jeff Sessions cite bible in controversial border policy. *CBN News.* Retrieved from https://www1.cbn.com/cbnnews/politics/2018/june/it-is-very-biblical-to-enforce-the-law-rsquo-sarah-huckabee-sanders-cites-the-bible-to-defend-controversial-immigration-policy

Jones-Rogers, S. (2019). *They were her property: White women as slave owners in the American South.* New Haven, CT: Yale University Press.

Jordan, M. (2018, December 26). 'A breaking point': Second child's death prompts new procedures for border agency. *The New York Times.* Retrieved from https://www.nytimes.com/2018/12/26/us/felipe-alonzo-gomez-customs-border-patrol.html

Kopan, T. (2018, May 15). DHS secretary defends separating families at the border. *CNN.* Retrieved from https://www.cnn.com/2018/05/15/politics/dhs-separating-families-secretary-nielsen-hearing/index.html

Mahdawi, A. (2018, May 29). Is Ivanka the worst Trump? Her tweeted portrait of 'perfect motherhood' seals it for me. *The Guardian.* Retrieved from https://www.theguardian.com/commentisfree/2018/may/29/is-ivanka-trump-worst-tweeted-portrait-border-agents

MAIA. (2006). Retrieved 10 December 2006, from http://mothersagainstillegalaliens.org

MAIA. (2007, September 30). Press release, MAIA, immigration policy.Retrieved from http://mothersagainstillegalaliens.org/site/php?option=com-content7task=view&id=24&Itemid=42

McElmurry, S. E. (2009). Elvira Arellano: No Rosa Parks, creation of 'us' versus 'them' in an opinion column. *Hispanic Journal of Behavioral Sciences, 31*(2), 182–203.

Pela, R. L. (2006, April 20). Minutewoman.Retrieved from http://www. phoenixnewtimes.com/2006-04-20/news/minutewomen

Riccardi, N. (2006, May 4). Anti-illegal immigration forces share a wide tent. *Los Angeles Times*. Retrieved from https://www.latimes.com/archives/la-xpm-2006-may-04-na-activist4-story.html

Roders, J., & Litt, J. S. (2004). Normalizing racism: A case study of motherhood in white supremacy, In A. L. Ferber (Ed.), *Home grown hate: Gender and organized racism* (pp. 92–107). New York, NY: Routledge.

Romero, M. (2008). 'Go after the women': Mothers Against Illegal Aliens (MAIA) campaign against Mexican immigrant women and their children. *Indiana Law Journal, 83*(4), 1355–1389.

Romero, M. (2011). Constructing Mexican immigrant women as a threat to US family, *International Journal of Sociology of the Family, 37*(1), 49–68.

Santa Ana, O. (2002). *Brown tide rising: Metaphors of Latinos in contemporary American public discourse*. Austin, TX: University of Texas Press.

Self, Z. (2018, November 27). Additional troops being sent to California border after migrants rush San Ysidro port of entry. Retrieved from https://www.10news.com/news/additional-troops-being-sent-to-california-border-after-migrants-rush-san-ysidro-port-of-entry

Shapira, H. (2017). *Waiting for José: Minutemen's pursuit of America*. Princeton, NJ: Princeton University Press.

Wells-Barnett, I. B. (1895). *The red record: Tabulated statistics and alleged causes of lynching in the United States*. Chicago, IL: Donohue & Henneberry. (Republished in 2015 by Cavalier Classics).

14

A Case for Academic Justice

Universities as Sites of Violence, Power (and Justice?)[1]

Nandini Sundar

Introduction

The growth of right-wing populist authoritarianism across the world has created an atmosphere where universities are directly under threat (*see:* Stanley, 2018). World leaders like Donald Trump, Viktor Orban, Erdogan, Narendra Modi, or Jair Bolsonaro frequently express contempt for academics, with the humanities and social sciences being particularly singled out for scorn. Soon after coming to power in Brazil, Bolsonaro proposed slashing public funding for higher education (Lloyd, 2018), while in India, Modi's regime has actively denigrated scholarship and scholars who are unpalatable to its ideological agenda.

In response, scholars have increasingly taken up the cause of academic freedom (*see:* Bilgrami and Cole, 2015; Butler, 2017). Academic freedom has mainly concerned itself with the freedom to teach and research, as well as extra-mural activities, or the right of faculty and students to engage in politics outside of the classroom (Post, 2015). On the one hand, there are McCarthy era-like restrictions being placed on what can be taught and who can be invited to campuses, with subjects like the human rights of Kurds, Kashmiris or Palestinians being treated as taboo. Funding has been cut to subjects like gender studies. On the other hand, the concept of academic freedom is being actively hijacked by bigots claiming free speech privileges in order to speak on campus. It is telling that Trump framed the issue of free speech on campuses across America in terms of the alleged stifling of conservative speech (*The Guardian*, 21 March 2019).

While academic freedom is indeed essential (*see* Kinzelbach et al., 2020; Sundar, 2018), especially in the face of the increasing levels of violence I describe below, I argue that this often ignores the material context through which academic work is produced – e.g. the high costs of publishing, global rankings and precarious employment – all of which reduce academic freedom in significant ways. It is hard to claim free and uncritical speech if one's job is precarious. It is difficult to pretend that you are part of a global academic community of ideas if journals charge so much, or engage in a significant critique of dominant ideas when no one is willing to publish you. As a consequence, academic life is unable to offer the space of freedom *within* knowledge that makes academic freedom worth defending. Academic freedom, both in its positive sense (in the freedom of students and faculty to grow); and in its negative sense (freedom from external constraint) should be of central concern.

There has, of course, been considerable work within the sociology of education on *inequality* and the manner in which it is enmeshed in syllabi, language, examining standards and so on. This includes recognition of the barriers to higher education expansion, and the extent to which higher education enables social mobility (*see*: Brown, 2018; Deshpande and Zacharias, 2013; Halsey et al., 1997). The problem is no longer just about access, since increasing numbers of working class, or, in the Indian context, lower caste youth, are now coming into higher education (Antonucci, 2016; Deshpande and Apoorvanand, 2018). The major concern, instead, is the commodification and privatization of higher education, with student fee increases and a decline in public funding, leading not just to the rise of a student precariat, but also reflecting and reinforcing inequality within the student population (Antonucci, 2016; Standing, 2011, pp. 78–90). This is quite apart from the manner in which elite universities continue to constitute 'fields of power' in reproducing bourgeois privilege (Bourdieu, 1989). The changing material and institutional contexts of universities – in terms of their global reach,[2] their jockeying for position in world rankings, the offering of Massive Open Online Courses (MOOCs), the cartelization of journal publishing and the star system in hiring and salaries – is also throwing up new challenges in addition to the older problems of how universities legitimate and reproduce class power (*see*: Altbach, 2016, 2013). Similarly, the rise of a few universities to global dominance is shaping inequality not just within but also between countries.[3] All of these have consequences for what is valorized as good scholarship, and affects academic freedom in that it marginalizes unfashionable issues, scholarship produced in the academic peripheries, as well as the work of those exploited by the university system, i.e. adjuncts.

It is time, therefore, that we expanded the conversation to speak of academic justice and not merely academic freedom. When scholars reflect on justice within the academy, it is usually to discuss social justice in the sense of access to underprivileged groups. This, quite often, is seen as antithetical to the pursuit of merit or knowledge. For instance, an article by Jon Haidt (2016) written for the Heterodox Academy, set up in response to what was felt as stifling political correctness in the academy, poses the issue thus: 'Why Universities Must Chose One Telos: Truth or Social Justice' (Haidt, 2016). In practice, of course, the two cannot be separated, and not only are truth and knowledge not transcendent, but social justice leads to new kinds of truth, as scholars from less privileged backgrounds bring new questions and new ways of answering them. The wave of feminist theory, race theory and post-colonial theory following the post-1960s expansion of the academy is an obvious example. However, academic justice goes beyond the question of social justice or greater representation, or even decolonizing the curriculum (*see*: Sanchez, 2018) to address the intrinsic links between equality, freedom and knowledge within scholarship and academic institutions.

In this chapter, I explore some of the different ways in which power and violence are experienced within the university setting today, and at the interface of the university and society, before going on to explore questions of justice. While power and violence are often inseparable, I start here with direct 'abnormal' violence before briefly touching upon how power encodes violence in 'normal' times.

Violence

While journalists, medics, and other professions are known to be vulnerable – leading to the setting up of organizations like *Medicin San Frontiers* or *Reporters San Frontier,* with explicit codes of neutrality that are meant to keep them safe, the academic profession with its ivory tower image has been seen, by comparison, as being a relatively safe profession. In principle, universities are meant to be sheltered spaces, where scholars can reflect in peace, or contest ideas without any serious repercussions. In fact, however, universities are hardly immune from the violence around them – including physical clashes between different student wings, the violence experienced by young women and students traversing unsafe cities.[4] In some areas there are also town and gown tensions, between elite universities with privileged, mostly white, students located amidst wider urban contexts of poverty and crime, which invest heavily in securing themselves from their neighbourhoods (*cf:*, Korn, 2009).

There are also direct attacks on universities and the ideals they represent. This is evident from just a quick look at the website, Scholars at Risk, which in 2020 alone listed 341 attacks on higher education in 58 countries, ranging from killings, violence and disappearance, to imprisonment, loss of position and travel restrictions (Scholars at Risk, 2020).

Turkey has recently seen the maximum number of arrests and dismissals of academics, mainly for signing a peace petition against the state's war on Kurds (*see:* Scholars at Risk, 2017, 2020; Özkirimli, 2017) and other articles in the same issue of the journal *Globalisations*). Israeli restrictions on Palestinian academics and Palestinian issues are a long-standing problem (Pappe, 2010), ranging from travel restrictions on Palestinian academics within and outside the country, to the setting up of Ariel university as part of a settler project on lands forcibly confiscated from Palestinians (Israeli Academics for Peace, n.d.), to surveillance of academics working on Palestinian issues in the United States (Salaita, 2015).[5]

Universities have also suffered during occupation and war. Scholarly associations have denounced the destruction of cultural heritage sites, like the Mosul museum (Archaeological Institute of America, 2015). However, the physical destruction of university infrastructure in places like Kabul, Iraq or Syria, or the dispersal of academic communities and research traditions, has been equally serious yet relatively neglected by governments and the media. Iraq had one of the best higher education systems in the region. Decades of sanctions meant no new journals, equipment etc., but the invasion made it worse. The United Nations University estimated that by 2005, 84% of Iraq's educational institutions had been 'looted, burned, or destroyed' (Schweitzer, 2013). By 2008, the Iraqi Ministry of Education recorded 31,598 violent attacks against universities and schools across the country (Schweitzer, 2013). The story of a country's subjugation may easily be told through the subjugation of its academics.

In India, the ruling Bharatiya Janata Party (BJP; 2014–2019) has recruited its own supporters into faculty positions as well as leadership roles in educational institutions, cut funding for subjects like women's studies and studies of social exclusion and discrimination, and reduced scholarships for postgraduates. It has promoted unscientific research, following the ruling regime's peculiar views. For instance, the Minister of State for Education claimed that Darwin's theory of evolution was scientifically wrong (Hariharan and Yusufji, 2019; Purkayastha, 2019). In addition, in keeping with its identity as a semi-fascist party, it has actively created an atmosphere of fear and silence on campuses through its student wing, the Akhil Bharatiya Vidyarthi Parishad (ABVP).[6] Between 2014 and 2020, the ABVP has repeatedly disrupted academic seminars, film screenings and public talks in universities across the country on the grounds that the speakers or topics were 'anti-national'. It has become almost impossible to hold seminars or show films on topics like human rights violations in Kashmir or the suppression of indigenous people accused of being involved in Maoist guerilla activities. Apart from using physical force against left students themselves, the ABVP and BJP have also invoked the law and police force against protesting students, charged them with sedition, denied them admission or rusticated and fined them. Jawaharlal Nehru University, long known for its leftist politics, has become a special object of capture (*see:* Sundar and Fazili, 2020).

The Hindu supremacist organization, the Rashtriya Swayamsevak Sangh (RSS), the parent body of the ruling BJP, insists that it is promoting Hindu culture. Their chain of schools is named after Saraswati, the Hindu Goddess of Learning. However, their reverence for learning and for teachers is selective. Teachers who have insisted on monitoring student elections to ensure fairness, or who have insisted on minimum academic standards, have been physically attacked by the ABVP.[7] More tellingly, the Hindu right killed M. M. Kalburgi, a rationalist, renowned Kannada scholar and former Vice Chancellor of Kannada University, Hampi, for his views on a heterodox Hindu sect. On 30 August 2015, two men posing as students knocked on the door of his house and shot him dead.

The physical violence of the ABVP is also increasingly combined with the conservatism of university authorities and the patriarchy students face at home, to police the behaviour of women students. Rather than becoming a space of freedom away from home, the university has become an extension of the home, but without the leaven of familial affection. In the last few years, there have been several protests by women students in India over restrictions on hostel timings, dress – not being allowed to wear jeans/or conversely, not being allowed to wear the hijab; not being allowed to use mobile phones, and even food – with female students in Banaras Hindu University (BHU) being denied non-vegetarian food (see Sundar and Fazili, 2020).

The Normal Violence of the University

While physical violence is a growing problem, it is important to remind ourselves of the more 'normal' forms of structural violence. For many students from exploited or oppressed backgrounds, whether due to caste, race, gender, sexuality or colonialism, the university holds out both promise and threat – the joy of learning and the fear of being unable to cope or compete, the excitement at meeting new people as well as anxieties about social comportment, fashion and sexual intimacy (*see:* Pathania and Tierney, 2018). While several studies have talked about the university's role as an ideological state apparatus, much less is known about what it means for an adult to internalize a fresh sense of inferiority; or the voluntary segregation that provides a sense of comfort on an alien campus. W.E.B. Du Bois's formulation of the double consciousness remains perhaps our best window into this feeling: 'It is a peculiar sensation, this double-consciousness, this sense of always looking at one's self through the eyes of others, of measuring one's soul by the tape of a world that looks on in amused contempt and pity' (Du Bois, 2006, p. 9). To understand this further, we often turn to writers and autobiographies of the ones who escape and become successful in their careers (Bama, 2012; Coates, 2015; Gidla, 2017; Hobbs, 2014). But what of those who do not, who drop out of the higher education system altogether?

Violence occurs when aspiration meets an impossibility, a crisis that is especially tragic when it comes to young people. Helm describes the growing number of suicides among students in Gaza:

> "It's like this," said Mustafa AlAssar, a 17-year-old Gazan who wants to study international law but can't, as there is no such course in Gaza, and he cannot leave. "You suddenly realise you can't be the person you want to be

in Gaza. And you can't show anyone outside who you are, because you can't get out. So you can't be the person you want to be." (Helm, 2018)

This longing to be a certain kind of person in a harsh system that doesn't allow it echoes in the suicide note of Rohith Vemula, a dalit (formerly untouchable) student, whose suicide in Hyderabad university in January 2016 was a major marker in raising the issue of caste discrimination on Indian campuses:

> The value of a man was reduced to his immediate identity and nearest possibility. To a vote. To a number. To a thing. Never was a man treated as a mind. As a glorious thing made up of star dust. In every field, in studies, in streets, in politics, and in dying and living ....My birth is my fatal accident. (Wire Staff, 2017)

Sadly, despite the momentary awareness created by Rohith's death, suicides by students from lower caste and indigenous communities have continued, especially in professional colleges where they face considerable discrimination (Acharya, 2019).

Finally, it is not only students who suffer from the inequalities, limitations and blockages of the university system. While the academic glass ceiling, especially for women and other minorities, is documented across countries, a topic that is less touched upon is the politics of citation (Ray, 2018). Reading Aldon Morris's forensic examination of how W.E.B. Du Bois was sidelined by Robert Parks and the Chicago sociologists should invite us to reflect on our own citational practices (Morris, 2015).

Power: The New Bureaucratic Global Context of Knowledge

Despite being embedded in bureaucracies, whether as part of large public universities and national ministries, or as part of corporate structures with their concomitant emphasis on auditing (Strathern, 2000), academics usually describe universities as spaces of academic freedom and intellectual exploration. The university is a space where students and teachers can learn truth, objectivity and speak truth to power. Much of the self-exploitation practiced by academics, as well as the real exploitation of the contract labour of colleagues, is justified by the belief that this is for some higher purpose, generating knowledge, training young minds etc. At its best, this is indeed what universities are for – engaging with the young for the sake of the future and engaging with knowledge for the sake of the world – but as with everything else, these ideals are embedded in a particular political economy, which threatens this superstructure constantly.

What is concealed by the ongoing discourse of global exchange, knowledge economies and access created through technology and MOOCs are the new forms of hierarchy that are set up within higher education and the increasing role of large universities as global players with enormous soft power. As Cedric Denis-Remis and Armand Hatchuel (2017) argue, in the *Paris Innovation Review*, there are dangers in the creation of an academic oligopoly, including corruption of ethics and values and academic wars. But the worst effect, as they note, is upon the knowledge systems of universities and people in less powerful countries, whose failure to meet global ranking standards means either intellectual oblivion or the diversion of scarce resources to 'catching up':

> The loss of autonomy of governments – and ultimately, of the people – in the control of knowledge and values, economic choices or development and in the recruitment of elites, should also be noted. Without prejudice to the survival of a certain pluralism, particularly in the competition between academic giants, the academic normative and prescriptive power will prevail and condition an increasing number of public choices – not necessarily in favor of the public.

> As for threats, we must also worry about the double penalty suffered by small countries whose universities are "killed" by the rankings – the best researchers, teachers and students will always prefer giants. Money will follow the same path, including public money: investments in local universities will be less and less profitable, less and less relevant, except in the case of hyper-specialization, with, in the case of research, global niche strategies at the expense of useful work for national development." (Denis-Remis and Hatchuel, 2017)

In India, entering the 'top 500' has become a governmental obsession, forcing the university system into absurd contortions. In 2017, the government declared it would list 20 'institutes of eminence', and give them enhanced funding and autonomy. When a whittled down list of six was announced, it was met with public disbelief because it included a university that was then non-existent, the Jio Institute, sponsored by Mukesh Ambani, one of Prime Minister Modi's biggest financiers. The New Education Policy introduced in

2020 speaks of autonomy but is vague and several provisions would regulate all existing universities even more tightly (Jayal, 2020).

If competing in global rankings means hiring star faculty who get grants and buy themselves out from teaching, this also means that universities are increasingly turning to contract labour for their regular teaching work. The globally increasing precarity of academic employment (*see:* Gill, 2009) has enormous implications for academic freedom, especially in the humanities, as contract faculty are unable to produce their own work or attempt radically new work, they are unable to be critical of their peers or the institution and are blamed for their predicament as part of the usual individualization of a capitalist problem. They do the same work, and bring the same standards to teaching, but get paid miserably compared to what tenured faculty make (Birmingham, 2017). As Berube and Ruth (2015) argue, the so-called crisis in the humanities is not a crisis of student numbers but a crisis of secure employment. Berube and Ruth (2015) estimate that contingent teachers make up 70% of all American faculty, or one million people (p. 14).

In Delhi University 40% of the teachers are ad hoc or temporary. As one such temporary teacher told Mallica Joshi of *The Indian Express*:

> As an ad hoc, I am supposed to work twice as hard as permanent teachers, pick up after them, make sure I am on good terms with the college principal and the teacher in charge. I have to be at every invigilation and answer sheet checking duty I am assigned so that I am not debarred from my job. To appease my principal and colleagues, I have to teach longer hours, do clerical work assigned to teachers and make the semester timetable. Even then, I can be removed from my position after four months if the college deems fit. (Joshi, 2016)

Journal publishing is another field where academics allow themselves to be exploited, as well as self-exploit through long working hours, in the belief that they are promoting knowledge, when in fact, the benefits are being passed on to journal publishers. Scholars do the research, peer review each other's papers for free and yet have to pay (or have their universities pay) exorbitant amounts to access journal articles. One of the more welcome steps in recent years has been the growing boycott of Elsevier,[8] the world's largest academic journal publisher, as well as the University of California's decision to end its subscription to Elsevier (Resnick, 2019).

In all these cases – increased auditing, global rankings, contract hiring - the commodification of education and its domination by a few academic multinationals is sharply reducing any meaningful idea of academic freedom.

Towards Justice

In conclusion, we need to move beyond academic freedom in the sense of (negative) liberty to teach, research, speak and write, towards securing the conditions that positively enable this freedom, not just for a few select individuals but for the academic community and society at large. This brings us to the question of academic justice.

Academic Justice would require secure employment, without which academic freedom, the raison d'être of the university system, is impossible. Justice would mean abolishing contract labour among faculty. It would mean giving students access to higher education by doing away with fees and making scholarships available. It would mean a safe, non-hierarchical working environment for students and faculty alike, with a constant questioning of how class, gender, caste or ethnic privilege is affecting our practice.

It would mean attention to making publications accessible, without prohibitively expensive paywalls, and without making open access publishing conditional on author payments. It would mean decolonizing our thought, our curriculum, our language and our memorials – in the words of African students: from Rhodes Must Fall to Fees Must Fall. In countries like India, it would mean being humble about our state salaries when peasants and workers get so little, and our knowledge often means so little compared to theirs.

But beyond this, we would still be left with the question of justice in our everyday practice. In fact, the question of justice – of fairness, objectivity, impartiality – haunts our practice as academics but is rarely acknowledged. We are constantly told that academic practice involves 'judgement' or 'judiciousness' in reading sources and making inferences. When we review manuscripts as peer reviewers, we ask ourselves whether we are doing justice to the author and her argument; when we try and capture an empirical situation involving live interlocutors, we ask ourselves whether we are doing justice to our field and to our informants. Justice is problematized in almost all our everyday encounters with students, especially over evaluations: are we as teachers doing justice *between* students; when students dispute the justness of a grade, teachers may well summon evidence, readings or logic, but students may feel that it is the *effort* that must be justly rewarded. As teachers in a multilingual country like India, we worry about the creeping dominance of English and yet appreciate the inter-translatability it provides. Now increasingly, as our, mostly but not always male, academic colleagues are being called out for sexual harassment in the MeToo movement growing on campuses and elsewhere, we worry about what due process means in doing justice to our young students and colleagues (*see*: Lukose, 2018; Pipyrou, 2018). In coming to terms with the materiality of our own practices and thought, we find that our struggles for justice have just begun.

Notes

1   A version of this was first presented at the presidential plenary of the International Sociological Association World Congress of Sociology in 2018.

2   The global reach is not new since universities in the metropoles have long attracted students from their colonies or post-colonies. However, the emphasis has shifted from the colonial goal of civilizing and educating the natives to running their own affairs to the post-colonial one of making money from overseas fees, and moving up the world rankings by showing internationalization of students and faculty.

3   Post-colonial critique, following Said (1978), has long emphasized the manner in which representation structures power and inequality between societies, but the current context runs across disciplines, and coopts nationals of different countries in markedly new ways, recreating dependency in new forms.

4   In 2012, a physiotherapy student in Delhi returning home after watching a film was brutally gang raped, leading to massive protests by students and others. This led to important changes in India's rape laws.

5   In April 2019, US authorities denied Omar Barghouti, a Palestinian leader, entry into the United States where he was to speak at a few campuses (Salem, 2019).

6   The ABVP was set up in 1949, as the student wing of the Hindu-nationalist RSS, with 'National Reconstruction' as its main goal (http://abvp.org/history). The RSS is the parent body of the current ruling party, the BJP.

7   In 2006 ABVP killed Ujjain professor HS Sabharwal after he cancelled student union elections. In 2009 all six students were acquitted. In 2016 in two separate incidents, ABVP students physically threatened and vandalized the office of the Dean, Faculty of Law, Delhi University for insisting on attendance norms. In 2018 ABVP attacked and blackened the face of Girin Baxi, Chemistry Prof in KSKVK University, Bhuj, Gujarat.

8   https://gowers.files.wordpress.com/2012/02/elsevierstatementfinal.pdf

References

Acharya, S. (2019, June 23). Student suicides – Why do numbers disproportionately tilt towards Dalits? *Bloomberg/Quint*. Retrieved from https://www.bqprime.com/opinion/student-suicides-why-do-numbers-disproportionately-tilt-towards-dalits

Altbach, P. G. (2013). *The international imperative in higher education*. Rotterdam: Sense Publishers.

Altbach, P. G. (2016). *Global perspectives on higher education*. Baltimore, MD: Johns Hopkins Press.

Antonucci, L. (2016). *Student lives in crisis: Deepening inequality in times of austerity*. Bristol: Policy Press.

Archaeological Institute of America. (2015). Joint statement on cultural destruction in Iraq. Retrieved from https://www.archaeological.org/news/aianews/18742

Bama. (2012, 1992). *Karukku* (translated by Laxmi Holmstrom). New Delhi: Oxford University Press.

Berube, M., & Ruth, J. (2015). *The humanities, higher education and academic freedom: Three necessary arguments*. Westport, CT: Palgrave Macmillan.

Bilgrami, A., & Cole, J. R. (Eds.). (2015). *Who's afraid of academic freedom?* New York, NY: Columbia University Press.

Birmingham, K. (2017, February 12). The great shame of our profession: How the humanities survive on exploitation. *The Chronicle of Higher Education*.

Bourdieu, P. (1989). *The state nobility: Elite schools in the field of power*. Stanford: Stanford University Press.

Brown, R. (2018). Higher education and inequality. *Perspectives: Policy and Practice in Higher Education, 22*(2), 37–43. doi:10.1080/13603108.2017.1375442

Butler, J. (2017). Academic freedom and the critical task of the university. *Globalizations, 14*(6), 857–861.

Coates, T. N. (2015). *Between the world and me*. New York, NY: Spiegel & Grau.

Denis-Remis, C., & Hatchuel, A. (2017, February 15). Top universities: New players in the global game of power. Retrieved from http://parisinnovationreview.com/articles-en/top-universities-new-players-in-the-global-game-of-power

Deshpande, S., & Apoorvanand (2018). *Exclusion in higher education today. India exclusion report 2017*. New Delhi: Centre for Equity Studies.

Deshpande, S., & Zacharias, U. (2013). *Beyond inclusion: The practice of equal access in Indian higher education*. New Delhi: Routledge.

Du Bois, W. E. B. (2006). *The souls of Black folk. Electronic classics series*. State College, PA: Pennsylvania State University.

Gidla, S. (2017). *Ants among elephants: An untouchable family and the making of modern India*. New York, NY: Farrar, Straus and Giroux.

Gill, R. (2009). Breaking the silence: The hidden injuries of neo-liberal academia. In R. Flood, & R. Gill (Eds.), *Secrecy and silence in the research process: Feminist reflections*. London: Routledge.

Haidt, J. (2016, October 21). Why universities must choose one telos: Truth or social justice. *The Heterodox Academy*. Retrieved 29 May 2019, from https://heterodoxacademy.org/one-telos-truth-or-social-justice-2/

Halsey, A. H., Lauder, H., Brown, P., & Wells, A. S. (Eds.). (1997). *Education: Culture, economy and society*. Oxford: Oxford University Press.

Hariharan, G., & Yusufji, S. (2019). *Battling for India: A citizen's reader*. New Delhi: Speaking Tiger.

Helm, S. (2018, May 18). A suicide in Gaza. *The Guardian*.

Hobbs, J. (2014). *The short and tragic life of Robert Peace*. New York, NY: Scribners.

Israeli Academics for Peace and Truth About the Ariel University. (n.d.). Retrieved from http://israeli-academics-for-peace.org.il/en/the-truth-about-the-ariel-university/

Jayal, N. (2020, September 4). NEP 2020 on higher education. *The India Forum*. Retrieved 25 November 2021, from https://www.theindiaforum.in/article/nep-2020-higher-education?utm_source=website&utm_medium=organic&utm_campaign=homepage&utm_content=Top-article

Joshi, M. (2016, November 28). Delhi University ad-hoc teachers: Four months at a time. *Indian Express*.

Kinzelbach, K., Saliba, I., Spannagel, J., & Quinn, R. (2020). Free universities: Putting the academic freedom index into action. *GPPI and Scholars at Risk*.

Korn, H. (2009, September 15). Safety in New Haven: A tale of two cities. *Yale News*.

Lloyd, M. (2018, November 2). Bolsonaro poses a serious threat to higher education. *University World News*. Retrieved 29 April 2021, from https://www.universityworldnews.com/post.php?story=20181102101957300

Lukose, R. (2018). Decolonizing feminism in the #MeToo era. *Cambridge Journal of Anthropology*, *36*(2), 34–52.

Morris, A. (2015). *The scholar denied: W. E. B. Dubois and the birth of modern sociology*. Berkeley, CA: University of California Press.

Özkirimli, U. (2017). How to liquidate a people? Academic freedom in Turkey and beyond, *Globalizations*, *14*(6), 851–856.

Pappe, I. (2010). *Out of the frame: The struggle for academic freedom in Israel*. New York, NY: Pluto Press.

Pathania, G. J., & Tierney, W. G. (2018). An ethnography of caste and class at an Indian University: Creating capital. *Tertiary Education and Management*, *24*(3), 221–231.

Pipyrou, S. (2018). #MeToo is little more than mob rule//vs//#MeToo is a legitimate form of social justice. *HAU: Journal of Ethnographic Theory*, *8*(3), 415–419.

Post, R. (2015). Academic freedom and the constitution. In A. Bilgrami, & J. R. Cole (Eds.), *Who's afraid of academic freedom?* (pp. 300–364). New York, NY: Columbia University Press.

Purkayastha, P. (2019). The curious case of RSS-BJP science. In G. Hariharan, & S. Yusufji (Eds.), *Battling for India: A citizen's reader* (pp. 240–248). New Delhi: Speaking Tiger.

Ray, V. (2018, April 27). The racial politics of citations. *Inside Higher Ed*. Retrieved 25 November 2021, from https://www.insidehighered.com/advice/2018/04/27/racial-exclusions-scholarly-citations-opinion

Resnick, B. (2019, March 1). The costs of academic publishing are absurd. The University of California is fighting back. *Vox*.

Said, E. (1978). *Orientalism*. New York, NY: Pantheon Books.

Salaita, S. (2015). *Uncivil rites: Palestine and the limits of academic freedom*. Chicago, IL: Haymarket Books.

Salem, O. (2019, April 12). US denies entry to BDS cofounder Omar Barghouti. *Al Jazeera*. Retrieved 29 April 2019, from https://www.aljazeera.com/news/2019/04/denies-entry-bds-founder-omar-barghouti-190411174724070.html

Sanchez, A. (2018). Canon fire: Decolonising the curriculum. *Cambridge Journal of Anthropology*, *36*(2), 1–6.

Scholars at Risk. (September 2017). Free to Think. Retrieved from https://www.scholarsatrisk.org/resources/free-to-think-2017/

Scholars at Risk. (November 2020). Free to Think. Retrieved from https://www.scholarsatrisk.org/resources/free-to-think-2020/

Schweitzer, M. (2013, October 1). The destruction of Iraq's intellectuals. *Al Jazeera*. Retrieved 29 April 2019, from https://www.aljazeera.com/humanrights/2013/10/destruction-iraqs-intellectuals-2013101114937748151.html

Standing, G. (2011). *The precariat: The new dangerous class*. London: Bloomsbury Academic.

Stanley, J. (2018). *How fascism works*. New York, NY: Random House.

Strathern, M. (2000). *Audit cultures*. London: Routledge.

Sundar, N. (2018, June 16). Academic freedom and Indian Universities, *Economic and Political Weekly*, *53*(24), 48.

Sundar, N., & Fazili, G. (2020, August 28). Academic freedom in India: A status report 2020. *The India Forum*. Retrieved from https://www.theindiaforum.in/article/academic-freedom-india

The Guardian. (2019, March 21). Trump threatens to cut funding for colleges 'hostile to free speech.' *The Guardian*.

The Wire Staff (2017, January 17). My birth is my fatal accident: Rohit Vemula's searing indictment of social prejudices. *The Wire*.

Index

A

Aboriginal Land Rights (Northern Territory) Act 1976, 41
Aboriginal peoples, 32, 33, 42
  Dubbo, 39
  making demands, 35
  Perth, 40, 40 (table)
  Tasmania, 34
  Terra Nullius, 34
Aboriginal Protection Acts and Ordinances, 34
'Aboriginal Protection' laws, 37
The Aboriginals Ordinance Act 1918 (NT), 40
Abraham, M., 106
Academic justice, 238
Acceleration theory, 133
Accountability, 184
Activists, 23
Afghanistan, 18
Afro-descendant communities, 65, 80
Akhil Bharatiya Vidyarthi Parishad (ABVP), 233
Amazon, 46
Ambani, M., 236
American Civil Liberties Union (ACLU), 50
Anchor baby, 214, 217
Anormative Regulation, 131
Anormative social regulation, 135–136
Anthropocene, 79
Anthropomorphizing nature, 76–78
Anti-gender movement, 87
Anti-homophobia, 91
Anti-immigrant campaign, 217–223
Anti-Mexican sentiment, 221
Anti-plurality, 18

Anti-subject, 198–199
Anti-violence, 25
Applied humanities, 199–201
Archer, M., 8
Arellano, E., 216
Argentina, 72, 87
Aryan myth, 164
Australia, 50, 162
  dispossession, 33–36
  Indigenous peoples, 32
  interdependency, 36–38
  land and social injustice, 35–36
  land justice and societal justice, 38–42, 39 (table)–41 (table)
  linking land justice and social justice, 42–43
  non-Indigenous peoples, 32
The Authoritarian Personality, 196
Auto genocide, 160

B

Banaras Hindu University (BHU), 234
Banfield, M., 180
Bangladesh, 23, 103
Barbarism, 70
Benedict XVI, 94
Berube, M., 237
Bible, 208
Bigotry, 26
Bipolar disorder, 128
Black, J., 134
Black Lives Matter movement, 26
Black Other, 163
Blacks, in New York City
  datavaillance, 49–56
  policing of, 49–56
  surveillance, 49–56

Blee, K. M., 211
Bloomberg administration, 55 (image)
Bolsonaro, J., 229
Brazil, 72, 87
  Afro-descendant communities in, 80
  disaster, 77
  Neopentecostal evangelicals, 90
  social fabric in, 124
Breeders, 215–217
Brexit syndrome, 22
Brigade, G., 212
Bright, J., 190
Broken Windows theory, 51
Browne, S., 61
Buddhist, 22
Burawoy, M., 8
Bureaucratic regulation, 131, 139–140
Burke, T., 24
Byfield, N. P., 6

C
Cambodia, 160
Canada, 36, 50
Capitalism, 16, 49, 125
Capitalist globalization, 1
Capitalocene, 79
Carceral state, 47–49
Carrolup Native Settlement, 39
Castro, E., 6
Catholic activists, 90
Catholic Church, 91, 94
Chavez, L., 209
China, 169
Christianization, 162
Civilizing process, 68
Climate change, 77
Cold War, 164, 165
Coleman, J., 184
Collective conscience, 130
Colombia, 87
Colonialism, 15, 165
  nature of, 162–164
Coloniality of power, 47
Colonization, 33
Command and control (CAC), 133, 134
Commission Regulation (EC) No 730/
    1999, 140
Commodification, 125–127
Communism, 96
CompStat, 51

Conflicts, 71–76
  internally displaced people by, 74
    (table)
  in Latin America, 75
  resolution, 191
  return of, 201–202
Conspiracy theory, 88
Convention on the Elimination of All
    Forms of Discrimination Against
    Women (CEDAW), 23
COVID-19 pandemics, 4
Crow, J., 210
Crutzen, P., 79
Cuba, 90
Culturocide, 160, 161
Czech Republic, 151

D
Dallacroce, M., 217
Daniels, J., 209
Data doppelganger, 46
Democide, 161
Democracy, 127
  gender equality, 23
  illiberal, 17–21
  justice, 23
  liberal, 16
De-subjectivation, 197
Digital data, 47
Digital platforms, 47
Dinkins, D., 51
Disasters, 73
  Brazil, 77
  internally displaced people by, 74
    (table)
  naturalizing, 76–78
Discrimination, 24
Dispossession, 33–36
Distributive justice, 181
Doctrine of Assimilation, 161
Domestic violence, 19, 107, 169, 172
    (figure), 202
Dubbo, 38
  demographic profile, 39, 39 (table)
Du Bois, W. E. B., 234
Duterte, R., 20

E
Ecocide, 160, 162
Ecological degradation, 162

Egypt
 Christian Copts in, 16
 Oriental peoples of, 164
Elcioglu, F., 128
Elias, N., 68
England, 50
Enlightenment, 70, 71
Environmental degradation, 77
Equity, 48
'Ethnic cleansing' strategy, 22
European Union, 145
Europhobic, 156
Eurosceptic, 156
Extended concept of violence, 67, 69
 (figure)
Extreme violence, 73

F
Facebook, 46, 208
Falsehood, 26
Fanon, F., 15, 127
Farmers Movement, in India, 26–27
Fear, 1, 18
Feminists, 23, 87, 92
Fictitious commodities, 125
2008 Financial crisis, 18
Food and Agriculture Organization
 (FAO), 166
Food insecurity, 76–77
Forcible commodification, 126
France, 50, 190
French Revolutionary law, 130

G
Galtung, J., 67, 79
Garelick, R., 224
Garland, D., 49
Gay marriage, 89
Gender, 3
 anti-homophobia and, 91
 violence against, 23–25
Gender Agenda, 88
Gender equality, 23
Gender ideology, 88, 89
 Catholic opposition to, 88
 moral crusade, 94
Gender inequality, 25
Gender violence, 169
Genocide, 34, 194
 defined, 160

Geological Time Scale, 79
Geo-politics, 1
Germany, 50
Giuliani Administration, 52
Giuliani, R., 51
Gledhill, J., 190
Glenn, E. N., 36
Global Age, 165
Global interdependence, 152
Globalization, 2, 16, 25, 152
Global Mapping of Sociologists for
 Social Inclusion (GMSSI), 27
Global North, 101
Global South, 114
Global Witness report, 75
Goffman, E., 185
GOLD DIGGER, 216
Gouldner, A., 179
Governance
 bureaucratic regulation, 139–140
 social institutions and, 137–139
 supranational, 157
 tactical, 136–137
The Great Transformation, 124, 125
Guerrilla movements, 192
Gurr, T. R., 166, 189, 196

H
Haberman, C., 110
Harff, B., 161
Harris, S. C., 215
Harvey, D., 126
Hawaii, 36
Helping professions, 181
Herbert, Z., 175
Hindu Rashtra of Hindutva, 21
Hindu supremacist organization,
 233
Hobbes, T., 186
Hobsbawm, E., 70
Homocentrism, 167
Homosexuals, 87, 96
Human Development Report, 170
Human insecurities, 111–116
Human rights, 21–23, 100, 114
Human society, 170
Hungary, 151
Huntington, S., 167
Hyper-nationalism, 18
Hyper-subject, 198

I

Illiberal democracies, 17–21
Imperial Presidency, 20
The Inconvenient Indian, 36
India, 20, 161
  Aryan myth, 164
  Bharatiya Janata Party (BJP), 233
  Farmers Movement in, 26–27
  female foetuses, abortion of, 169
  muslims in, 16
  Oriental peoples of, 164
  refugees, 103
Indigenous community, 65
Indigenous land justice, 36–38
Indigenous movements, 26
Indigenous peoples, 32
  British colonized, 35
Inequality, 76, 230
Information capitalism, 47
  carceral state, 47–49
Injustice, 3
Interconnectedness, 79, 152
Interdependency, 36–38
Internal Displacement Monitoring
  Centre (IDCM), 73
Internally Displaced People (IDPs), 73
International Sociological Association
  (ISA), 123. *See also* XIX
  International Sociological
  Association World Congress of
  Sociology
Intersectionality, 4, 25, 169
Intersectional violence, 3, 23–25
Iraq, 197
  Kurds in, 16
Islam, 190
Islamic fundamentalism, 18, 154

J

Jews, 194, 196
Jihadis, 190
Johnson, J., 212
Jones-Rogers, S., 210
Joshi, M., 237
Justice, 2, 16, 100, 101, 181, 238–239
  arc of, 111–116
  distributive, 181
  gender equality and, 23
  interlocking practices, 113 (figure)
Justice Cascade, 113

K

Kannabiran, K., 106
Kelsen, H., 130
Keynes, L., 159
Kim Jong-un, 20
King, T., 36
Kuhar, R., 93
Kunbidji people, 41
Kurds, 16, 232

L

Labour Party, 126
Land, 35–36, 40, 43, 65, 66, 75, 126,
  223, 232
  Aboriginal peoples, 34, 37
  destruction of, 109
  dispossession, 2, 42
  Indigenous, 33, 36–38, 43
  injustice, *See* Land injustice
  justice, *See* Land justice
  non-Aboriginal peoples, 35, 37
  Noongar people, 39
  Pitjantjatjara people, 32
  power and wealth, 36
  social injustice and, 38
  tenure, 33
  Torres Strait Islander peoples, 37
  Yankunytjatjara people, 32
Land injustice, 35–36, 38, 42–43
Land justice, 5, 33, 44
  Indigenous, 36–38
  vs. societal justice, 38–43, 40 (table)–
  41 (table)
Landless People's Movement, in South
  Africa, 27
Latin America, 75, 87, 193
  Catholic Church, 91–92
  colonialism and, 165
  gender ideology, 94
  LGBTI + Rights in, 89
  sexual and reproductive rights in, 88
Law and order, 48
League Tables, 138
Legitimacy, loss of, 195
Leninism, 128
Levien, M., 126
Levi, P., 197
LGBTI+, 87, 89, 92, 95, 96
LGBTQ, 24, 26
Liberal democracies, 16, 18, 50

Liberation, 25
Litt, J. S., 213
López, V., 110
Loyalty, 179
Lutrawita, 34
Lyon, D., 51
Lyon, K., 61

M
Mahdawi, A., 207
Majoritarian, 18, 19
Makarrata Commission, 32
Malinowski, B., 179
Maningrida, 40
  demographic profile, 41 (table)
Mapping, 9, 51, 128, 171, 171 (figure)–
  172 (figure). *See also* Violence
Market fundamentalism, 125
Marketization, 16, 125
  mass media, 154
Martinelli, A., 8
Marx, K., 159
Massive Open Online Courses
  (MOOCs), 230
Mass killings, 161
Mauss, M., 179, 180
McQuillan, D., 60
Mead, G. H., 185
Media, 25–26
Mercantilism, 47
Merian people, 36
#MeToo movement, 24
Mexico, 87
Migrants, 101, 102, 114, 209
  classifications of, 104, 104 (figure)
  economic, 104
  foreign born, 103
  geographic congurations, 103
  illegal, 105
  jurisdiction, 115
  temporary, 104
  violence, 108
Mikoyan, A. I., 165
Minuteman Civil Defence Corps
  (MCDC), 211
Miskolci, R., 7
Modi, N., 20, 229
Mohai, P., 67
Monopoly, 68
  legitimate, 194
Moral capital, 184
  benefits of, 186
  function of, 185

Moral crusade, 92, 94
Moral culture
  accountability, 184
  axio-normative coherence *vs.*
    'anomie,' 183
  familiarity, 184
  personal contacts, 184
  social order *vs.* traumatogenic change,
    183
  transparency, 183
Moral values, 177
  justice, 181
  loyalty, 179
  reciprocity, 179
  respect, 181
  solidarity, 180
  trust, 178–179
Morphostatic, 131
Mothers Against Drunk Driving's
  (MADD), 219
Mothers Against Illegal Aliens (MAIA),
  10, 212–215
  'educational' mission, 217–223
Multiculturalism, 132
Multinationalism, 136
Myanmar, 18
  horrendous atrocities, 22
  Rohingyas, 16, 22

N
Napoleonic Code, 130
National Census of Population and
  Housing, 38
National Council of La Raza (NCLR),
  222
Nationalism
  defined, 145
  functions, 146
  securing cohesion, 147
National justice, 115
National populism, 145
  alternative to, 155–157
  causes, 151–153
  challenge of, 157
  in contemporary Europe, 150–155
  digital and social media, 154
  global interdependence, 152
  globalization, 152
  interconnectedness, 152
Nation building, 191
Natural disasters, 162
Naturalizing 'disasters,' 76–78
Neoliberalism, 3, 125

Neo-orientalism, 165
Neopentecostal evangelicals, 90
New York Police Department (NYPD), 51, 55
Non-Aboriginal population
    Dubbo, 39, 39 (table)
Non-Indigenous peoples, 32
Non-subject, 198
Non-violence, 15
Noongar people, 39
Normativity, 130
The Northern Territory National Emergency Response Act 2007, 41
NT Liquor Act, 41

O
Oommen, T. K., 9
Orban, V., 17, 229
Organization for Economic Cooperation and Development (OECD), 80
Orwell, G., 14
Oslo Agreement, 201

P
Pandey, G., 106
Paradox of pacification, 79
Paraguay, 65
Park, S., 110
Pascale, C. M., 108
Pastoral Land Commission, 80
Patternote, D., 93
Peacekeeping, 191
Pentecostal church, 91
Persian Gulf War, 70
Personal somatic violence, 67
Physical violence, 159
    ABVP, 233
Pitjantjatjara people, 32
Poland, 151
Polanyi, K., 124–126, 128
Political correctness, 137
Political instability, 76
Political pluralism, 149
Political violence, destructuration of, 195
Politics without conviction, 136–137
Polycentricity, 133
Populism, 21–23, 124
    European, 149
    ideological elements, 148
    nationalism and, 149

National populism. *See* National populism
political pluralism, 149
Portugal, 26
Poverty, 76, 170
Power, 15, 19, 235–238
    defined, 2, 14
    media, 25–26
    monopoly, 16
Predictive policing, 58–61
Primary socialization, 196
Primitive accumulation, 126
Protest movements, 26–27
Przeworski, A., 127
Purkayastha, B., 7
Putin, V., 20

R
Racialization, 56–58
Racism, 18, 48
Radical feminist ideology, 88
Rashtriya Swayamsevak Sangh (RSS), 233
Ratzinger, J. A., 88
Reciprocity, 179
Recommodification, 126
Refugees, 23, 104, 110, 111, 114, 209
Regulations, 134–135
Renan, E., 203
Restorative justice, 112
Re-subjectivation, 197
Revolutionary Armed Forces of Colombia (FARC), 91
Right of Breathing, 67
Right of Hunger, 67
Right of Thirst, 67
Right to Sleep, 67
Ristanovic, V. N., 169
Roders, J., 213
Rohingya Muslims, 16, 22, 23
Romero, M., 10
A Room of One's Own, 87
Rousseff, D., 96
Rousso, H., 203
Rummel, R. J., 160
Russia, 129
Ruth, J., 237
Rwanda, 169, 190

S
Same-sex marriage, 88
Savage Beasts, 162

Scholars, 23
Scotland, 50
Self-defense, 15
Sexual assault, 24
Sexual harassment, 24
Sikkink, K., 113
Simmel, G., 186
Slovakia, 151
Social activism, 18
Social change, 131
Social cohesion, 15
Social injustice, 35–36
  interdependency of, 36–38
Social institutions, 137–139
Social justice, 18, 19, 126
  women and, 25
Social media, 26, 46, 92
Social normativity, 130
Social processes, 67–71
Social resistance, 66
Social sciences, 199–201
Social theory, 175
Societal justice, 38–42, 49
  land justice and, 42–43
Society, 175
  agency of, 176
Socio-ecological violence, 66, 71–76,
  78–81
Sociological analysis, 199–201
Sociology, 1, 27–28, 175
Solidarity, 180
Somalia, 18
South Africa, 128
  Landless People's Movement in, 27
South Sudan, 18
  horrendous atrocities, 22
Spain, 26
Spitzer, E., 55
Sri Lanka, 169
  ethnic Tamils in, 16
State fragility, 76
Stop-and-Frisk practice, 59
Street Crime Unit (SCU), 52
Structural Adjustment Programme
  (SAP), 166
Structural violence, 3, 159, 166
Sundar, N., 10
Sweet family moment, 206
Symbolic violence, 159
Syria, 16, 18
  horrendous atrocities, 22
Sztompka, P., 9

T
Tactical governance, 136–137
Tasmania, 34
Tastsoglou, E., 106
Technology, 167–168
Telus, 46
Terra Nullius, 33, 34, 37, 43
Three-world schema, 9
  emergence of, 164–167
Tilly, C., 189, 196
Time's Up, Say Her Name, 27
Tischner, J., 185
Toepfer, K., 72
Torres Strait Islander, 32, 33, 37
Transparency, 183
Truganina, 34
Trump, D., 8, 19, 20, 145, 224, 229
Trust, 178, 179
Truth-telling commission, 44
Tugal, C., 127–128
Turkey, 129, 232
Twitter, 46

U
UF-250 form, 52
  in terry stops, 53 (image)–54 (image)
Uluru, 32
UN Economic Commission for Latin
  America and the Caribbean
  (ECLAC), 80
UnidosUS, 222
United Nations Environment
  Programme (UNEP), 71, 72
United Nations High Commission on
  Refugees (UNHCR), 102
United States, 21, 36, 100
  Black Lives Matter movement, 26
  Blacks, in New York City, 49–56
  civil rights, 48
  criminal justice systems, 49
  disasters, 75
  equity, 48
  forced conformity, 47
  migrants, 102, 105, 110
  Mothers Against Illegal Aliens
    (MAIA), 217
  police, racialization and social
    sciences, 56–58
  predictive policing, 58–61
  socialization, 47
Universal Declaration of Human Rights
  (UDHR), 100

Unregulated commodification, 126
U.S. Immigration and Customs
    Enforcement (ICE), 110

V
Valentino, B., 161
Vatican, 89
Venezuela, 72, 90
   horrendous atrocities, 22
Verizon, 46
Victims, emergence of, 192–195
Vietnam, 162
Violence, 2, 15, 22, 100, 101, 231–234
   adjectivation of, 69 (figure)
   analysis of, 195–197
   commodification, 126
   communities, 105
   conflicts and, 73
   defined, 189
   domestic, 169
   extended concept of, 67, 69 (figure)
   gender, 3, 23–25
   interlinked, 106, 107 (figure)
   internally displaced people by, 74
     (table)
   intersectional, 3, 23–25
   language, 108
   LGBTQ, 24
   mapping, 171, 171 (figure)–172 (figure)
   micro level, 168–171
   migrants, 108, 113
   physical, 159
   prevention and exit, 195–197, 202–203
   routinization of, 116
   social processes and, 67–71
   socio-ecological, 66, 71–76, 78–81
   State-facilitated, 109
   structural, 3, 159, 166
   symbolic, 159
   systematic theorization of, 67
   technology and, 167–168
   types of, 162–164
   university, 234–235
   weaponized language in, 108
   women, 23–25
von Clausewitz, C., 70
von Holdt, K., 106
Vulnerability, 114

W
Walby, S., 105
Wales, 50
Walter, M., 5
War, 71–76
War on Crime, 47
War on Drugs, 47
Water stress, 76
Weaponized language, 108
Weber, M., 15, 68, 159, 193
Wells-Barnett, I. B., 210
Western democracies, 65, 145
Western liberal democracy, 16
WhatsApp, 108
White supremacist movements, 211
White women, 210
   Mothers Against Illegal Aliens
     (MAIA), 212, 213
   right-wing movements, 211
   white supremacist movements, 211
Wieviorka, M., 10
Wolfe, P., 36
Women
   emancipation, 87
   violence, 168, 169
   violence against, 23–25
Women's March on Washington, 25
Woolf, V., 87
World Bank, 71
World Migration Report, 102
World War I, 167, 169
World War II, 27, 72, 164, 167, 171

X
Xenophobia, 180
XIX International Sociological
   Association World Congress of
   Sociology, 4, 14. *See* also
   International Sociological
   Association (ISA)

Y
Yankunytjatjara people, 32
Yemen, horrendous atrocities, 22
Yoo-rrook Justice Commission, 44

Z
'Zero tolerance' policy, 206